FAMILY BUSINESS

FAMILY BUSINESS

ERNESTO J. POZA

Weatherhead School of Management
Case Western Reserve University

THOMSON
™
SOUTH-WESTERN

Australia · Canada · Mexico · Singapore · Spain · United Kingdom · United States

THOMSON
━━━━★━━━━ ™
SOUTH-WESTERN

Family Business
Ernesto J. Poza

Editorial Director:
Jack W. Calhoun

Editor-in-Chief:
Michael P. Roche

Executive Editor:
John Szilagyi

Senior Developmental Editor:
Judith O'Neill

Senior Marketing Manager:
Rob Bloom

Production Editor:
Emily S. Gross

Manufacturing Coordinator:
Rhonda Utley

Production House:
Lifland et al., Bookmakers

Compositor:
Pre-Press Company, Inc.

Printer:
Phoenix Color
Hagerstown, MD

Design Project Manager:
Anne Marie Rekow

Cover Designer:
Anne Marie Rekow

Cover Photographer:
Joe Cornish, Digital Vision

To Karen and Kali
because creating is a family venture

———————————■———————————

BRIEF CONTENTS

CONTENTS

PREFACE

Family business is a vibrant area of growing interest today among researchers, theorists, investors, policymakers, practitioners, and many others—with good cause. The excesses of the "deal era" of the late 1990s have been worked out, and the dot-com bubble has burst. With the demise of the dot-coms has come an increasing awareness that speed, sustainability, flexibility, quality of product and service, brand, customer relationships, employee care, and patient capital are the only genuine sources of competitive advantage for firms faced with the economic challenges of the global economy. Family businesses, to be sure, confront substantial challenges, but they often possess unique advantages on all of these fronts.

Many of the assets that differentiate a family-owned or family-controlled business from other forms of enterprise revolve around the relationship between the family and its business, especially the guidance that family members exert as managers and as shareholders. In the aftermath of recent corporate meltdowns, business schools are engaging in a broader range of research and dialogue on governance and the role of shareholders and boards. In this same vein, the potential value of family ownership, stewardship, and control have been convincingly demonstrated in recent years. Consider the Hewlett and Packard families, who opposed the merger between HP and Compaq Computer. And consider the Ford family, who, during a period of turmoil at the large auto producer, appointed William Clay Ford, Jr., as CEO of the Ford Motor Company, to replace Jacques Nasser, a key nonfamily executive.

Why didn't the Hewlett and Packard families just diversify the family portfolio, reallocating assets to other companies' equity in pursuit of risk management and net-worth protection? Perhaps it was because the heirs cared about the enterprise and accepted the responsibility of stewardship, instead of operating as average investors in publicly traded firms so often do. They saw the value of the family legacy embedded in the enterprise and wanted to preserve it—not to arrest progress, but rather to create a future wisely built on a very worthwhile past. Some analysts have suggested that the Hewletts and Packards continue to hold a vision of an enterprise that adapts, succeeds, and continues to build value and wealth for its many stakeholders: its employees, its suppliers, its customers, the communities in which it does business, and its shareholders.

Alongside these very visible examples of family ownership and family leadership are hundreds of smaller, lower profile, privately held family businesses with the same commitment to continuity from generation to generation. From the United States, Europe, Latin America, Asia, Australia, and the Middle East comes compelling evidence of the commitment of business families to building firms that last.

In the media industry, which has seen much family ownership replaced by corporate ownership, the owners of a few great enterprises have exhibited singular commitment in the face of generational transitions and turmoil wrought by economic, natural, and technological forces. Katharine and Don Graham, of the *Washington Post*, amply displayed their commitment during the Watergate and Pentagon Papers crises and throughout the generational transfer of power. The Blethens, of the *Seattle Times*, exemplified true stewardship responsibility when the family (down to the fifth generation) recommitted itself to continuity in the face of a financially debilitating strike. The Ferré Rangel family, of *El Nuevo Día* in Puerto Rico, created a model for succession in Latin America by transferring power and the entrepreneurial spirit to a new generation that is looking for success in the technological world of the Internet, amid the convergence of multiple media forms.

Yet, most family businesses (approximately 67 percent) do not survive beyond the founding generation under the control of the same owning family, and only about 12 percent make it to the third generation. However, few businesses of any type enjoy long, successful lives today. When the Standard and Poor Index of 90 major U.S. companies was created in the 1920s, companies on the list stayed there for an average of 65 years. But, by 1998, a firm's expected tenure on the expanded S&P 500 list was a mere 10 years.

Family businesses are extremely important to the economic well-being of the United States and the other free economies of the world. Between 80 and 95 percent of businesses in the United States and Latin America and over 80 percent of businesses in Europe and Asia remain family-owned and family-controlled. These same businesses, small and large, young and old, account for more than 50 percent of the gross domestic product of the world's most advanced economies and employ a majority of the population. It is unfortunate that the stereotype of nepotism in family businesses tends to overshadow, in the eyes of media, academic researchers, business schools, and the government, the significant contribution these enterprises make day in and day out.

In the past year alone, several top-ranked academic journals (including the *Academy of Management Journal*, *Organization Science*, and the *Journal of Business Venturing*) have published articles exploring the unique agency costs, strategic resources, features, and issues of family businesses. Quality research in established periodical literature is sure to generate more knowledge of the exceptional challenges and advantages of family businesses, with the prospect of very useful implications for practice. The fact that family business is becoming the focus of research in management, economics, law, and the behavioral sciences also bodes well for the possibility of positively influencing current dismal survival statistics.

Educational programs in family business at the undergraduate and graduate business school levels have grown tremendously in the past several years. This book captures that progress by pointing to key leadership tasks and a set of management, ownership, and family practices that can help mediate the relationship between a family and its enterprise. Adopting an optimal mix of these practices will ensure that the unique strengths and competencies of the family enterprise (for example, speed and long-term orientation)—and not its much-heralded vulnerabilities (for example, nepotism and family conflict)—retain the upper hand. Leading, managing, and governing family enterprises are tasks that increasingly require a set of skills, abilities, and practices that serve sustainability and continuity.

APPROACH

Written with the next-generation family business owner in mind, *Family Business* is the result of an interdisciplinary appreciation of the advantages enjoyed and challenges faced by family businesses. By focusing on the best practices available to family firms, it promotes the capacity of family members to better lead family-owned businesses into succeeding generations. The book also offers advice to the next generation of service providers to family enterprises (such as consultants, attorneys, bankers, financial planners, and family therapists) and to corporate partners in the supply chain (such as managers of dealership networks in the automotive, appliance, and industrial equipment industries), who depend on family-owned businesses for distribution and sales.

It should be noted that *Family Business* is a scholarly book. Rooted in theory, research, and practice, it goes beyond traditional textbooks by not only fostering understanding of family business theory and family dynamics but also exploring its subject with a managerial action orientation. *Family Business* includes a diverse collection of real-life (not composite) cases and exercises. Based on actual family business documents, these cases and exercises disclose concepts and practices that have benefited other family businesses. Moreover, *Family Business* goes way beyond basic "how-to" books by reviewing both theory and recent research, thus supporting informed and context-relevant planning and decision making.

Reading and working through this book provides an opportunity to better understand the unique opportunities and challenges faced by family businesses. These businesses are, after all, important to millions of enterprising families, to 85 percent of the employee population, and to the future of free economies around the world. Family businesses continue to be the primary engines of global economic activity.

It would be a disservice to the next generation to continue to dwell on the problems and stereotypes of family firms; these are already quite prevalent in the business and family business literature. Instead, my goal is to pass on the torch of accumulated knowledge (much of it quite recent) about family firms. It is my hope that readers will take away from *Family Business* a variety of sound managerial, governance, and family practices that will increase the odds that their family-owned or family-controlled corporation will continue from generation to generation.

ORGANIZATION

Part 1 defines the particular characteristics of family-owned and family-controlled businesses and describes the unique challenges faced and advantages enjoyed by these companies. Part 2 personalizes these concepts by presenting the critical leadership tasks for both generations involved in succession and continuity efforts: the CEO, who builds institutions of governance, promotes shareholder loyalty, and then passes the torch to a successor; the CEO spouse or other trusted third party, who promotes trust and family unity and communication; and, finally, the next-generation leaders, who perform the delicate task of respecting the past while advocating change and adaptation with a new vision for the company.

Part 3 is a collection of the family, management, and governance practices that recent research has identified as both protecting family firms from the unique hazards they face and providing for the deployment of their unique sources of competitive advantage. These practices include planning the estate so as to ensure business agility in the next generation, planning strategically for the rejuvenation and continued growth of the business, complementing the skills of the owning family with those of capable nonfamily managers in the top management team, using advisory boards or boards of directors to provide a benchmark and hold management accountable to shareholders, and holding frequent family meetings to facilitate communication and planning.

Part 4 provides glimpses of the future of family businesses, addressing the need for change and adaptation and the leadership required. Recognizing that competitive fitness is not limited to large, management-controlled multi-nationals, it also presents a strategic perspective on growth opportunities for family businesses. Its optimistic assessment of the future of family business is rooted in facts that emerged from the economic developments of the early part of the 21st century.

DIVERSE CASES AND EXERCISES

Cases about family businesses are provided for each major segment of the book. The nine carefully screened cases are as diverse as family businesses themselves. They show both male and female CEOs in the process of passing the torch to female and male next-generation leaders. The businesses represented are geographically diverse, with locations in North America, Latin America, and Europe. They range in size from $15 million to close to $4 billion in annual revenues, and they operate in a wide variety of industries. Owning families are of diverse ethnic backgrounds. The cases are not meant to illustrate either effective or ineffective practices but rather to promote reflection, discussion, and active learning of the concepts presented in the book. Consequently, questions accompany each case to provide a framework for discussion.

I gratefully acknowledge the support that the Fairfax Foundation and the Conway family provided in the preparation of the Fasteners for Retail cases. I am similarly indebted to the Ferré Rangel family for their candor and support in preparing the Ferré Media Group case. For permission to publish "The Cousins Tournament," I am indebted to Kelin Gersick. For reasons of privacy, others who gave consent to publish cases about their family businesses must remain anonymous. Finally, I would like to acknowledge my debt to John H. Davis and Louis B. Barnes, whose study of the Graham family raised some of the notions included in my work.

Exercise questions based on actual company documents, such as a family business constitution, and current family business situations are provided at the end of several chapters. In addition to being used to launch robust class discussions, these exercises, along with the case material, can be assigned as papers, projects, or homework.

TEACHING AND LEARNING

A group of PowerPoint™ presentation slides accompany every chapter, providing instructors with a complete set of basic notes for lectures and providing students with a helpful set of review materials. These slides, which highlight and synthesize key concepts for greater recall, are available for download at http://poza. swlearning.com.

An Instructor's Manual is also available to faculty who adopt *Family Business.* Prepared by book author Ernesto Poza, it has the dual objective of reducing preparation time and making your teaching more effective. It provides comprehensive and integrated teaching support, including notes for all cases. Visit the book's Web site at http://poza.swlearning.com, where you will find links for downloading resources related to this book.

TEXTCHOICE

TextChoice is the home of Thomson Learning's online digital content. TextChoice provides the fastest, easiest way for instructors to create their own learning materials. You may select content from hundreds of our best-selling titles, choose material from one of our databases, and add your own material. Contact your South-Western/Thomson Learning sales representative for more information.

ACKNOWLEDGMENTS

Family Business is ultimately the expression of a community of learning in the field of family business. Back in the early 1980s, this community met often in New York City and included innovators, scholars, and practitioners, like the late Richard Beckhard, then an adjunct professor at the Sloan School of Management at M.I.T.; the late Barbara Hollander, a family therapist; Iván Lansberg, a family business heir and assistant professor at Yale University; John Ward, then professor at Loyola University in Chicago; Elaine Kepner; Matilde Salganicoff; and family business owners George Raymond and Rod Correll. I am indebted to them all. Dr. Léon Danco, the father of family business education and consultation, and Donald Jonovic, at that time Dr. Danco's associate and now an independent family business speaker, consultant, and author, have also influenced my work. Their friendship has been constant and knowledge inspiring.

My practice, as a family business advisor and board member, has vested this book with a unique point of view. My first consulting assignments with family-owned businesses took place in 1979. I owe a world of gratitude to those pioneers—the Grupo Alfa and the Garza family, Thetford Corporation, the Grupo

Salcedo and the Salcedo and Arosemena families, and the M&M Mars division of Mars, Inc. Since then, many other family enterprises have entrusted, to our mutual explorations, their succession planning, strategic growth plans, leadership development, family meetings, and unique approaches to governance. In all cases, these family businesses have been in search of more than solutions—they have been in search of continuity and of excellence. I respect their desire for privacy and thank them all immensely for the opportunity to make a difference. Many of their stories can be found throughout this book.

True innovators in academia have also shaped this book. Dean Emeritus Theodore Alfred, Dean Scott Cowen, and Professor Richard Osborne, all at the Weatherhead School of Management at Case Western Reserve University, invited me to join the faculty, challenged me to perform as a scholar and educator, and provided me with the opportunities for research, teaching, and service that are most responsible for the contents of *Family Business*. Michael Horvitz and the Horvitz family made *Family Business* possible through a generous gift that established the Partnership for Family Business and the Discovery Action Research Project for Family Business. I also want to thank Michael for his continued personal support and encouragement. For reviewing various chapters of the manuscript and preparing helpful critiques, I thank Frederic J. (Rick) Hebert, East Carolina University; Ken Preston, Berkley Center for Entrepreneurship and Innovation, New York University; and Alan G. Weinstein, Canisius College.

Professors Richard Boyatzis, Robert Hisrich, José Rosa, and William Schulze have been important guides in the latter part of my journey. Laura Watt, assistant director of the Partnership for Family Business, organized and supported all the educational programs and the Discovery Action Research Project for Family Business. This book could not have happened without her. Laura's and Michelle Snevel's exceptionally high standards and tremendous commitment to the families in family businesses are responsible for the success of the unique program Family Business: The Next Generation Leadership Institute. The baton is now in Teresa Kabat's able hands. I also want to thank Tracey Messer and Reiko Kishido, doctoral students and research associates who helped with the collection and analysis of Discovery data. Tracey was also a key associate in the writing of two of the cases and one of the chapters in *Family Business*. I am indebted to Associate Professor Susan Hanlon, University of Akron, for her contributions to Chapter 1.

Several chapters of this book were written on the quiet island of Mallorca, Spain. Antonio Barderas, Fernando Casado, and Marilena Jover made it all possible—thank you.

At South-Western/Thomson Learning, I would like to recognize the high standards and extraordinary efforts of John Szilagyi, Judy O'Neill, Emily Gross, and Jeanne Yost. The deadlines were aggressive, and everyone did his or her part to make it all happen.

As a teacher, I always have in the top of my mind the contributions of fellow scholars and practitioners. I want to particularly thank John Davis, Kelin Gersick, and Iván Lansberg. Their groundbreaking social and systemic appreciation of family businesses and their governance is evident throughout the book.

I also want to thank the following people for their thoughts, ideas, encouragement, discussions of pedagogy, and clinical and casual case conversations over the past 20 years: Rick Aberman, Clay Alderfer, Mauricio Alvarez, Craig Aronoff, Joseph Astrachan, Glenn Ayres, Antonio Barderas, Louis B. Barnes, Sidney Barton, Otis Baskin, Peter Baudoin, Nan-b de Gaspé Beaubien, Carmen Bianchi, Vivien Blackford, Anthony Bogod, David Bork, Joyce and Robert Brockhaus, Bonnie Brown, Fredda Herz Brown, Ira Bryck, John Bullard, Katiuska Cabrera-Suárez, Randy Carlock, Fernando Casado, Guido Corbetta, Edwin Cox, Thomas Dandridge, Leslie Dashew, Thomas Davidow, Philip Dawson, Francois deVisscher, Richard Dino, Ernest Doud, Nancy Drozdow, Dennis DuBois, Ann Dugan, Barbara Dunn, Gibb Dyer, John Fast, Michael Fay, Jack Fitzpatrick, Roberto Floren, Alicia Turner Foster, Ellen Frankenberg, Louisa Frederiksen, Claudio Fuchs, Miguel Gallo, Leonard Geiser, Joseph Ginsburg, Joe Goodman, Salo Grabinsky, Bruce Grossman, Sara Hamilton, Wendy Handler, Lee Hausner, Ramona Heck, Edwin Hoover, Frank Hoy, Thomas Hubler, Cindy Iannarelli, Dennis Jaffe, Roxanne Johnson, Sandra Johnson, Ema Juárez, Dirk Jungé, Carlos Kaplún, Paul Karofsky, Robert Kauer, Andrew Keyt, Scott Kunkel, Kacie LaChapelle, Sam Lane, Alden Lank, Peter Leach, Gerald LeVan, Paul Lippert, Mark Litzsinger, Jon Martínez, Gregory McCann, Ruth McClendon, Stephen McClure, Marion McCollom, Christopher McCracken, Drew Mendoza, John Messervey, Robert Middleton, Moni Murdoch, Howard Muson, Ross Nager, Richard Narva, Patricia Nelson, Sharon Nelton, Joseph Paul, Nina Paul, Patrice Persico, David and Joseph Pistrui, George Rimler, Leo Rogers, Mark Rubin, Bruce Sanford, William Sauer, John Schoen, Amy Schuman, Paul Sessions, Pramodita Sharma, Michael Shulman, Marc Silverman, Jordi Solé Tristán, Ritch Sorenson, Olga Staios, Eleni Stavrou, Stephen Swartz, Albert Thomassen, John Troast, Michael Trueblood, Nancy Upton, Marta Vago, Francisco Valera, José Villareal, Karen Vinton, René Werner, Mary Whiteside, Kathy Wiseman, Thomas Zanecchia, Alberto Zanzi, and Gary Zwick.

To my extended family—Hugo, Carmen, Hugo II, Karen, Carlos, Heidi, and the nephews and nieces—I want to say thank you for your love. And to Karen and Kali, I want to express all my love and my thanks for the sacrifices made in support of the writing of this book, for their love, and for their commitment to growth, change, and family unity.

Ernesto J. Poza
Professor for the Practice of Family Business
Director, Partnership with Family Business
Weatherhead School of Management
Case Western Reserve University
Cleveland, Ohio, United States

ABOUT THE AUTHOR

Ernesto J. Poza (BS, Yale University; MBA/MS, Massachusetts Institute of Technology) is an internationally recognized, top-rated speaker and consultant to family-owned businesses. He is Professor for the Practice of Family Business at the Weatherhead School of Management, Case Western Reserve University, where he is also Director of the Partnership with Family Business. As a speaker, he challenges business owners to revitalize mature businesses through strategic thinking, succession planning, and change management. His work has been featured on CNN, NBC, and NPR, as well as in *Fortune Small Business, Family Business Magazine, Inc., Industry Week,* and *Nation's Business.* Poza is on the editorial board of *Family Business Review* and is a contributing editor of *Family Business Magazine.*

In recognition of his contribution to the field of family business, the Family Firm Institute awarded him the Richard Beckhard Practice Award in 1996. His research interests are in the areas of family business continuity, new venture creation, family business governance, leadership of change, and family entrepreneurship. As head of E. J. Poza Associates, a consulting firm based in Chagrin Falls (Cleveland), Ohio, he has advised family-owned, family-controlled, and Fortune 500 companies, including Huber & Co., Mars, Scripps, Grupo Alfa, Grupo Femsa, Grupo Ferré, General Motors, Goodyear, and Atlantic Richfield. He is the author of *Smart Growth: Critical Choices for Business Continuity and Prosperity* (Jossey-Bass Publishers) and *A la sombra del roble: La empresa privada familiar y su continuidad* (Editorial Universitaria).

He is a founding member and Senior Fellow of the Family Firm Institute (http://www.ffi.org) and the creator of a unique program for successors, Family Business: The Next Generation—A Leadership Institute for Owner-Managers and Family Businesses. He serves on the boards of several family-controlled corporations and helps private companies plan for continuity from generation to generation.

PART

DEFINING THE FAMILY BUSINESS

1

FAMILY BUSINESS
WHAT MAKES IT UNIQUE?

Family-owned and family-controlled firms account for between 80 and 95 percent of all incorporated businesses in the United States, where approximately 17 million family firms (including sole proprietorships) operate.[1] A full one-third of all *Fortune 500* companies are family-controlled, and about 60 percent of all publicly traded firms remain under family influence. While many family businesses are small, as of 2001 there were 138 billion-dollar family firms in the United States alone, with 19 such firms operating in France, 15 in Germany, 9 each in Italy and Spain, and 5 each in Canada and Japan.[2] In the United States, family firms account for 49 percent of the gross domestic product, 85 percent of private sector employment, and, along with entrepreneurial firms, about 80 percent of all jobs created in the last two decades. Arguably, family businesses are the primary engine of economic growth and vitality not only in the United States but in free economies all over the world. The contributions of family businesses to the United States and world economies are summarized in Exhibit 1-1.

On the downside, approximately 85 percent of all family businesses fail within their first five years of operation. Among those that survive, only 30 percent are successfully transferred to the second generation of the founding family owners. This high failure rate amounts to the squandering of a significant opportunity for job and wealth creation in many communities. Not all family businesses that are not passed down to the next generation go on to close their doors, but many do.

For her contributions to this chapter, I wish to thank Susan Hanlon, a research scholar at the Weatherhead School of Management, Case Western Reserve University, and associate professor at the University of Akron, who reviewed the literature and provided a fresh perspective on the field.

EXHIBIT 1-1	FAMILY BUSINESS: THE STATISTICAL STORY	
Family businesses constitute	80%–98%	of all businesses in the world's free economies.
Family businesses generate	49%	of the GDP in the United States.
Family businesses generate more than	75%	of the GDP in most other countries.
Family businesses employ	85%	of the U.S. workforce.
Family businesses employ more than	85%	of the working population around the world.
Family businesses created about	80%	of all new jobs in the United States in the last two decades.
A total of	37%	of *Fortune 500* companies are family-controlled.
A total of	60%	of all publicly held U.S. companies are family-controlled.
Number of family-owned businesses in the United States:	17 to 22 million	
Number of U.S. family-owned businesses with annual revenues greater than $25 million:	35,000	

SOURCES: Dreux, Dirk, "Financing Family Business: Alternatives to Selling Out or Going Public," *Family Business Review 3*(3), Fall 1990; Daily, C., & Dollinger, M., "An Empirical Examination of Ownership Structure in Family and Professionally Managed Firms," *Family Business Review 5*(2), 1992; Beehr, T., Drexler, J., & Faulkner, S., "Working in Small Family Businesses: Empirical Comparisons to Nonfamily Businesses," *Journal of Organizational Behavior 18*, 1997; Astrachan, J., & Carey, M., "Family Businesses in the U.S. Economy." Paper presented to the Center for the Study of Taxation. Washington, D.C., 1994; and Oster, S., *Modern Competitive Analysis*, New York: Oxford University Press, 1999.

And the odds get worse in the transition between second and third generations, when only 12 percent of such businesses remain in the same family, seeming to prove true the old adage "from shirtsleeves to shirtsleeves in three generations."[3]

Today, there is a widespread myth that a company is prehistoric and on the road to extinction unless it is "high tech" or has grown to be a very large, diversified multi-national corporation. Ironically, this myth is often promoted by news media that are largely family-controlled; such leading newspapers as the *New York Times* (the Sulzbergers), the *Washington Post* (the Grahams), and the *Wall Street Journal* (the Bancrofts) come to mind. Yet, on the basis of global hypercompetition, many forms of family businesses are thriving. They are the agile, niche-focused, high-quality customer service providers—precisely the profile of so many successful family-controlled businesses. You might be surprised to learn that Smucker's, Perdue Farms, Gap, Levi Strauss, L.L. Bean, Motorola, Mars, Anheuser-Busch, Hallmark, Fidelity Investments, Timken, Marriott, American Greetings, Ford Motor, Kohler, Nordstrom, SC Johnson, Bigelow, and Wal-Mart are all family-owned or -controlled. And then there are thousands of smaller and less well known, but just as successful, family-owned businesses—companies that build homes and office buildings, manufacture unique products, and provide custom services; that are the backbone of most supply chains and distribution channels; and that retail much of what consumers buy.

WHAT CONSTITUTES A FAMILY BUSINESS?

What do we mean by the term *family business*? Its definition is not as easy to come by as you might think.

- In a comprehensive study of family businesses, Chua, Chrisman, and Sharma cited 21 different definitions of *family business* found in their review of 250 research articles.[4]

- Family businesses come in many forms: sole proprietorships, partnerships, limited liability companies, S corporations, C corporations, holding companies, and even publicly traded, albeit family-controlled, companies. That is why estimates of the number of family businesses operating in the U.S. economy range between 17 and 22 million. In the free economies of the world, estimates of all enterprises considered family businesses range between 80 and 98 percent.

- In a large-scale study of the role of family contractual relationships within the Spanish newspaper industry, a business was considered to be a family business if the last name of the CEO and/or the editor was the same as that of the owners.[5]

- Another recent empirical study took the position that family firms are theoretically distinct from other closely held firms because of the influence of altruism on agency relationships (relationships between shareholders and management). The authors of this study went on to say that family firms are differentiated by both the active involvement of family in firm management and the intent of family members to retain ownership of the firm. They ultimately defined a family business as an enterprise where two or more family members hold 15 percent or more of the ownership, where family members are employed in the business, and where the family intends to retain control of the firm in the future.[6]

- A more recent article ascribed the uniqueness of a family business to the very different influence that family has on ownership, governance, and management participation; the experience reflected in the generation in charge; and the organizational culture embedded in the enterprise.[7]

Taking into account this full range of research and analyses, this text considers family businesses as constituting the whole gamut of enterprises where an entrepreneur or later-generation CEO and one or more family members influence the firm. They influence it via their participation, their ownership control, their strategic preferences, and the culture and values they impart to the enterprise. *Participation* refers to the nature of the involvement of family members in the enterprise, whether as part of the management team, as board members, as shareholders, or as supportive members of the family foundation. *Control* refers to the rights and responsibilities family members derive from significant voting ownership and the governance of the agency relationship. *Strategic preferences* refers to the direction family members set for the enterprise through their participation in top management, consulting, the board of directors, or even family councils. *Culture* is the collection of values, defined by behaviors, that become embedded in an enterprise as a result of the leadership provided by family members, past and present. Family unity and the nature of the relationship between the family and the business also define the culture.

This book, therefore, adopts an inclusive theoretical definition of a family business that focuses on the vision, intentions, and behaviors, vis-à-vis succession, of the owners. Ownership structure aside, what differentiate family businesses from management-controlled businesses are often the intentions, values, and strategy-influencing interactions of owners who are members of the same family. The result is a unique blending of family, management, and ownership subsystems to form an entire family business system. This family-management-ownership interaction can produce significant adaptive capacity and competitive advantage. Or it can be the source of significant vulnerability in the face of generational or competitive change. The dominant decisions in a family business, according to this inclusive theoretical definition, are "controlled by members of the same family or a small number of families in a manner that is potentially sustainable across generations of the family or families."[8]

Thus, we arrive at a working definition of a family business. A family business is a unique synthesis of the following:

1. Ownership control (15 percent or higher) by two or more members of a family or a partnership of families
2. Strategic influence by family members on the management of the firm, whether by being active in management, by continuing to shape the culture, or by serving as advisors or board members
3. Concern for family relationships
4. The dream (or possibility) of continuity across generations

The following characteristics define the essence of the distinctiveness of family firms:

1. The presence of the family
2. The owner's dream of keeping the business in the family (the objective of business continuity from generation to generation)
3. The overlap of family, management, and ownership, with its zero-sum (win-lose) propensities, which render family businesses particularly vulnerable during succession
4. The unique sources of competitive advantage derived from the interaction of family, management, and ownership, especially when family unity is high

BUILDING FAMILY BUSINESSES THAT LAST

Without vision and leadership from members of two generations and the use of select family, management, and governance practices, the future is bleak for family-controlled enterprises. The blurring of boundaries among family membership, family management, and family ownership subjects family businesses to the potential for confusion, slow decision making, or even corporate paralysis. An inability to adapt to changes in the competitive marketplace or powerlessness to govern the relationship between the family and the business will ultimately undermine the enterprise. As a result, a family business that lacks multi-generational leadership and vision can hardly be positioned to retain the competitive advantages that made it successful in a previous, often more entrepreneurial, generation.

Building a family business so that it continues takes ongoing dialogue across generations of owner-managers about their vision for the company. Family businesses that have been built to last recognize the tension between preserving and protecting the core of what has made the business successful on the one hand and promoting growth and adaptation to changing competitive dynamics on the other.[9] Family businesses capable of succession planning, confident that each generation will responsibly bring a different but complementary vision to the business, have a foundation on which to build continuity. A set of best management and governance practices has been identified by studying such businesses.

FAMILY BUSINESS RESEARCH

The field of study of family enterprises goes back only to 1975, when entrepreneur, family business educator, and consultant Dr. Léon Danco published his pioneering work, *Beyond Survival: A Guide for the Business Owner and His Family*.[10] Two watershed events played key roles in turning the study of family business into a field:

1. The publication of a special issue of the journal *Organizational Dynamics* in 1979[11]
2. The launching of a specialized journal, *Family Business Review*, in 1986[12]

Still, between 1975 and the early 1990s, most of the published work on family businesses was anecdotal, rooted in the stories of consultants and observers of these mostly privately held enterprises. Only in the last decade has research begun to both address the unique characteristics of family-owned and family-controlled businesses and struggle with the definition of this form of enterprise.

Notwithstanding the absence of research on this unique form of organization, family businesses most likely constitute the earliest form of enterprise. Whenever parents, engaged in making a craft, cultivating the soil, or even ruling a country, welcomed members of the next generation as helping hands in the pursuit of that enterprise, a family business was born.

Today, family businesses are considered by many to be on the cutting edge of corporate performance, job creation, return on investment, quality of product and service, flexibility, customization capability, and speed to market.[13] They are also well known for their vulnerability to decline after the retirement or demise of the founding entrepreneurial generation.[14] The agency cost literature has traditionally argued that, when owners hire managers or agents, additional oversight and control mechanisms are required, resulting in an increase in enterprise management costs.[15] More recent literature argues that agency costs are significant for family companies as a result of CEO entrenchment, conflict avoidance, and altruism.[16] Measuring the perceptions of different stakeholders, monitoring executive performance, and implementing a particular set of managerial and governance practices all contribute to controlling the proposed costs and to procuring resources that can actually accrue competitive advantage to family firms.[17]

The Discovery Action Research Project is a longitudinal study, conducted in the form of "action research," with companies participating in the Partnership with Family Business at the Weatherhead School of Management, Case Western Reserve University, and in family business programs at the University of Pittsburgh and the University of St. Thomas. Its findings suggest both safeguards that can prevent higher agency costs and resources and capabilities that can provide unique benefits to family firms. Both the safeguards and the sources of competitive advantage will be discussed in the chapters that follow, but it seemed appropriate to introduce the project here and to say something about its scope since we will connect many of our later discussions to it.

The action research conducted by project researchers constituted an iterative process of diagnosis, feedback, and collaborative action with members of participating firms and families. The sample for this study included 868 executives and family members who were involved over the past eight years in 90 businesses. Specifically, the sample was made up of 303 family members in the business (68 percent of family members), 145 family members not active in the management of the business (32 percent of family members), and 420 nonfamily managers. Of those family member respondents who identified their position in the family, 90 were CEOs (22 percent), 48 were CEO spouses (12 percent), 111 were sons (27 percent), 73 were daughters (18 percent), and 84 were "other" (21 percent). This "other" category included siblings of the CEO, sons- and daughters-in-law, nephews, and nieces.

THE SYSTEMS THEORY PERSPECTIVE

Systems theory is the theoretical approach first used in the scholarly study of family business. It remains pervasive in the literature today. In the systems theory approach, the family firm is modeled as comprising the three overlapping, interacting, and interdependent subsystems of family, management, and ownership.[18] According to the open-systems model graphically represented in Exhibit 1-2, each subsystem maintains boundaries that separate it from the other subsystems and the general external environment within which the family firm operates.[19] In

EXHIBIT 1-2   THE SYSTEMS THEORY MODEL OF FAMILY BUSINESS

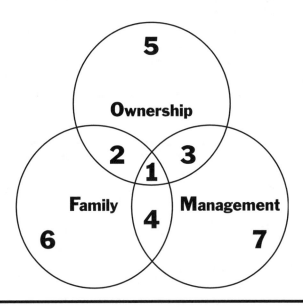

SOURCES: Adapted from Gersick, K., Lansberg, I., Davis, J., & McCollum, M., *Generation to Generation,* Boston: Harvard Business School Press, 1997; and Churchill, N., & Hatten, K., "Non-Market-Based Transfers of Wealth and Power," *American Journal of Small Business 11*(3), pp. 51–64, 1987.

order for the organization to perform optimally, the subsystems must be integrated so that there is unified functioning of the entire system.[20] General systems theory also suggests that, in order to reverse the natural progression toward entropy or decline, the three subsystems and the larger family business system all have to increase their requisite variety (internal capabilities) in order to successfully cope with increasing variety in the environment.

This model suggests that a family firm is best understood and studied as a complex and dynamic social system in which integration is achieved through reciprocal adjustments among subsystems. For this reason, the family subsystem is expected to have a strong impact on the ownership and management subsystems, and vice versa. One subsystem cannot be understood separate from the entire system within which it exists. Understanding comes when all three subsystems, with their interactions and interdependencies, are studied in their totality as one system. Emphasis in this research stream is appropriately focused on the interactions of the three subsystems and on the integration mechanisms used to determine outcomes of the larger system that provide mutual benefits to all system members.

Depending on the positions they have in the system, individual perspectives of members of the family and the firm will understandably be different. That is, a parent who is CEO and 100-percent owner of the firm (represented by position 1 in Exhibit 1-2) will likely view things very differently than will a family member who is not active in management and does not own any shares in the business (position 6). Similarly, a nonfamily manager (position 7) is likely to have a very different perspective on whatever situation the firm or family is facing, as a result of her or his unique placement in the family business system.

In its more extreme forms, this phenomenon leads to categorization of family businesses based on their propensity to have a family-first, ownership-first, or management-first perspective on issues. As a result of this propensity, priority may be given to that particular subsystem over others, and even over the entire system. In other words, in its most extreme forms, this phenomenon can lead to significant suboptimization of the family-ownership-management system commonly known as a family business. This suboptimization leads, theoretically, to a lower level of performance than the family business is capable of achieving.

BLURRED SYSTEM BOUNDARIES

Because of the complexity implicit in a system that is composed of three subsystems, each potentially with different goals and operating principles, family businesses are vulnerable to suffering the consequences of blurred boundaries among the family, ownership, and management subsystems. Research in the social sciences—both psychology and economics, for example—suggests that emotion can lead to behaviors and actions that rational thought would seldom support. As a result, family patterns or dynamics, replete with emotional content, can easily override the logic of business management or ownership rents.

Lack of awareness on the part of company employees or family members that the particular assumptions that go into decision making are based on whether an issue is considered a family, ownership, or management issue may create incongruent policies and untenable decisions. In the most extreme, but still quite common, circumstances, family rules may overtake the business. For instance, suppose a younger son insists on starting work after 10 A.M. every day, despite the requirement that, as a customer service manager, he report to work by 7 A.M. His father or aunt, to whom he reports, may choose to avoid the conflict and anxiety his tardiness provokes by ignoring it and allowing it to go on. Avoiding resolution of this disagreement out of fear or altruism only diminishes problem-solving ability; unchecked, problems can grow for years. Succession hurls many of these avoided and unsettled issues to the forefront of family business management, often at a very vulnerable time in the life of a family business.

The absence of balance and clear boundaries between family, ownership, and management is not always resolved by putting the family first. To the contrary, business management or ownership could just as easily be favored in decision making and action taking, again to the detriment of the whole family business system.

FAMILY-FIRST BUSINESSES. In family-first family businesses, employment in the business is a birthright. The stereotype of nepotism, which still dominates most people's views of family businesses, derives from this not-so-infrequent suboptimization of the family business system. Clearly, if employment is based solely on the applicant's last name, merit and other important criteria in the selection and succession processes are devalued or entirely irrelevant. Understandably, nonfamily managers with high career aspirations are often reluctant to join family businesses out of concern for their future prospects. Unless their exercise of due diligence assures them that their career ambitions will not be thwarted by a lack of family connection, high-potential nonfamily managers may choose never to join family-owned or family-controlled firms.

Because a family-first family business exists primarily for the purposes of the family, perks that transfer from the business to family members are often extensive. Financial systems may be obtuse by design, and secrecy is often paramount. After all, lack of transparency supports the ability of family members to reap rewards beyond what would be deemed reasonable under standard human resource, compensation, and benefit policies. Consequently, the business often becomes part of a lifestyle. The Rigas family and Adelphia Communications were ultimately prosecuted by the SEC and other federal and state authorities as a result of a tangled web of relationships between the business and the family that were deemed to represent extensive self-dealing to the benefit of Rigas family members. (See the Adelphia Communications case in the Cases section at the end of Part 2.)

While well-managed and well-governed family businesses may have sound reasons for paying all the members of the next generation in top management equal or nearly equal salaries, family-first businesses are prone to equalize compensation regardless of responsibility, results, and overall merit. Ironically, because their primary concern is family, the level of commitment of family-first businesses to the continuity of the business across generations depends on the agendas of individual family members and the levels of conflict associated with running the business. Family-first businesses are likely to choose continuity only if members of both generations aspire to this goal and if the current generation has sufficient resources in retirement to make this possible. In cases where neither generation dreams of continuity or sees value in having the enterprise be a legacy for the next generation, the business will most likely be sold at the end of a generation. And, even if family members aspire to perpetuate the company, family-first businesses have great difficulty in providing for continuity, since successor selection, strategic renewal, and governance of the relationship between family and business all require a strong commitment to sound business management principles.

MANAGEMENT-FIRST BUSINESSES. Management-first family businesses are likely to actively discourage family members (especially in-laws) from working in the business and/or to require work experience outside the business as a prerequisite for employment. The performance of employed family members is reviewed in the same manner as the performance of nonfamily managers, and human resource policies generally apply equally to family and nonfamily employees. Compensation is based on responsibility and performance, not position in the family hierarchy. And the scorecard on business performance is all business; for example, the focus is on profitability, return on assets, market share, revenue growth, and return on equity. Once in the company, next-generation family members are often viewed in terms of how they will be able to manage and grow the firm—in other words, in terms of their utility and potential contribution to the business.

When family members meet socially, the conversation often turns to business subjects. Family events—even weddings and honeymoons—are sometimes arranged (as in the movie *Sabrina*), canceled, or delayed for business reasons. There is no automatic commitment to family business continuity among management-first companies, because the enterprise is seen as a productive asset. As an asset, it could just as easily be folded into a larger company through a tax-free exchange of stock with a publicly traded corporation or sold through an employee stock ownership plan.

OWNERSHIP-FIRST BUSINESSES. In ownership-first family businesses, investment time horizons and perceived risk are the most significant issues. When shareholders come first, the priority is risk-adjusted economic returns or owner rents—for instance, shareholder value, EBITDA, earnings growth rates, and debt/equity and debt/asset ratios.

Ownership-first family businesses have shorter time frames within which financial results are evaluated. Just as impatient and greedy investors on Wall Street, aided by analysts and the media, can pressure well-managed publicly traded companies into short-term thinking, family shareholders inactive in the business, with little understanding of management and the time cycles involved in new strategies or new investments, can hamper effective operation of a family-controlled business. They can cause it to lose the founding culture, which valued the role of patient capital.

Patient capital—one of the significant advantages of many family businesses—disappears at the hands of greedy shareholders. Siblings and cousins, caught in the web of high expectations for short-term returns via dividends, distributions, or the creation of shareholder value, are prone to second-guess family members in management. Family managers, who better understand the limited capabilities of the business to deliver on the promise of high returns, are most likely managing in the long-term interest of shareholders. If family unity suffers as a result of this pressure by some family members for high returns and short time frames, a loss of will and vision may result. Family business continuity may be abandoned in favor of immediately recapturing, via sale of the company, the value created by previous generations.

THE ALTERNATIVE TO BLURRED SYSTEM BOUNDARIES: JOINT OPTIMIZATION

Implicit in systems theory is the capacity to jointly optimize interrelated subsystems in such a way that the larger system can be most effective and successful in the pursuit of its goals. Intuitively, reaching this state would seem akin to reaching nirvana and equally difficult. Yet thousands of family businesses, many of them featured throughout this book, achieve precisely that. They balance the goals and needs of each of the subsystems in what appears to be a masterful walk across a tightrope. Through family forums, governance bodies, strong cultures, family unity, strategic planning, fair policies, and solid managerial practices, they inspire a commitment to something larger than the self—the greater good.

Companies facilitate joint optimization of family, management, and ownership subsystems by writing employment policies that guide the employment of family members in the business. They further optimize the relationship by developing participation policies that guide the involvement of family members in nonmanagement roles—for example, board service, philanthropy, and family council leadership. As a result, some family members join the business as employees, while others become responsible shareholders and stewards of the family's resources.

In these companies, the performance of employed family members is reviewed in the same manner as that of nonfamily managers, with compensation decisions based on both level of responsibility and performance. Siblings or cousins in the same generation may, therefore, receive quite different salaries and benefit packages. Other firms engaged in joint optimization may pay a team rate, equalizing compensation in the interest of promoting overall corporate—and not just divisional or business unit—responsibility. Family members are encouraged to work outside the business first to get some experience. If they later join the family business, their development for top leadership is often a priority. When family members meet, the pendulum is allowed to swing back and forth between family and business priorities. These families realize that such a flexible and balanced approach allows them to invest in the subsystems in ways that, in the long run, benefit the larger system: the family business.

These families and firms have a commitment to family business continuity. Efforts to jointly optimize ownership, family, and management systems often indicate the family's desire to use the business as a vehicle for the transfer of important values and a proud history and at the same time strive for continued improvement and growth. In these companies, ownership and organizational structures accommodate both the family-ownership strategy and the competitive strategy of the business.

Edgepark Surgical, a leading family-owned medical device distribution company led by the Harrington family and a team of very capable nonfamily managers, has developed a statement of company culture and values that displays a deep understanding of the powerful effects of joint optimization. Its culture and values statement says:

We are:

- Family-Owned, Professionally Managed. We are a family acting in the Company's best interest.

We believe in:

- Integrity: We do what we say we will do.
- No Walls: We have no barriers to communication.
- Tenacity: We have an unrelenting determination to reach objectives.
- Profitability: We are committed to performance and results.
- Improvement: We are never satisfied.
- Service: We are loyal to our customers and respect them.

THE AGENCY THEORY PERSPECTIVE

Traditionally, agency theory has argued that the natural alignment of owners and managers (the agents) decreases the need for formal supervision of agents and for elaborate governance mechanisms, thus reducing agency costs of ownership in family firms. More recently, however, agency theory has been used to support the opposite position. Researchers have concluded that family firms have one of the more costly forms of organizational governance. They posit that the altruism of owner-managers leads to increased agency costs emanating from their inability to manage conflict among owners and between owner-managers and nonfamily managers.[21] Other researchers have concluded that the relational contract created when family ties exist between owners and agents is a source of increased agency costs due primarily to executive entrenchment.[22] Other potential sources of agency costs are attributed by both sides to goal incongruity between the CEO and the rest of the family: (1) the CEO's ability to hold out, based on his or her status within the family, (2) avoidance of strategic planning because of its potential for fostering familial conflict, (3) lack of career opportunities for nonfamily agents, (4) lack of monitoring of family members' performance, (5) lack of monitoring of firm's performance, and (6) preference for less business risk. Strategic decisions that could highlight potential conflicts of interest between a firm's shareholders and its owner-managers include decisions about diversification, rate of growth, debt intensity, investment, CEO compensation, and CEO tenure or entrenchment.

Research suggests that such costs may be controlled or avoided through the use of certain managerial and governance practices. Some researchers recommend a mechanism that would enable a family business to monitor the performance and decision making of family executives.[23] Others believe that a set of managerial practices, as opposed to any one specific practice, will facilitate control of these unique agency costs.[24]

According to agency theory, a firm's board is an important mechanism for limiting managers' self-serving behavior in situations where a firm's managers and its owners have conflicting goals. For this reason, experts on corporate governance recommend inclusion of outside directors as lead or presiding directors on corporate boards to ensure the board's independence from top management. This recommendation is based on the belief that inside directors, by virtue of their employment with the firm, are beholden to a CEO for their careers and are therefore unlikely to monitor the CEO's actions effectively. In contrast, outside directors are expected to provide more vigilant monitoring in order to maintain their reputations and avoid liability lawsuits.

COMPETITIVE CHALLENGES FACED BY FAMILY BUSINESSES

My experience both as a scholar and as an advisor to over 100 family-owned businesses for the past two decades substantiates what business owners often perceive as a set of perils posing unique challenges to their businesses. For example, many owners see shrinking product life cycles as requiring their companies to innovate more and to adapt and renew their strategies more frequently. They also perceive intense cost competition and rapid change in distribution and value chains as requiring tremendous agility and, thus, as representing serious challenges to their firms.

Family business owners are also well aware of the increasing individualism of younger generations, who often relate to the concepts of extended family and legacy as if they were alien constructs. Owners are equally concerned by the media's version of who the winners are in globally competitive markets. According to the media, large multi-national, publicly traded companies (and, until 2000, dotcoms) are the only possible winners in the increasingly competitive landscape. This bias concerns many family owners, who fear that the next generation of owners is growing up thinking that family businesses are defunct and the exciting career opportunities lie elsewhere.

On the other hand, next-generation members are often concerned about what they perceive as the entrenchment of the current-generation CEO. In an age where life expectancy has increased significantly, fears about entrenchment may be difficult to displace. Both generations worry that the growing complexity and severity of tax and estate tax laws may predispose owners to make tax minimization a priority, to the detriment of other important considerations like agility and corporate control.

It is important to note that the agency cost studies referred to earlier did not include a comparative nonfamily business sample. Thus, these studies highlighted possible agency costs of altruism and CEO entrenchment in family firms but failed to address the relative impact of a different set of agency costs on nonfamily firms (e.g., the increased costs of sophisticated financial and auditing systems and staff). Indeed, an equally viable possibility is that the unique differences provided by family ownership and control are a source of competitive advantage. In other words, the agency cost literature has not yet helped to resolve the quandary of whether agency costs hinder family firms or whether the interaction between business and family represents a potential competitive advantage.

COMPETITIVE ADVANTAGE: THE RESOURCE-BASED VIEW

The competitive advantages inherent in family businesses are best explained by the resource-based view of organizations. From this theoretical perspective, a firm is examined for the specific complex, dynamic, and intangible resources that are unique to it. These resources, often referred to as organizational competencies embedded in internal processes, human resources, or other intangible assets, can provide the firm with competitive advantages in certain circumstances. In a family firm, one of these resources may be overlapping owner and manager responsibilities, which can lead to advantages derived from streamlined and efficient monitoring mechanisms. The advantages could include reduced administrative costs, speedy decision making, and longer time horizons for measuring firm performance.

Other resources unique to family firms may be customer-intense relationships, which are supported by an organizational culture committed to high quality and good customer service, and the transfer of knowledge and skills from one generation to the next, which makes it easier to sustain and even improve firm performance.[25] Ownership commitment (willingness to hold on and fight) over the long term, rather than shareholder apathy and capital flight (readiness to switch from IBM shares to GE shares in the portfolio), is yet another possible source of competitive advantage. The Ford, Hewlett, and Packard families have all recently exemplified this potentially unique resource in their ownership stance vis-à-vis CEO performance.

The unique resources that family businesses can call on to create competitive advantage are summarized in the following list:

- Overlapping responsibilities of owners and managers, along with small company size, enable rapid speed to market.
- Concentrated ownership structure leads to higher overall corporate productivity.
- Focus on customers and market niches results in higher returns on investment.
- Desire to protect the family name and reputation often translates into high product/service quality and higher returns on investment.
- The nature of the family-ownership-management interaction, family unity, and ownership commitment support patient capital, lower administrative costs, skills/knowledge transfer, and agility in rapidly changing markets.

For a comparative view of the data supporting the unique competitive advantages of family firms, refer to Exhibit 1-3. The ability of a particular family business to capitalize on these advantages depends on the quality of the interaction between business and family. It is precisely this interface that agency theorists suggest needs to be addressed with a series of managerial and governance practices that will safeguard the firm from any family-based hazards. Measuring the perceptions of different stakeholders, monitoring executive performance, and implementing a particular set of prescribed managerial and governance practices can all contribute to controlling the hypothesized costs and turning the unique features of family firms into resources that actually produce competitive advantage.

The importance of (1) jointly optimizing the ownership, management, and family subsystems, (2) controlling agency costs, and (3) ultimately exploiting the unique resources available to family businesses in order to achieve competitive advantage provides the theoretical framework for this textbook. In the chapters that follow, managerial, family, and governance practices aimed at achieving competitive advantage are explained and discussed. Because of the

EXHIBIT 1-3 COMPETITIVE ADVANTAGES OF FAMILY BUSINESSES ON SEVEN DIMENSIONS

I. Speed to Market

Market	Company Size (in sales)	Time to Bring New Product to Market (in months)
United States	> $100 million	22.6 months
	< $100 million	16.0 months
In Japan	> $100 million	19.1 months
	< $100 million	14.0 months
In Europe	> $100 million	23.4 months
	< $100 million	15.9 months

SOURCE: Boston Consulting Group, http://www.bcg.com.

II. Strategic Focus on Niches

Market Size	Business Performance (as measured by ROI)*
<$50 million	28.1%
$50 to $100 million	26.8%
$100 to $250 million	24.2%
<$1 billion	10.9%

*4-year average ROI.

SOURCE: Clifford, D., & Cavanagh, R., *The Winning Performance: How America's High Growth Midsize Companies Succeed*, New York: Bantam, 1985.

III. Ownership Concentration and Corporate Productivity

Stock concentration is positively correlated with

- Related diversification
- R&D expenses/employee
- Training expenses/employee
- Overall corporate productivity

SOURCE: Hill, C., & Snell, S., "Effects of Ownership Structure and Control on Corporate Productivity," *Academy of Management Journal* 32(1), pp. 25–45, 1989.

IV. Relative Quality and Return on Investment

Relative Product Quality	Return on Investment (as measured by ROI)*
High	27.1%
Medium	19.8%
Low	16.8%

*4-year average ROI.

SOURCE: Clifford, D., & Cavanagh, R., *The Winning Performance: How America's High Growth Midsize Companies Succeed*, New York: Bantam, 1985.

(continued)

| EXHIBIT 1-3 | COMPETITIVE ADVANTAGES OF FAMILY BUSINESSES ON SEVEN DIMENSIONS *(continued)* |

V. Patient Capital and Long-Term Perspective

- Average tenure of 18 years for owner-managers vs. 8 years for public company CEOs is correlated with commitment to the long term and making efficient long-term investments in the family business.[1]

- Company continually optimizes the mix among family, management, employees, customers, and ownership for higher long-term profitability.[2]

[1]Daily, C., & Dollinger, M., "An Empirical Examination of Ownership Structure in Family and Professionally Managed Firms," *Family Business Review* 5(2), 1992; and James, H., "Owner as Manager, Extended Horizons and the Family Firm," *International Journal of the Economics of Business* 6(1), 1999.

[2]Adapted from Waterman, Robert H., Jr., *What America Does Right*, New York: W. W. Norton and Company, 1994.

VI. Total Costs

	Family Businesses	Other Businesses
Lower cost of capital[1]	When the business owner controls 100% of the stock and the stock is in the hands of family shareholders enjoying family harmony, the effective cost of capital is nearly 0%. While there is an opportunity cost, cash flow from the business can be reinvested for growth without paying out high dividends or taxes or incurring high interest on debt.	Financing costs for other businesses can range from 25–30% for venture capital to 17–20% for mezzanine financing to the prime rate for bank financing.
Lower administrative costs[2]	According to the agency cost literature, the overlap between owner and manager or principal and agent allows family-owned businesses to enjoy lower administrative costs because of lower CEO compensation, reduced levels of supervision, and reduced investment in financial systems and controls.	

[1]deVisscher, Francois, "When Shareholders Lose Their Patience," *Family Business Magazine*, Autumn 2000.

[2]Gomez-Mejía, L., Larraza-Kintana, M., & Makri, M., "The Determinants of Executive Compensation in Family-Controlled Public Corporations," *Academy of Management Journal* (in press).

VII. Agility and Customization Capability in Rapidly Changing Markets

- Inventory and quality costs of capital-intensive, long-run manufacturing have increased in the last decade. The greater flexibility of new manufacturing and distribution-retail-service technology (including numerical control equipment in the factory and low-cost PCs in distribution centers and retail points) makes smaller runs economically attractive.

- Increasing demand for customization, rapid changes in consumer preferences, and shorter product life cycles lead to rewards for opportunity-seeking owner-managers who can make decisions fast.

- EDI/Internet-based, value-added partnerships in the supply chain make agility possible across the value chain. An early example was the Milliken–Levi Strauss–Dillards supply chain agreement in the early 1980s.

SOURCE: Poza, E., "Look Who's Out There on the Cutting Edge," *Family Business Magazine* 4(1), Winter 1993.

key role that the CEO plays as the architect of the platform for competitiveness and continuity, Chapter 2 will address the mandate of current-generation CEOs to build institutions of governance and manage the transfer of power in family businesses.

SUMMARY

1. Family businesses are the primary engine of economic growth and vitality in free economies all over the world. Being unique in their attributes, they are unique in the assets and vulnerabilities that they bring to the marketplace.

2. Family businesses constitute the whole gamut of enterprises where an entrepreneur or next-generation CEO and one or more family members influence the firm via their participation, their ownership control, their strategic preferences, and the culture and values they impart to the enterprise.

3. Family businesses that have been built to last recognize the tension between preserving and protecting the core of what has made the business successful and promoting growth and adaptation to changing competitive dynamics.

4. The Discovery Action Research Project is a longitudinal study whose findings suggest both safeguards that can prevent higher agency costs and resources and capabilities that can provide unique benefits to family firms.

5. In the systems theory approach, the family firm is modeled as comprising three overlapping, interacting, and interdependent subsystems of family, management, and ownership, making possible significant adaptive capacity and competitive advantage through joint optimization. The boundaries between these subsystems present unique challenges, with migration across the boundaries being seldom illegal but often highly problematic for the long-term financial health, competitive fitness, and continuity of the business across generations of the same owning family.

6. Agency theory has recently been used to argue that family firms have one of the more costly forms of organizational governance. Increased agency costs result from owner-managers' inability to manage conflict, executive entrenchment, lack of performance monitoring, and a preference for less business risk, among other things. A firm's board is an important mechanism for limiting managers' self-serving behavior in situations where a firm's managers and its owners have conflicting goals.

7. The resource-based view of family businesses holds that competitive advantages result from (1) overlapping responsibilities of owners and managers and small company size, enabling rapid speed to market; (2) focus on customers and market niches, resulting in higher returns on investment; (3) concentrated ownership structure, leading to higher corporate productivity; (4) desire to protect the family name and reputation, translating into high-quality products/services; and (5) family-ownership-management interaction, family unity, and ownership commitment supporting patient capital, lower administrative costs, skills/knowledge transfer between generations, and agility in rapidly changing markets. A prescribed set of management and governance practices will help the firm capitalize on these resources.

LEADING THE FAMILY BUSINESS

∎

2

FIRST LEADERSHIP IMPERATIVE

THE MANDATE TO BUILD INSTITUTIONS OF
GOVERNANCE AND MANAGE THE TRANSFER OF POWER

Clearly, CEOs of family businesses have a mandate to drive the success of their businesses. Without the commitment to optimizing potential, any enterprise is likely to wither. But are family business CEOs fulfilling the longer term mandate of institutionalizing the enterprise?

THE CEO AS ARCHITECT OF GOVERNANCE

Blurred system boundaries, as discussed in Chapter 1, present the strongest case for the need to build institutions to govern the relationships among family, ownership, and management of the business. If family rules become business rules, or vice versa, conflict is avoided; however, problem-solving ability is diminished, and agency costs are incurred. And if this pattern continues for too long, no amount of succession planning can ensure the continuity of the business to the next generation.

Unfortunately, the critical need to build institutions of governance is often lost on the CEO. That CEOs of family businesses perceive both the business and the family much more favorably than do the rest of the family and nonfamily managers is the most statistically significant finding of the Discovery Action Research Project, a longitudinal research study of close to 100 family businesses, conducted by the Partnership for Family Business at the Weatherhead School of Management, Case Western Reserve University.[1] The findings further indicate that CEO-parents perceive the business significantly more positively than do other family members along all these dimensions: business planning, succession planning, communication, growth orientation, career opportunities, and the effectiveness of their boards.

On the family front, these same owner-managers are more satisfied with how the employment of family members and their participation in the business are being handled. CEOs perceive greater clarity and understanding among family members of succession standards and processes and the manner in which the estate and business ownership will be transferred across generations. CEO-parents also perceive the relationships among family members more positively and feel that expression of differences are encouraged to a greater degree than do other family members. CEO-parents are significantly more positive in their assessment of the extent to which younger generation managers in the business are listened to and their ideas given consideration. These findings indicate that older-generation managers may well be unaware of the concerns harbored by other members of the firm and the family—or perhaps they just appreciate them with a perspective unavailable to the rest of the usually younger family members and nonfamily managers.

It is not surprising that the more positive perceptions held by CEOs apply not only to the firm but also to family-related subjects. This highly congruent finding suggests that any efforts by advisors on the board or by consultants to family businesses will face resistance from the CEO on two interrelated fronts—family and firm—both of which are relevant to continuity planning in the firm.

These are not surprising findings, given the tremendous autonomy of CEOs of family-owned businesses and how little feedback these CEOs generally receive on their performance from either family members or key nonfamily managers. The power implicit in being the top manager, principal owner, and head or partner of the family limits and changes the nature of the information provided to the CEO-parent.

CEOs are also significantly more sure that the length of time the present chief executive officer will continue in this role is understood. This finding supports the observation that many more CEOs *think* about retiring or changing their responsibilities than *act* on it. Few actually make announcements or behave in a way that commits them to a transfer of power within a specified period of time.

On all of the dimensions measured, CEO-parents have a more positive perception than do younger members of the family, particularly those 41 to 50 years old who are working in the business. CEOs' perceptions may be skewed by their own success, and they may have difficulty seeing problems in what they have created and continue to manage. Or they may be in a life stage where the problem-finding/ solving efforts in which others continue to engage assume a less important role than making peace with one's dream and one's family.

Recognizing the existence and magnitude of the differences between CEO owner-managers and the rest of the family and nonfamily managers in the business is an important step in increasing a CEO's understanding of his or her firm and family. Results of the Discovery study consistently reinforce the central role of the CEO and parent as architect of the systems, culture, and practices of both firm and family. Thus, a CEO's positive bias may implicitly depreciate others' views, resulting in a decreased ability to detect problems. It may also threaten the retention of key nonfamily managers and members of the next generation of owner-managers and thus even thwart the adaptation and very survival of the business.

It may be that, simply because CEOs know more about what is in place and planned, they perceive things more positively than do those who lack that knowledge and are dissatisfied with not knowing. Another, perhaps more important implication is that they are much more satisfied with what they have created than are others key to the business. They are also much less likely to experience sufficient dissatisfaction with the status quo to want to change anything, even if it is in the best interests of family business continuity. This lack of motivation by the CEO may thwart efforts to promote the readiness of the next generation and to build the institutions necessary to govern the relationship between the family and the business in the future.

What kinds of governing institutions do CEOs need to build? Research on best practices indicates that a board of directors/advisory board, a family council, a family assembly, an annual shareholders' meeting, and a management team that includes a number of top-notch nonfamily managers can all play a role in improving the family-management-shareholder interaction. (These institutions of family business governance will be thoroughly discussed in the chapters that follow, so no additional detail will be provided here.) Only after constructing an infrastructure founded on these governing institutions can the CEO architect confidently proceed with his or her plan to transfer power to the next generation.

THE TRANSFER OF POWER

Chief executives preparing to transfer power do not, single-handedly, have to make succession happen. They may not even have to be among those working hard to make it happen. But, to be sure, they have to be the architects of the transition and then know when to get out of the way, letting the engineers, contractors, and tradespeople (advisors, staff, and next-generation members) take over. There is evidence from several studies, however, that CEOs in family-controlled companies are prone to longer tenures and even entrenchment. By not making way for the torchbearers of the future, these CEOs tend to create serious weaknesses in the company's ability to continue across generations.[2]

Transferring power has never been easy in any setting. Successful, smooth transitions are one of the reasons General Electric is such an admired company. GE develops general management thoroughly and broadly. And, periodically (though not very often), it supports the orderly transfer of power to the next-generation manager, as Jack Welch did in 2001.

For many, the drive for power is as much a life force as the need to achieve and to be loved. In the family business, transfer of power is further complicated by the demands of family relationships and the sheer potency of ownership. In other words, transfer of power in the family business is not just a matter of passing the managerial baton on to the next generation, as at GE, but also a matter of passing on the flaming torch of family leadership and the golden mallet of ownership control. Many stories of failed successions in privately held and family-controlled companies reflect the difficulty of doing all three of these things within a reasonable period of time. The Bingham dynasty of Louisville, Kentucky, ended in 1986. Barry Bingham, Jr., had been appointed president of the Louisville *Courier-Journal* years earlier, but in the mid-1980s his father, Barry Bingham, Sr., still retained majority control, voted his daughters onto the board of directors, and eventually decided to sell the company, all without consulting Barry, Jr.

In other cases, some of which I have personally observed in my work as a family business advisor, significant ownership stakes have been passed on to the next generation but no real power. Motivated by a desire to minimize the effect of estate tax laws that threaten the continuity of the business unless transfers begin early, owner-managers did little to prepare next-generation members for responsible ownership and stewardship. Leaving controlling ownership (a majority of the voting stock) and top management posts in the hands of the previous generation makes a mockery of the presumed transfer of power.

These out-of-phase transfers of management and ownership create extremely difficult leadership challenges for new CEOs. This is especially true when succession is triggered by the unexpected illness or sudden death of the CEO-parent.

You will find no advocacy of early transfer of ownership in these pages. My desire is to promote understanding that the transfer of power needs to be uniquely designed for each family and business in such a way that family leadership, ownership control, and company management are all part of the transfer. Congruency in the transfer of power, as represented by management, family, and ownership shares, is at the heart of an effective transition across generations of owner-managers.

THE CEO AS ARCHITECT OF SUCCESSION AND CONTINUITY

Having studied and followed the lives and careers of chief executives of family-controlled companies over the years, I think it important to note that those who have crafted a successful succession in a business do not necessarily fit the profile of a hero, as depicted by the larger-than-life charismatic characters in a Hollywood production. Instead, most are modest, substantive entrepreneurs or serious professionals (usually in second-, third-, or fourth-generation firms) with a mission. They are hard-working plow horses, not show horses. They care more about doing the right thing for the company and its continuity than about promoting their own egos or agendas. In this sense, they are very similar to successful chief executives of well-known publicly traded companies, the so-called Level 5 leaders.[3]

But CEOs of family businesses are building companies to last, so they cannot afford to become narcissistic, spotlight-hungry performers. These owner-managers are stewards of a legacy that has a life of its own, with a value beyond that of the individual CEO. Recognition that the business is not bound to the life span of its current leader leads many CEOs to once again assume the role of architects, as they confront succession and continuity. Architects realize that, for their vision to become a reality, they must enlist the right people and then execute the right strategies to ensure both sustainability and continuity. The "right people," by the way, usually have to be in the top management team and among the governors of the shareholder group; they may be complemented by board members and outside advisors.

Samuel Curtis Johnson III, retired fourth-generation chief executive of SC Johnson: A Family Company, rather easily arrived at the realization that he had to be the architect of transition—it was part of the family's legacy. Herbert Fisk Johnson, second-generation president of SC Johnson, died suddenly in 1928, without leaving a will. The battle that ensued between siblings ultimately gave 60–40 majority control to Herbert Fisk Johnson, Jr. (Samuel Curtis's father). Samuel Curtis still remembers the 10 long years that it took his father to settle his grandfather's estate. Consequently, his father vowed not to do that to his son, and Samuel Curtis, in turn, vowed not to do it to his sons and daughters either.[4]

Assuming the responsibilities of the chief architect, he assembled a continuity construction project team for the $5 billion, 100 percent family-owned enterprise. Team members included not only his capable heirs but also key nonfamily managers, one of whom served as bridging president for several years while the next generation of Johnsons got ready to succeed Samuel Curtis. Independent outsiders on the board and a small cadre of family, estate, and family business consultants assisted the project team. Over a span of more than 10 years, Johnson family members (undoubtedly assisted behind the scenes by their spouses) planned with these key nonfamily professionals the building of a unique structure for the Johnson family and the SC Johnson company, much as Frank Lloyd Wright and his team had designed a unique headquarters for the company in Racine, Wisconsin, back in the late 1930s.

What went into the continuity plan? The planning consisted of many conversations, much soul-searching and reflection, a variety of developmental assignments for next-generation members, the appointment of interim nonfamily presidents, and the re-enactment of a trip that Herbert Fisk Johnson, Jr., had made to Brazil back in the 1930s to study carnauba wax. This trip was sponsored in the interest of reclaiming the legacy and sharpening the vision for next-generation members.

Wills, shareholder agreements, an organizational structure that gave each sibling a division to run, and ownership stakes that gave each sibling controlling interest in his or her division were all part of the plan. Also, an ownership board was created, consisting of all four siblings and three external advisors (in case conflicts should arise). A soft family culture, with all its subtleties and nuances, was coupled with the business equivalents of structural beams and a knowledge of physics.

Once the right people were in place, the strategies for the various divisions were working, and the institutions for governing the relationship between the business and the family existed, Samuel Curtis Johnson III decided it was time to retire. He was 72, and he knew he could not run the company forever.[5]

CEO EXIT STYLES

This section draws heavily on research done by Jeffrey Sonnenfeld and P. L. Spence, as reported in their 1989 article in *Family Business Review*.[6] In fact, the first four departure styles discussed in this section—monarch, general, ambassador, and governor—are the products of their research. Observation and direct involvement in over 100 succession and continuity processes over the past 20-some years have led me to adapt Sonnenfeld and Spence's original typology to include two additional CEO exit types: the inventor and the transition czar. Herewith, then, are descriptions of the six most common CEO exit types.

THE MONARCH

Kings and queens rule for life; they have no retirement provision in the law. They have no expectation of early departure to compensate them for years and years of presiding over wars, calming social unrest, and (contrary to public opinion lately) leading very visible and demanding socio-political lives. Because succession cannot take place while the monarch is alive, many Greek and Roman tragedies and several of Shakespeare's better-known works feature palace revolts and death by poisoning. Monarchs rightly operate on the assumption that they will die with their crowns on.

Many business owners rule as if guided by the same principle. Years after the generally accepted retirement age of 65, they still show up daily at work, to read the mail, to make or receive a few calls, and to reverse or second-guess decisions made by next-generation or key nonfamily managers over the last 24 hours. Effectively, they rule the company during a 3- to 4-hour workday.

Monarchs hire and fire a whole series of aspiring general managers, presidents, and chief operating officers. The better they are, the sooner they go, because monarchs do not imagine that anyone could ever replace them. In this context, Dr. Franz Huebel, CEO of Precista Tools, comes to mind. With Huebel hiring and firing four different bridging presidents in the span of five years and resisting the participation of next-generation members in top management, succession came only after Huebel had a fatal heart attack.[7]

Monarchs in business do not talk about succession, nor do they set a date for departure or a deadline for change in responsibility. They genuinely seem to believe that illness and death are things that happen only to others—those poor souls who never ran their own empire. Monarch types are prevalent among business owners because having lifelong control over their own lives, careers, and companies, as well as the lives and livelihoods of their employees, leads them to be the last to accept that time is no longer on their side and what lies ahead may more easily be measured in months than in years.

They refuse to talk about letting go, even to their closest advisors. As a result, succession planning never takes place, responsibility that would help to develop the next generation of managers is never delegated downward, and information is closely controlled through the assistance of a loyal accountant or CFO. Consequently, the secret ingredients of the company's success are never fully revealed.

If a monarch rules the family business, chaos will likely follow his or her death. In the vacuum created upon the monarch's departure, greed and a thousand hidden agendas will flourish, destroying in months what took a whole lifetime—or even several generations—to create.[8] The daughters, sons, nieces, nephews, and in-laws of a monarch had best be prepared for conflict, political turmoil, and loss of both individual self-worth and company net worth. A coup d'etat seldom works in a family business. Advisors or service providers to royalty find out, sooner or later, that there is no timely way to help a business monarch when succession and continuity are the goal. In the business world, there are no moats large enough, no technology slow enough, and no competition genteel enough to allow sufficient time for mourning and re-coronation to take place.

The General

Unlike monarchs, generals partly retire in a display of self-discipline, per the rules of the military. But these chief executives leave office reluctantly and plot a return. Generals wait patiently, hoping that the younger officer or popularly elected leader will demonstrate his or her sheer inadequacy. When that happens, they return triumphantly to right the wrongs and rescue the unit that lesser people could not save. Today's general lives six months out of the year in Florida, California, or Arizona but plays golf with a cell phone on standby, hoping for the call suggesting that Junior has just made the biggest blunder of his life. Why? Because it is precisely that piece of news that will bring the general back into service, making his or her heart beat strongly and passionately again. He or she flies back to town, reappears in the office, and retakes control, as if never having missed a day of work.

Generals live for the day when they will be called back into service to right the real or fabricated wrongs committed by next-generation managers. (Unfortunately, the wrongs are sometimes fabricated by a group of loyalists; they may be key nonfamily managers who never had much use for the young scion, or they may be siblings and cousins who are still jealous about not having been chosen for the leadership position.) Since businesses are hardly ever problem-free or steadily successful, odds are that the general, much like the monarch, will continue to rule, undermining the capacity of anyone else in the organization to succeed at the helm.

If a general runs the family business, other officers and enlisted personnel need to know that their new responsibilities and authority will be only part-time, because the general will be back soon to take full-time possession of all available power. Heirs to a general should learn to enjoy the times when they are in control of the business, because the feeling will be short-lived. Willingness to drop a new information systems project, advocacy of a human resource issue, or a new strategic plan as soon as the general reports back to duty is a must. Advisors and consultants to the part-time regime should build or maintain bridges with the general. Otherwise, their consulting project will be considered useless and too expensive the minute she or he returns to the company.

The Ambassador

Most family business owners take on the role of either a monarch or a general when they exit their business. Fewer owners become ambassadors. Ambassadors exit the business by delegating most of the operating responsibilities to next-generation members and/or key nonfamily managers but hold on to their diplomatic or representational duties on behalf of the corporation. In the fast-food industry, both Dave Thomas, founder of Wendy's International, and Colonel Harlan Sanders, Thomas's one-time mentor at Kentucky Fried Chicken, chose this path. They became marketing spokespersons—the personas, or public images—for their businesses and, through ads and personal appearances, reinforced the power of the brand that they embodied. In both cases, business operations were delegated to key nonfamily members of the top management team.

George Soros of Soros Fund Management is becoming an ambassador, as he turns to writing a book and leading his charitable foundations. At the same time, he is making room for his son Robert, the eldest of five children and the only one to join the family business. Robert's preparation in the financial industry occurred outside the family company. He worked for several investment firms and banks between 1986 and 1994, when he joined the Soros Fund.[9]

Ambassadors make room for top-notch nonfamily managers and next-generation members. They allow others to learn the business first-hand and to eventually take over responsibility for running the enterprise. The CEOs prone to become ambassadors include those who enjoy people, like to travel, and have always entertained the idea of living several months of the year in a city that is also a key market, such as London, Paris, or New York. CEOs who discover another calling in philanthropy or public service (say, the Salvation Army, the Jewish-American Committee, or the U.S. Senate) are candidates for this exit type as well. Ambassadors make good board members for a few years after their exit.

Ambassadors should proceed slowly with their exit, making sure that the next generation and/or key nonfamily managers are indeed capable and ready to take over day-to-day operations. An ambassador who rushes to the exit may have no option but to return as a general, in order to fix the problems of the corporation. The heirs of an ambassador-type CEO are lucky indeed. They merely need to prepare themselves thoroughly and avoid competing with the CEO for visibility outside the business. Advisors to this type of CEO should build bridges with key nonfamily management and the next generation because, without such relationships, they are likely to be replaced by a younger and less expensive service provider.

THE GOVERNOR

It is an unfortunate fact of family business that less than 5 percent of all family business owners exit after having set a deadline for the transfer of power. In the interest of a smooth succession and continuity of the business, Jack Welch, the largest individual General Electric shareholder, left his post that way, after naming Jeff Immelt to replace him. GE is one of the best-managed companies in the world. Perhaps more than any other company, GE enjoys a competitive advantage derived from a core competence known as management expertise. Its management—more than its products, technology, marketing, or financial prowess—is what gives GE an edge. Few public or private management-controlled companies have CEO succession take place in such an orderly fashion that the company's sustainability or continuity is not threatened.

Governors set a departure date and announce it publicly, thus committing themselves to the goal of transferring power within a pre-established time frame. By making the date public, they lend a sense of urgency to planning for the inevitable transition and enlist other key management personnel, employees, suppliers, and customers in the process. As chairman and CEO of *El Nuevo Día* and the Grupo Ferré-Rangel (a newspaper, media, and industrial conglomerate in Puerto Rico), Antonio L. Ferré did just that. During the eight-year period following his departure date announcement, family members both in and out of the business and key non-family managers worked feverishly and tenaciously to accomplish a smooth succession that would ensure sustainability and continuity for the enterprise.[10]

THE INVENTOR

Jack Bares, CEO emeritus of Milbar Corporation and current CEO of Meritool, a hand-tool product development company, is a great example of another CEO exit type: the inventor. More than anything else, Jack had always enjoyed developing hand tools for new applications. So when Jack, his daughter, the board, and other heirs decided that they were ready for succession, Jack started an engineering and product development company. Milbar was purchased by Jack's daughter in a clear demonstration of her commitment to the enterprise and its continuity. While she succeeded him at Milbar, the inventor moved across the street to continue developing new tools, his life's work.[11]

The inventor designation is really a metaphor for an exiting CEO who takes on a satisfying key position in another enterprise. The inventor could just as easily be called the marketer, the private investor, or the tinkerer. Frank Mars, who ran Mars Inc. for many years, transferred power to sons Forrest and John Mars and created a small gourmet chocolate company. He named the new enterprise and its products Ethel M as a gesture of love for his wife and built a whimsical "chocolate factory" that I and thousands of tourists in Las Vegas have visited to learn about chocolate and the making of premium chocolate confections.

Inventors are creative people. Once they have built systems and institutions that will help the next generation lead successfully, they are usually ready to pursue their next dream. Heirs to inventors are very fortunate. They can request coaching and negotiate for advice on an as-needed basis. It helps to schedule breakfasts, lunches, or "wisdom meetings" with the CEO on a regular basis. Advisors and service providers to an inventor should build bridges to the next generation but be aware that successors will more than likely want to choose their own advisors.

THE TRANSITION CZAR

Because it is very difficult to do so, very few CEOs choose to exit by becoming the lead agent in the multi-year transition known as succession. However, transition czars can add significant value to succession across generations, particularly when family companies are complex and multi-national and owning families are large and multi-generational.

CEOs may choose the role of transition czar out of a desire to consult during the managerial and political processes that a complicated transition requires. While some CEOs enjoy being an ambassador for the company, others prefer being the shuttle diplomat, or the "Henry Kissinger," of the company and its shareholders.

Samuel Curtis Johnson III, retired CEO of SC Johnson: A Family Company, took this responsibility on as much to ensure a successful succession as to begin his process of transitioning out of the CEO role. In this role, he both coached the next generation and supported their development in unique and differentiated ways. Eventually, as a skilled architect would, he crafted a succession and continuity plan that structurally divided the business in such a way that the siblings in the next generation would remain united in friendship.[12]

Transition czars need to be aware of the difficulties inherent in being at the center of changing what they created. It often helps to seek outside advice from both a board and family business consultants. Because of the propensity for blurred boundaries among family, management, and ownership, transition czars need to be sure that they are wearing the CEO hat when dealing with a management or ownership issue and the father/mother/uncle/aunt hat when a family matter is at stake. It is difficult leadership work.

Transition czars often carry out the succession and continuity responsibility with significant assistance from the CEO spouse. This team effort allows the CEO to concentrate on codifying the institutional memory of both the business and the family (through a family constitution, for instance) and building the institutions that will ensure effective family business governance (like boards and family councils). Meanwhile, the CEO spouse works to create trust and family unity in such a way that visions about the firm's future are further understood and agreed upon and the unique and complementary contributions of different family members and key nonfamily managers are better appreciated. The role of the CEO spouse is discussed further in Chapter 3.

Heirs to a transition czar need to be patient and very self-aware in their relationships with the CEO. Whether the person they are relating to is in the CEO role or the parent or relative role makes a huge difference in how they should act. Keeping the right "hats" on the right people is particularly tricky but also particularly worthwhile for an heir to a transition czar.

Transition czars realize the risks posed by a power vacuum and provide active leadership of the entire succession process with family members, key nonfamily managers, customers, and suppliers. Through boards of directors with independent outsiders, advisory boards, family meetings, and family constitutions, they help build institutions and legacy principles that will govern the family enterprise after succession.

IMPLICATIONS OF CEO EXIT STYLES FOR SUCCESSION AND CONTINUITY

What do CEO behaviors say about the most likely exit type? What do the CEO's spouse and children and key nonfamily managers think is likely to be the CEO's departure style?

Monarchs and generals are the worst enemies of succession. They deny the facts and stonewall, refusing to engage key nonfamily managers and the next generation in building readiness for sustainability and continuity across generations. Little preparation can take place and little hope maintained when so many questions remain unanswered: Will the family keep or sell the business? Will family or nonfamily members run it? Will they run it successfully or right into the ground?

Monarchs and generals may be the reason why the average tenure of CEOs in family-owned businesses is more than double that of CEOs in management-controlled companies (17 vs. 8 years).[13] However, it can be argued that the difference in tenure is due to the tendency of senior executives in publicly owned firms to think more about retiring wealthy at 40 or 50 and less about legacy, while family business CEOs consider the long-term interests of shareholders to be paramount.

Clearly, management theory and research on best practices do not support short CEO tenures or quarterly scorecards that distort the concept of shareholder value. Nor do family business theory and practice particularly encourage extremely long CEO tenures (30 to 40 years, for example), which may represent CEO entrenchment. A monarch or general is not likely to be working for the long-term sustainability and continuity of the business. Nor is he or she likely to be concerned about the hidden costs of such long tenure to the business, to next-generation members, and to family health and harmony.

Monarchs and generals must seriously consider changing their ways or face destroying what is often their most important creation. If change is out of the question, appointing a bridging president and an effective board of directors or advisory board with independent outsiders may help ameliorate the negative impact of these exit types on succession and continuity.

Ambassadors, governors, inventors, and transition czars all allow for a generational transition to be planned and eventually executed. They also provide for time to realistically assess the company's unique situation and evaluate successors' capabilities and developmental needs. Ultimately, the CEO is the architect not only of the unique business he or she created but also of the most appropriate structure for succession and continuity.

These best family business practices will be discussed in Chapters 5 through 9, but first we turn, in Chapter 3, to the key leadership role of the CEO spouse in the succession and continuity process.

SUMMARY

1. CEOs of family businesses perceive both the business and the family much more favorably than do the rest of the family and nonfamily managers.

2. To ensure both their ability to govern and the business's continuity, CEOs must enlist competent people both in the top management team and as the

governors of the shareholder group; these individuals can be complemented by board members and outside advisors.

3. The six most common CEO exit types are the (1) monarch, (2) general, (3) ambassador, (4) governor, (5) inventor, and (6) transition czar.

4. CEOs who want their companies to continue to be successful beyond their lifetimes allow for a generational transition to be planned and eventually executed. They also provide for time to realistically assess the company's unique situation and evaluate successors' capabilities and developmental needs.

5. As architects of trusting relationships and institutions for the governance of the family–business relationship, successful CEOs implement the following best practices:

   ■ Plan the estate with business agility, not just tax minimization, in mind (Chapter 5).

   ■ Pursue strategic growth by building on the firm's core competencies (Chapter 6).

   ■ Leverage the family's skills and abilities by hiring capable and dedicated nonfamily managers in leadership roles (Chapter 7).

   ■ Welcome the review of outside board members who continuously raise the bar for the owner-manager (Chapter 8).

   ■ Promote communication and accommodation among family members through frequent family meetings or an ongoing family council (Chapter 9).

EXERCISE

HOW TO SAFELY PROMOTE A SOMETIMES DIFFICULT CONVERSATION

Try this: After having someone explain the six different exit styles in a family or management meeting, invite students to write down the likely exit style of the current CEO of their family firms. [If implementing this exercise at an actual family meeting, understand that secret balloting often works best. Before revealing the results of the poll, clue in the CEO as to the result (to avoid the surprise factor, which sometimes increases resistance and denial).]

Ask students to suggest ways in which a family could follow the result of the poll not with an "I told you so" type of confrontation, but with a discussion as to why it is so, what makes it so, and what could be done to either reinforce this exit approach, change it, or ameliorate its negative implications.

Second Leadership Imperative
Promoting Trust Among Family Members

CEO spouses play a key, if often invisible, role in most family-controlled corporations. They are in the background of most stories of successful (e.g., SC Johnson), stressful (e.g., *New York Times*), and troubled (e.g., Wang Laboratories) generational transitions.[1]

Family business research has largely ignored the role of the CEO spouse. Of the tragic tale of the Louisville *Courier-Journal* (discussed in Chapter 2), owned by the Bingham family, the *New York Times* states, "In the drama there is no single villain, nor a hero or healer who might have bridged the gulf of distrust and anger."[2] Although the writer does not refer exclusively to Mary Bingham, the CEO spouse, her role in the family's tragedy is woven throughout this and various other reports about the end of the Bingham dynasty.

The multiple levels on which CEOs influence succession planning and the ensuing dilemmas have been acknowledged by CEOs themselves, their advisors, and scholars. But people other than the incumbent CEO also significantly influence leadership succession and continuity in the family firm. The CEO spouse, in particular, is an important actor in both of these processes. The media and the more scholarly literature seldom address or acknowledge the roles and perspectives of CEO spouses. Yet recent studies have identified CEO spouses as being central to succession and continuity processes in family-controlled companies.[3]

I wish to thank the student research team that conducted the inquiry process with CEO spouses. The team members from the Partnership for Family Business Program at Case Western Reserve University were Gina Burk, Kim Hastings, Betty Moon, Karen Magill, and Susan Spector. [Some of the material in this chapter was first published in an article by Ernesto J. Poza and Tracey E. Messer in *Family Business Review* 14(1), March 2001.]

THE UNIQUE ROLES OF THE CEO SPOUSE

This chapter discusses the CEO spouse's unique roles as steward of the family legacy, facilitator of communication, and touchstone of emotional intelligence in family relations. CEO spouses often play a determining role in successful generational transitions, but not without facing tensions and dilemmas. This chapter also explores the blurring of life, career, and family roles by the CEO spouse. Looking at the options available to CEO spouses and the choices made by some spouses has the potential to enrich our understanding of the variety of leadership roles essential to family business continuity.

The findings discussed here are the direct result of structured conversations with CEO spouses.[4] However, the motivation for the inquiry and some of the perspectives offered in this chapter were influenced by my personal observations and consultations with more than 100 family-controlled corporations, as well as candid conversations with their CEOs and CEO spouses. Such observations and conversations revealed the central, yet often invisible, part that CEO spouses play in the generational transition process. Over and over again, in seldom-recognized ways, these spouses assume a key role in initiatives to improve the relationship between the family and the management of the business and to further orderly governance of the ownership system.

The discrepancy between the spouse's degree of influence and his or her degree of visibility to the firm and its ownership group were illustrated by my conversation with one CEO spouse. This spouse complained about the small and rather unimportant role she played in her family's business. Then, a few minutes later, she told me that she was the reason her brother and her son were now working for the firm. Significantly, company employees credited her brother with increasing profits through disciplined inventory management. And they credited her son, who had worked outside the family business after earning an MBA degree, with building a financial infrastructure that enabled better management of operating costs. This CEO spouse neither recognized nor was recognized for her significant impact on the business and its capacity for continuity.

The research team interviewed CEO spouses to learn more about their role as co-architect of succession and continuity. The interview questions focused on the spouse's contributions to the business as a parent and as a partner, as well as his or her role as co-architect of the unique relationship between family and business. The authors of an article reporting preliminary findings from Case Western Reserve University's Discovery Action Research Project called the CEO spouse one of the chief architects of the family's culture and the business's practices.[5]

The Discovery study found that spouses assume different leadership functions, depending on their relationship with the CEO, their knowledge of and interest in the business, and their commitment to a vision that includes continuity of family participation in the business. Three other factors influence the role adopted by a spouse in a family-controlled business: (1) the perception of need, described by spouses as dependent mostly on the quality of the relationship between the CEO and next-generation member(s); (2) the spouse's ability to perform the needed leadership role; and (3) the availability of others to perform communication-promoting and trust-enabling functions. The study found some traditional spousal types but also found many CEO spouses comfortably assuming multiple leadership roles as needs changed.

Regardless of the role played, CEO spouses repeatedly described themselves and other spouses as:

- Being stewards of the family legacy.
- Keeping "family" in the family business.
- Instilling a sense of purpose, responsibility, and community in family members.
- Embodying a spirit of cooperation and unconditional support.

ROLE TYPES OF THE CEO SPOUSE

Interview data from the sample of CEO spouses were analyzed in the context of the original research question: What unique contributions do CEO spouses make to the family-owned business? Six leadership or role types emerged: (1) jealous spouse, (2) chief trust officer, (3) business partner, (4) vice president, (5) senior advisor/keeper of family values, and (6) free agent.

THE JEALOUS SPOUSE

Many entrepreneurs and family business owners, particularly those who are first or second generation, have a mistress-like relationship with their business. The family has to compete with the business for the CEO's recognition, affection, financial resources, and time. In this context, many spouses experience jealousy; competition with the business for time and affection is a prominent theme in their lives. One spouse, who personalized these competitive dynamics and saw herself as competing with her spouse rather than with the business, said, "I think he wanted someone who was not going to compete with him. If I do, that could be a source of conflict for us. I don't like talking about it."

Jealous spouses feel that the CEO loves the business so much that it has become her or his first priority. Jealousy of a spouse's commitment to her or his work is not limited to spouses of family business owners. Spouses of attorneys, doctors, executives in public companies, and others in extremely demanding professions can all suffer the same fate. Yet in family-owned businesses, the often-observed overlap of family and business makes the jealous spouse a particularly hearty type. Reflecting on her role over the years in the family business, one spouse said, "I am the political pawn. . . . I was an only child and often events connected to me, such as school events, graduation, and my wedding, were used as opportunities to cement relationships with important family shareholders." Today, she is the spouse of a third-generation CEO, and the pattern continues. On the other hand, jealous spouses may provide the motivation for greater delegation and professionalization of the business so that its success and survival depend less on the superhuman efforts of the CEO.

THE CHIEF TRUST OFFICER

Some CEO spouses see their major contribution to the family-owned business as providing the glue that keeps everyone united through the predictable challenges that families who work together face. These spouses, known as chief trust officers, act as healers, mediators, facilitators, and communication conduits for their families. They are the fence-menders in business and family relationships. Individuals performing this role are sometimes referred to as trust catalysts.[6] The following statements from CEO spouses illustrate this role:

- "You've heard the term *pillow talk*? I listen to my husband, I listen to my daughter, I listen to my son, and I put it all together."
- "I am the peacekeeper, the troubleshooter, and fence-mender."
- "I bring intuition, insight, discernment. I am the spiritual captain, the nurturer of love, respect, and honor. I also bring an ability to see things in context."
- "What I bring to this process is creativity and a kind of glue. I bring a staying quality that rides through rough or smooth times, consistent and dogged. I also bring an ability to keep an eye on a distant spot, rather than focusing on pieces. It's about focusing. If you can do that even in the squabble of the short term, then you can keep your balance."

These spouses often remind family members of the need for balance between work and family. They may also take responsibility for family initiatives, like creating a family council, writing the family's history, hosting weekly or monthly family gatherings, being the contact person for facilitators of semiannual family retreats, and planning family vacations and multi-generational celebrations. Sometimes polar opposites of their business-first CEO spouses, chief trust officers try to balance family and business by advocating a family-first agenda.

Chief trust officers often have a unique appreciation of the interpersonal and developmental challenges in family business continuity. Through their ability to understand and articulate various stakeholders' points of view, they are frequently able to broaden the dialogue from an exclusive focus on facts to a wider view, encompassing both facts and feelings, so that better decisions can be made. These spouses are often effective at putting succession planning and transition to retirement on the CEO's agenda.

THE BUSINESS PARTNER

Some spouses are critical to the business, whether through their financial investment in the business or because of their professional, technical, or administrative skills. Some of these spouses begin as business partners during the start-up and early stages of company development and then move on to a different role. Others remain active business partners. Among those who move to a different role later in life, their presence and determination in those early days is the subject of family anecdotes and family pride.

One business partner started a new division in a business run by the fourth-generation CEO. She told us, "My husband had wanted me to join the company for a long time. The custom decorative hardware business I started within the company has grown to where many women are working at home and earning an extra $1,000 a month for their families. We need to have opportunities like this in our economy."

The business partner's advice is often sought, both on and off the job. He or she shows up regularly for work and is responsible for a variety of projects. Business partners may be the lineal descendants of the owning family and have effectively employed the CEO spouse to run their inherited business. Or they may be large shareholders (e.g., 50-percent owners) and therefore act as a full partner of the CEO.

The economic advantages of having two highly committed owner-managers working side by side can include a more flexible and lower cost management structure. Such benefits seldom come without complications, however. One business partner acknowledged the unique challenges of this type when she said, "You want to be sure what role you want to play. Do you want to play marriage or business partnership, or both? For me, it is difficult to do both."

THE VICE PRESIDENT

Much like the business partner, the vice president plays a critical role in running the family-owned business. This spouse's technical, professional, or administrative skills are essential to managing the business in such a way that the family's interests are pursued and safeguarded. Unlike the business partner, this type of CEO spouse acts as a trusted employee, not as an owner, and therefore limits contributions and involvement to the function or project that he or she performs. The vice president's functional expertise does not necessarily give him or her a voice or a vote on broader company management or ownership issues.

If customer relations are this spouse's strong suit and a needed skill, that's where his or her contributions may be made. Acting as an ambassador of goodwill, the vice president may attend functions and play a key role in the development of new approaches to managing customer loyalty. Margrit Blever Mondavi, spouse of the former CEO of Mondavi Wines, Robert Mondavi, eloquently performed this role, bringing innovations like wine festivals and other promotional opportunities to the marketing function at Mondavi.

If, on the other hand, this spouse's capabilities lie in relations with employees, she or he may help develop a performance appraisal system, a health insurance plan, a company newsletter, communication meetings, recognition events, the summer picnic, or the Christmas party. "If somebody passes away, . . . I am the mother, so one of the things that I do is that I make sure we send out a personal condolence letter, which is signed by me. I also make sure that if somebody moves into a new home or has a baby, I send a personal gift."

If architecture or design comes naturally to the spouse, any work on facilities and their redesign may become her or his project:

> I was the person who persuaded my husband to take some steps to improve the office and plant working conditions. I think that it has had a very uplifting effect on the spirits of people working in the company. I worked as a consultant on the restoration project. I found the architects, was involved in the selection of the materials and furnishings used, and managed the relationship with city hall. The feedback from employees tells me that we have pleased them at a very personal level. And it's not about luxury, because the renovations have created a comfortable but not luxurious space. But the renovations have shown them respect.

Among the vice president–type spouses interviewed, accounting and finance were also common functional roles. Sometimes the spouse is the accountant or CFO, depending on his or her skills and the size and complexity of the business. Sometimes the spouse is the family's financial officer and overseer of the family's wealth: "Financial planning, I am very much in the middle of that. Because that, in a sense, is the other side of the business that has nothing to do with what the company manufactures. It has more to do with managing family affairs, and I am very much involved in that."

Although the advantage of having a trusted family member in these functional roles is evident, the spouse's adoption of these roles may enable a culture of secrecy to persist in the family business. Having problems or difficulties relating to company finances, relations with customers, or employee relations handled privately by one of the business's most trusted members—the CEO's spouse—enables secrets to remain "in the family." Another drawback is that the spouse may take credit for things done by other employees and thus negatively impact the culture of the organization.

As vice president of human resources, finance, marketing, or facilities, the CEO spouse may serve on the company's statutory board as secretary or treasurer of the corporation but not act as a senior advisor or influence strategic decisions by top management or the board.

THE SENIOR ADVISOR/KEEPER OF FAMILY VALUES

Although akin to the chief trust officer, the senior advisor is more than a relationship problem solver; he or she helps the children grow up with a sense of the business, its history, and its customers. Also known as the keeper of family values, the senior advisor instills a sense of what the business stands for and what it means to the family. While nurturing a love for the business among family members, senior advisors often have no visible role in the business. Their independence and lack of visible influence over business issues enhance the respect they command in matters of great importance to the family and the business.

These spouses are deans of the intangible crossovers between family and business. Katharine Graham, former CEO and chairwoman of the *Washington Post*, attributed to these crossovers much of the commitment to quality shown by family-owned newspapers. She said, "I don't think it's an accident that the newspapers best known for quality in this country—the *New York Times*, the *Wall Street Journal*, the *Los Angeles Times*, the *Boston Globe*, the *Washington Post*, and outstanding papers in Dallas, Sacramento, California, St. Petersburg, Florida, and elsewhere—are, or were until recently, family controlled. It seems that certain attributes essential to quality are more easily provided by families than by public companies."[7]

Besides a commitment to quality, senior advisors may bring an antidote to the CEO's propensity to create a culture of secrecy with its corresponding sense of loneliness. One senior advisor believes that the role she plays is that of an anti-isolation agent in continuity efforts in the family business: "When you live in a relatively small town and you know people who have a family business, they don't talk about [it]. So you are very isolated. You might think you are the only person having a certain kind of problem. No one is ever going to tell you you are not unique."

Senior advisors often promote family values that advocate family business continuity. One spouse told us, "In the end, it isn't dad's business. The business belongs to the children. And if the business continues, it will belong to the grandchildren. So what I can do for the business is love them all." This same spouse added, "A family business is an extension of your family. It is an extension of your love, your trust and respect. You can't separate them."

Some CEO spouses recognize that they are role models for the next-generation, the builders of new legacies—legacies the preceding generation may not have considered important. One senior advisor–type spouse in a third- to fourth-generation business stated it this way: "In a very male-oriented culture in the business, it's good if there are roles there for women to follow because of me. There are now more than male role models. Three out of our four grandchildren are girls; this new legacy is important."

Senior advisors are keenly aware that for the family legacy to remain vibrant and alive, it has to change and adapt itself to the present and the future. After all, "The business that my husband runs isn't the business that his father ran, and the same will be true for the next generation."

A spouse's obvious interest in and support of the business family may play a part in predisposing the spouses of next-generation members to seek the top leadership role. The phrase "Behind every great man, there is a great woman" (or its converse, "Behind every great woman, there is a great man," sometimes heard during Prime Minister Thatcher's noteworthy leadership of England) applies to many CEO spouses, highlighting once again the influence that even less visible spouses have on the family business.

Despite the wide-ranging influence they have, senior advisors often are not interested in controlling the business or in gaining recognition or appreciation of the role they play. They know, as do others close to the action, that in the areas of love for the business and the family, commitment to legacy, and intangible crossovers (e.g., love in the family evidencing itself in quality of products), these spouses are masters. The most visible roles that senior advisors/keepers of family values are likely to play include leading the effort to document and publish a family business history and speaking eloquently during the 100th-anniversary celebration of the family-controlled company.

THE FREE AGENT

The free agent is often very aware of both family and business matters, having perhaps served the family-owned business in some capacity earlier in life. But this spouse chooses to develop an identity separate from the CEO and the family business: "My role is being me, not the wife and not the mother. I believe it is very important for a spouse to maintain a separate sense of self. I feel so sad when I see a woman who feels so lost when her husband dies because he was her whole life. A woman can't be the most helpful and supportive she can be if she does not have some understanding of who she is separately."

Free agents often believe that there is no need for them to be any more involved with the business or the family than they are, as other people are satisfactorily performing the role of chief trust officer or trust-facilitator:

> Paul never had a peer discussion with his dad about the real estate development business he had started. That is why when we went on vacation, about twice a year, at 4:00 p.m. every day, Paul would have a session with the kids. When they were young, it was with cookies and milk, then pop, then beer and wine. Paul would talk to them about the business, about different memories, where the grandparents came from and similar topics. It was a fun family meeting. It was an important foundation of respect. No one else's father talked to them about the business. Another thing that Paul did was to sit down with the kids at the beginning of the school year and discuss what they [thought] their expenses [would] be. Then Paul would write them a check, and they had to manage it. Paul wondered sometimes if the kids ever got extra money from me. Never did we give them extra. They had to manage the money and they did. You have to trust them. Parents tend to hold money as control. I think Paul thought of it because his father never did it with him.

Another free agent described her role in relation to her CEO spouse in this way: "I think I provide a home that is a refuge, a social life that is not business-oriented, and travel around the world which is enlightening and broadening." Still another spoke of her relationship with the next generation: "I show my adult kids that they're loved. They benefit by my not being involved. I am not a 'buttinski.' They have the freedom and latitude to do what they have to do."

Free agents are usually available for consultation and advice during particularly trying or challenging times in the life of the family and the business. But, in general, these spouses thrive on their marginality vis-à-vis the business. One spouse confided, "She [my daughter] is now the CEO, her brother reports to her on some things but also runs his own division, [and] it is entirely up to the two of them to make it work. Other than being supportive of her, I have nothing to do with the management of the business." Another free agent recognized that for succession and continuity to go smoothly, both she and the CEO had to leave their roles: "Our job is to teach them to walk and then walk away. We both must walk away."

Free agents are the polar opposites of jealous spouses, with their constant reactiveness to the business. One free agent told the researchers, "Claire, who I met in one of the sessions, is jealous of her husband. It's her family's business, but the husband is running it. So she, and others like her, is constantly involved in intermediating. If they had a life of their own, . . ."

Still another free agent–type spouse, aware of her role in leading through marginality, said, "My involvement is I am married to my children's father. Initially, when the children were old enough to consider the possibility of working in the business, they would come to me and complain about the way my husband was doing something or other. I used to accept the burden and make myself the messenger. Now I refuse to and remind them that it's their job to report to him directly."

These spouses often have active lives as community leaders, volunteers, grandparents, and bearers of the legacy for multi-generational family-owned businesses. As free agents, they are available to fulfill other roles (e.g., chief trust officer or even business partner) should the business and/or the family urgently need their contributions.

THE BROADER VIEW

This chapter has focused on the CEO spouse because of the many instances where, even in the presence of other resources, these spouses have engineered outcome-changing feats in the processes of succession and continuity. However, spouses are not the only individuals who can perform these roles. Family business literature and my own experiences and research include examples of others' performing these functions, including the CEO, an uncle or aunt, a consultant, and a minister, priest, or rabbi who is close to the family.

Still, CEO spouses tend to have a special sense of calling about their role and a self-awareness about the type of individual who can perform the role successfully: "It is not any easy place to be. You must manage your ego and go for the whole picture."

Also, changes may occur in the CEO spouse's role type across her or his own life cycle as well as across the life cycles of the CEO, the family, and the business. Sometimes CEO spouses who were once business partners migrated to the roles of chief trust officer or free agent. There was no single cause for these shifts, which sometimes simply reflected changing needs. At other times, the shifts were the result of personal development phases or just the personal preference of the CEO spouse. Whatever the cause, CEO spouses were clearly aware of changing roles over time.

Whether CEO spouses are in formal or informal positions, recognized or unrecognized for their contributions, they often adopt a role in preserving and strengthening family unity and the feasibility of family business continuity. CEO spouses, along with the CEOs, were co-architects of family unity, family communication, and business practices. The CEO spouses found ways to make contributions they felt were important—even when standing on the margin of the business—whether or not they were recognized for those contributions. Marginality need not result in invisibility, provided the overall family business agenda stresses love, legacy, and continuity over power. Theirs is an important leadership role.

SUMMARY

1. The CEO spouse plays unique roles in the family business, including steward of the family legacy, facilitator of communication, touchstone of emotional intelligence in family relations, and co-architect of successful generational transitions.

2. The six role types of the CEO spouse are (1) jealous spouse, (2) chief trust officer, (3) business partner, (4) vice president, (5) senior advisor/keeper of family values, and (6) free agent.

3. Shifts may occur in the CEO spouse's role type across her or his own life cycle as well as across the life cycles of the CEO, the family, and the business.

THIRD LEADERSHIP IMPERATIVE
THE NEXT GENERATION

Any observer of the world of industry and finance over the last decade has to be impressed by the number of high-profile companies that have selected a next-generation member of the owning family as president or chief executive. The decade was characterized by globalization, quantum technological change, the upending of business models implicit in dot-coms, and the restructuring of the value chain. As a result, many industries are consolidating, many manufacturers are choosing to go directly to the customer, and competition is intense everywhere. Yet, much like the forecasted demise of paper with the advent of the paperless office, the demise of family-owned/controlled companies has been wildly exaggerated.

The belief widely held in the United States that family business is an oxymoron and that "the kids are not good enough to run the business" has to be countered with the facts. Competent, hard-working, visionary yet practical leaders of the next generation are taking over the reigns of great companies all over the world.

In Italy, third-generation Agnellis now control Fiat. In France, the Peugeot heirs work at the company, serve on its board, and control the company. In Germany, second-generation Quandt family members own 46 percent of BMW shares. In Japan, the Toyoda family still has much influence on Toyota through potential successor Akio Toyoda, the youngest member of its board. And in the United States, fourth-generation Ford chairman William Clay Ford replaced nonfamily CEO Jacques Nasser, after Nasser's managerial revolution failed. Note that all of these examples come from a highly capital-intensive industry, requiring multiple sources of external capital. During the last decade, the auto industry has also had to deal with intense competition and global consolidation.

In other industries, too, family successors are taking over in record numbers. Third-generation Blake Nordstrom became president of the elegant retail chain; James Hagedorn, whose family controls much of Scotts, recently became the lawn-care company's chief executive; Rupert Murdoch at Fox and George Soros at Soros Fund Management are both grooming members of the next generation to take over the business. At Fidelity Investments, the largest mutual fund company, Abigail Johnson was named president of investment management operations and will likely succeed her father, Edward C. Johnson III, as chairman. In the food industry, Jim Perdue, a member of the third generation, has become chairman of Perdue Farms, succeeding Frank Perdue; and John Tyson has taken over the running of Tyson Foods from the largest shareholder—his father, Don. Two brothers, who represent the next generation of Mondavis, have taken over from Robert Mondavi and are furthering Robert's mission to make Napa wines as well known for their quality as those of Bordeaux, Burgundy, and Tuscany.

Still, no trend is a trend if it does not have exceptions. Leon Gorman, grandson of the founder of L.L. Bean, has stepped down as president and chief executive officer and found a successor outside the family, for the first time in the company's history. Gorman's three sons chose not to work at L.L. Bean, but the family is careful to point out that the new CEO worked at the company for 18 years before this promotion and shares the company's core values and traditions, which presumably came from founder Leon Bean and his descendants. Perhaps, as Ford Motor Company has done in previous generations, L.L. Bean will skip this generation but remain on the lookout for capable members of the next generation who want the challenge of running the family business. At Anheuser-Busch, the new CEO is on interim assignment until a fifth-generation member, August Busch IV, is fully ready for the demanding post of running this publicly traded but family-controlled $12-billion corporation. When August A. Busch III turns over the roles of president and chief executive officer to Patrick Stokes, a 59-year-old loyal employee, Stokes will be Anheuser-Busch's first non-family chief executive in 140 years.

ARE THE KIDS GOOD ENOUGH TO RUN THE BUSINESS?

Before her death, Katharine Graham proclaimed that, notwithstanding the fact that many of the large newspapers had become management controlled, family control was still the name of the game for most of the high-quality newspapers, like the *Washington Post*, the *New York Times*, and the *Wall Street Journal*. Her son, Don Graham, whom she chose to succeed her as CEO and publisher, had a lengthy developmental journey. Don served his country in Vietnam and then returned to the United States to work a beat in Washington, D.C., as a policeman, not a reporter. A couple of years later, he joined the *Washington Post* and began to amass experience in the news and media industries with a variety of assignments at the *Post* and a business education from Harvard Business School.

Empirical deduction from a systematic review of such succession experiences has led me to the following conclusions:

1. Many next-generation members of business-owning families want to lead and are ready to work hard and make the sacrifices necessary to be responsible leaders. Determining whether this is true of the next generation in your own family is key. Evidence can be found in work hours, flexibility, adaptability, willingness to serve, commitment to a mission larger than themselves, education, respect for what has made the business successful so far, and overall discipline in both thought and action.

2. The multi-year succession process of many next-generation executives has included a number of challenging assignments, particularly those where outcomes are measured in profit or loss and are clearly attributable to the successor. Early in their development, these next-generation executives usually worked outside the family business, where results are more objectively and exclusively attributable to performance, unbiased by family influences. After they joined the family enterprise, assignments generally included profit center and general management responsibilities that replicate the often-conflicting demands on the chief executive, who is ultimately responsible for profit or loss and the creation of shareholder value. Given the flexibility of the financial software now available, even small, single-unit family businesses can create successor accountability for profit or loss. Information on results—the bottom line—and the discipline created by this accountability determine readiness and capability far more effectively than bloodline does.

   In larger companies, with only United States operations, these early assignments were often far from company headquarters. In the case of multi-national businesses, many early experiences happened abroad. For example, after running his own Fort Worth real estate empire, Ross Perot, Jr., worked in the London office of Perot Systems before succeeding his father as Perot Systems chief executive.[1]

3. Through solid performance and interpersonal skills, next-generation members have earned the respect of nonfamily employees, suppliers, customers, and other family members, often shareholders, whom they will serve and lead. Evan Greenberg, son of Maurice Greenberg, is being groomed to run American International Group (AIG), an insurance company that has been very successful in creating shareholder value. Evan is not admired for his polished interpersonal skills; he has acquired the reputation of being as tough and aggressive as his father. But key AIG executives around the world and AIG shareholders respect this about the successor, while competitors fear it. Evan has earned this respect without taking the traditional career path of college and an MBA. Upon graduation from high school, he skipped college to work odd jobs. Only after joining an AIG branch office in Denver did he return to college and

industry-specific coursework before running small and then larger profit centers for AIG overseas.[2]

4. In most cases, the successor development process included much education—college, industry-sponsored programs, and business schools. MBAs helped many successors gain both the skills and the confidence they needed to steer a responsible professional or middle management career into top management echelons. Unfortunately, MBA programs do not usually address ownership and the unique role that it plays in the leadership of family-led companies. Programs acknowledge trading and perhaps investment, but seldom patient long-term ownership. Graduating students often head to Wall Street and consulting firms, which seldom advise on the owner-manager relationship from a long-term perspective. However, ownership education is increasingly becoming available at leading business schools through entrepreneurial and family business curricula. At the Weatherhead School of Management at Case Western Reserve University, for instance, a year-long post-graduate program called Family Business—The Next Generation: A Leadership Institute for Owner-Managers and Family-Controlled Companies fulfills this mission.

5. Coaches and mentors, both inside and outside the family, have been an important feature of the developmental journey. Gina Gallo, of Gallo Wines, credits both Julio Gallo, her grandfather, and Marcello Monticelli, a 35-year Gallo veteran, with being her mentors. A third-generation family member, she has assumed primary responsibility as winemaker and marketer for the Gallo of Sonoma line of premium wines. She is attempting to do one of the hardest things in business—reposition a brand identified with low price and fair quality to a much higher value price point. Marketers had suggested that Gallo launch the wines under a different name precisely because of the image problem, but a sense of pride in the family and the name decided the issue for Gina.[3]

6. The process of deciding whether the potential successor was right for the job, for the company, and for the company's strategic needs took many years. Sometimes, it included an assessment by an outside professional, such as a psychologist, who coached the successor through evaluations by peers, supervisors, subordinates, customers, suppliers at work, and relatives at home. In the post-graduate next-generation leadership program at Case Western Reserve University, every participant begins the year-long developmental journey by having a dozen reviewers fill out the Goleman-Boyatzis Emotional Competencies Inventory, which focuses on 52 behaviors linked to executive success. Participants then receive feedback and coaching as appropriate. Successor candidates who have experienced this process and been accountable for profit and loss know themselves and their strengths and weaknesses well (see Exhibit 4-1). Such a degree of self-awareness is often hard for next-generation members to achieve because of the large shadow cast by their family predecessors.

| EXHIBIT 4-1 | A PROFILE OF SUCCESSFUL SUCCESSORS |

Successful next-generation leaders share the following characteristics:

- They know the business well; ideally, they like or even love the nature of the business.
- They know themselves and their strengths and weaknesses, having had the necessary outside experience and education.
- They want to lead and serve.
- They are guided responsibly by the previous generation, by advisors, and by a board of outside directors.
- They have good relationships and the ability to accommodate others, especially if part of a successor team (siblings, in-laws, or cousins).
- They can count on competent nonfamily managers in the top management team to complement their own skills.
- They have controlling ownership or can lead, through allies, as if they did.
- They have earned the respect of nonfamily employees, suppliers, customers, and other family members.
- Their skills and abilities fit the strategic needs of the business.
- They respect the past and focus their energies on the future of the business and the family.

SOURCE: Adapted from Davis, J., "Successor Development," a presentation at the International Family Enterprise Institute meeting in Montreal, 1998.

7. A board of directors—or a committee of that board made up primarily of independent outsiders—performed the final review of successor performance and company-strategy fit. These directors also offered advice on the timing of the succession. In companies that created advisory (nonstatutory) boards composed of independent outsiders, in lieu of having independent outsiders on their board of directors, these boards provided a forum for many discussions about selecting and anointing the CEO successor. Throughout the several years over which the succession process occurred, board members, individually and collectively, were very active in the assessment, the facilitation of difficult conversations, the review of pertinent information, and the ultimate appointment of the successor.

Including a committee of outside directors or an advisory board not only ensures more thorough and objective data gathering, analysis, and decision making but also suggests to other candidates, nonfamily executives, and both family and nonfamily shareholders the independent and objective nature of the decision. Shareholder support of the decision is always important but is especially so in publicly traded family-controlled firms.

THE VERY YOUNG MEMBERS OF THE NEXT GENERATION

Experienced advisors to family businesses, as well as family business owners themselves, are adamant about the need to start the children's education early. From the time they are seven or eight, heirs to the family business need to begin receiving de-entitlement training. Through stories and anecdotes of the sacrifice and commitment of the founders during the early days of the business, heirs will begin to understand that, more than privilege and wealth, a family business means stewardship and responsibility. Clearly communicating the enjoyment and the pride associated with the business is also important. The idea is not to discourage them from thinking about joining the business later in their lives but to ensure that, if this is what they want to do, they know they will earn their position rather than inherit it. Since much learning derives from direct experience, in their teen years these members of the next generation need to be exposed to working for a salary or performing family chores, both of which promote the development of a work ethic.

A work ethic is the most influential counterbalance to any experiences with the advantages of wealth. But besides a work ethic, young next-generation members need an understanding that the family's estate requires stewardship in order to be preserved and grown for subsequent generations. Through family meetings, special education for the young heirs, and/or early experiences in financial management, the children will begin to realize that the company is not simply a source of cash for their checkbook but, instead, a responsibility requiring stewardship. The presence of heirs who approach an operating company with a checkbook mentality certainly increases the probability that the business and the family will both be destroyed. In fact, experienced business owners argue that the risk of business failure rises exponentially with the development of a sense of entitlement and aspirations of liquidity.

A good way to develop a sense of financial responsibility among very young next-generation members is to provide them with their own expense account, based on quarterly or semiannual budgeting—and no possibility of additional deposits in the case of overspending. Chapter 3 described a business owner who held one-on-one business education sessions with the next generation during family vacations and gave the children their own checking accounts for school and life expenses, after determining with their input an appropriate budget. Actions such as these reduce the propensity of parents to use money to control their children as they grow. At the same time, they help children assume personal responsibility for financial matters early in life.

When young next-generation members come to work in the business, their compensation needs to be market-based. Using compensation to communicate love, to respond to personal needs, to communicate equality, or even to engender a sense of sacrifice on behalf of the corporation is not helpful. Along with market-based compensation should come performance reviews. Performance reviews help assess results against goals. By treating next-generation members the same way nonfamily employees are treated, they reinforce a merit rather than an entitlement culture. Most importantly, they provide next-generation members with developmental feedback at a time in their careers when it is most useful.

Results of the Discovery study indicate that performance reviews are least often done with members of the owning family.[4] The reasons are easy to understand: A family member is not the person best qualified to do a performance review of another family member, and key nonfamily managers are hesitant to hold next-generation members of the family to high standards because, after all, they may someday end up working for them. Yet next-generation members are seriously handicapped when their careers proceed in a performance feedback vacuum. Senior nonfamily executives who enjoy much security in the company and are personally confident and independent are ideal candidates for carrying out this task, even if they are not the direct supervisors of the family members. In this case, the supervisor, the senior nonfamily manager, and the next-generation member all meet to review performance and to establish a new set of goals for the next relevant period.

SIBLING AND COUSIN TEAMS

Cases in which a team of siblings or cousins assume power, through an "office of the president" or an "executive committee," represent only a tiny minority of all CEO successions. In those cases where no individual team leader is chosen, the concern is that the choice may represent not the CEO-parent's informed decision as architect of the firm's continuity but, rather, his or her inability to decide. Making such an important decision tugs at the heart of any father or mother. While most chief executives in family businesses are also parents, clearly they need to wear their CEO hat when confronting this decision.

The family leader may love everybody equally, but the CEO is compelled by administrative tradition and current management practice to choose one individual from among many loved ones. Sometimes, next-generation members collude in this dynamic. Rather than be denied the top spot, next-generation members may suggest structures that minimize the differences among them. Assisting in making this emotionally charged decision is another way in which a board can help the chief executive with the succession decision-making process.

As an experiment, one smart, successful, and well-intentioned CEO created an office of the president. The three third-generation members' abilities, contributions, and capacity to work together were tested under this structure for about three years. Two siblings ran independent divisions and the other was the chief financial officer, but all three were part of the office of the president. Notwithstanding the significant attention given to developing and facilitating the concept, the office of the president did not, in the end, significantly help the three siblings manage their interdependence successfully. The CEO, on the advice of his board and with the support of all but one next-generation member, decided to appoint a single successor CEO of the corporation. Currently, all three siblings are board members, and five independent outsiders ensure review and accountability at the holding company level.

NEXT-GENERATION PERSONALITIES. As they grow up, siblings often adopt very different but complementary personalities; one son may be great at marketing, while a daughter may excel in operations or finance. Such differences present unique opportunities for staffing a growing business. On the other hand, these differences may constitute grounds for much disagreement and conflict. The past is perhaps the greatest forecaster of the future, so evidence of collaboration rather than competition among a group of siblings is the best predictor of their capacity to work together as a team. When it comes to teams that include cousins or in-laws, the differences are often even more pronounced because these next-generation members grew up with different parents, who influenced their development differently. Parenting the next-generation members of one team, for example, were one brother who liked to spend his money and live well, another brother who was frugal, and a sister who was extremely religious and charitable.

INTERDEPENDENCE OF TEAM MEMBERS. Interdependence, or coordinated independence, is a central issue for sibling and cousin teams and a very difficult one to manage. It is at the root of most disagreements between and across generations. The best way to minimize the difficulties that may arise is to design an organizational structure that establishes very different roles for the different members of the next generation. For example, one sibling might be assigned to run the London office, another to run operations, and the other to run the sales division. You may recall that this was the approach chosen by Samuel Curtis Johnson III at SC Johnson. Of course, he also built a board at the holding company level, where all four sons and daughters, plus three independent outsiders, could meet and work through the unavoidable issues of interdependence, such as capital allocation decisions.

A Top Management Team. Only rarely do sibling and cousin teams in family businesses share an office (as in the office of the president concept) or split the positions of CEO and COO between them. More often, they function as a top management team. In other words, several members of the family, whether in marketing, finance, or general management of a division, report to one chief executive officer. This is the case at the Gallo and the Mondavi wineries. It is also true of the Estée Lauder Companies, where Aerin Lauder, the granddaughter of the founder of the cosmetics giant, has joined with members of the previous generation and cousins in a team effort. Clearly, family members were chosen based on their skills and how those skills complement each other, with some members working in marketing, others in operations, and still others in the international arena.

Managing Interdependence. After a CEO has taken great care to create different posts, with clearly differentiated roles, what else can be done to avoid second-guessing, working at cross-purposes, sending multiple signals to employees, and general wear and tear on family relationships? Some guidelines for managing interdependence follow:

1. Establish common goals.
2. Reflect those different roles in an established organizational chart.
3. Develop procedures that reduce relationship wear and tear. For instance, establish a process for role negotiations between parties, a process for team building, and a code of conduct or list of ground rules to be observed by all parties.
4. Establish forums for discussing relationships and sharing feelings on an ongoing basis so that bad feelings are not allowed to fester and multiply unchecked. Disciplined communication in regularly scheduled meetings where the participants address the question "How are we doing?" and not just "What are we doing?" makes a huge difference in the success of sibling and cousin teams.
5. Transfer ownership with full recognition that the next-generation CEO needs to have not only the job and the title but also the ability to lead, whether alone or with true allies, as if she or he had 51 percent of the voting stock. Anything less could easily create paralysis and deprive the new leader of the ability to be nimble and agile, a competitive advantage of many entrepreneurial and family-owned businesses.

The fact that so many family-owned and family-controlled businesses today are enjoying successful transfers of power to next-generation members may be a direct result of more sophisticated use of management practices like performance reviews and governance practices like reliance on boards of directors, advisory boards, and family councils. All of these techniques assist the CEO in ensuring that succession is not about nepotism and privilege but rather about demonstrated capabilities and accountable execution of managerial and/or ownership responsibilities by the next generation.

A VISION FOR THE COMPANY: TAKING IT TO THE NEXT LEVEL

Each generation has the responsibility of bringing to the business their own vision for the future of the business.

—Samuel Curtis Johnson III, Retired Chairman, SC Johnson: A Family Company

Compared to their predecessors, younger members of a business family are often more inclined to accept new technologies and more prone to assume the risks that go along with promoting growth of the business. If their chosen profession is management, next-generation members are likely to want to engage in strategic planning, redesign information/financial systems, and pursue digital strategies or e-commerce opportunities. How can the skills and visions of the next generation be most usefully tapped by the family enterprise?

Earlier in this chapter, it was observed that in successful successions the heir often found employment outside before joining the family business. Next-generation members interested in developing their own capacity to lead the firm and the family would be well served by following that example.

But once next-generation members have performed a three-to-five-year stint in a professionally managed, leading-edge global corporation, are opportunities created for them to play a change-agent role on behalf of the family's business? Many times, they are not, and the reasons are evident. It is hard enough for a CEO to embrace and accept change at a stage in life when enjoying the fruits of one's labor seems more appealing. It is significantly harder to do so when the agent of change is a son or daughter, nephew or niece—the same "child" who only a few years ago, it seems, was so prone to say "No" to everything.

The business reason for welcoming the next-generation's ideas is that their complementary skills and perspectives are precisely what a family business often needs as it struggles to update itself in order to grow and continue to create value for its customers. When the fourth-generation members of Sidney Printing Works in Cincinnati joined the family company, they provided the necessary skills for the business to become a strong contender in the new era. In this case, the two generations were fundamentally in agreement on their vision for company growth—a situation that does not happen all that often. While continuing to use traditional methods to print labels, signs, maps, and product literature in their plant, Sidney Printing Works, with the aid of its fourth-generation family members, now assists customers with Web materials, helps them submit designs digitally for production in multiple media, and customizes and archives those designs for multiple end uses. Ultimately, a new business unit called SpringDot, Inc., was created, acknowledging this innovative use of next-generation skills.[5]

AT&T Comcast provides another example in which a vision of company growth was supported by two generations, but on a much larger scale. In 2002, Ralph Roberts helped his son Brian snag the cable business from AT&T, and Brian became the CEO of AT&T Comcast, the number-one cable company, serving 22 million homes. Even with concessions made to AT&T management, the Roberts family will have control, and Brian will have the opportunity of a lifetime to make his father's and his vision a reality. Certainly, it is not always this easy.

DISAGREEMENTS: HAVING THE DIFFICULT CONVERSATIONS

> My father forced me to think and to present my ideas in a forceful way because he said no to everything. He took the position of devil's advocate. And everything I brought in for approval—to buy a hotel, build a hotel, grow a hotel business, to change the strategies—he'd say no.
>
> —J. W. Marriott, Jr., CEO and Chairman of the Board, Marriott International[6]

If there is a disagreement worth having in a family-controlled company, it is a disagreement about the vision and future direction for the firm. Implicit in conversations about strategy across generations is the tension between fully appreciating and respecting what has made the business successful so far and fully accepting that, given the accelerated rate of change in today's global marketplace, the firm will be overtaken by the competition and eventually driven to extinction unless it is willing to adapt.

Consider the experience of a family company I will call by the fictitious name of Madco Industries. Madco found itself in a strategic dilemma. The CEO's son, who was vice president of finance, was convinced that Madco, a regional distributor of high-priced industrial equipment, could grow and prosper if it complemented its existing operations with the creation of a new channel of distribution via the Internet. His father, the CEO, was equally convinced that doing so would be a bad idea on two counts. First, it would set up a competitive situation between the new company and the existing one and, potentially, between father and son. Second, it could damage relationships with distributors in other parts of the country with whom, in the absence of competition, relationships were cordial and competitive dynamics gentlemanly.

The situation first came to our attention when the son and potential successor called with the news that he was leaving the firm. After obtaining his MBA and then returning to the family firm, he had implemented a new financial information and control system. Since that assignment was now done and he wanted to have a little entrepreneurship in his life, the idea of starting a Web-enabled company fit him fine. He described how he had suggested the new digital strategy to the CEO and how the latter had quickly dismissed it, with the words "over my dead body." The son could not refrain from responding to this ultimatum, so he said, "If we don't do it, somebody else will, and then somebody outside our family will be eating our lunch." So, perhaps coincidentally, I suggested that he have his father give me a call to arrange a lunch meeting for the three of us.

At the beginning of the meeting, the two generations could hardly speak to each other, even with my assistance. Emotions were running high. By the end of the afternoon, though, we had crafted what seemed like a reasonable plan. The potential successor would write a business plan for his new idea, price shares in the new company on the basis of the seed capital required, and get a 20-minute slot on the agenda of the next meeting of the eight distributors from around the country. This meeting was held every year in the hometown of one of the distributors. That year, it was Madco's turn to host, and the meeting was scheduled to take place in two months. Because the eight distributors had assigned territories and competed not with each other but with others throughout the country, this meeting provided a forum for learning and candid conversation. The potential successor would thus get his opportunity to present the business plan and see whether the other distributors considered it a viable idea and would buy shares in the new venture. The CEO closed our extended lunch meeting by telling his son, "If you manage to sell as little as one share in the project, I am in too."

While this plan represented quite a challenge to the young man, it seemed like a reasonable turn of events. The potential successor might get an opportunity to be an entrepreneur; in the meantime, his decision to leave the family business was at least delayed. His father felt strongly that the only way he would be willing to consider changing his mind was if the idea passed the marketplace test, especially among people he respected and with whom he had a relationship he wished to protect.

At the group meeting, the son successfully sold several shares in the new business venture. The e-commerce company was launched as a collaborative venture between several of the distributors, and the son became the new venture's president. About a year and a half after its successful launch, the publisher of a trade publication in their industry made an offer to acquire the new company. On the basis of that offer, it appeared that the successor had managed to create more shareholder value in 18 months than the CEO had created in a whole generation. Very impressed with the offer and cognizant that it could take another lifetime to achieve such returns in the absence of the transaction, the son and his partners, including his CEO father, decided to sell.

While the new venture did not remain in the family company's fold for long, it represented great growth and creation of shareholder value for the company and a tremendous learning opportunity for the successor. He is again looking for entrepreneurial opportunities and is a little better financed this time around.

In conflict-averse families, parents often attempt to squelch sibling rivalry or intergenerational conflict. They seek to alleviate conflict because they feel anxious about the expression of differences or aggression by the now-adult children. In these families, next-generation members remain dependent on parents to resolve their differences well into adulthood. Controlling parents join in creating an unhealthy equilibrium, a dismal dance in which next-generation members operate primarily out of their dependency and powerlessness—the exact opposite of the entrepreneurial and enterprising behavior desired of next-generation business leaders.

RESPECTING THE PAST AND FOCUSING ON THE FUTURE

The tension across generations around the issues of growth and innovation is neither new nor exclusively a product of new technology or the e-commerce revolution. Many years ago, as a young chemist working in the company's lab, Samuel Curtis Johnson III, recently retired chairman of SC Johnson: A Family Company, tried to convince his father that he had the formula for a breakthrough product, an insecticide. Reports are that several attempts at convincing his father of the soundness of the idea were rebuffed with a simple "Remember, son, we are a wax company." Samuel Curtis continued to faithfully perform his assigned job at the lab and carry out his "skunk works" project on the side. He also continued to bring up his idea and advocate its merits in subsequent meetings with his father, only to receive the same admonition. Finally, young Samuel Curtis reportedly added a tiny amount of wax as an inert ingredient to his formulation for the insecticide. When he once again took the new product, now part of the wax family of products, to his father, it received the go-ahead; after all, the insecticide was now wax-based.

A fourth-generation member of the family insists that it was not the adding of wax that changed the father's mind but rather the young chemist's persistence and continued hard work on the new product formula. Whatever the reason for the change of heart, S. C. Johnson II finally became convinced that the idea was sound and that the product did not stray too far from the company's established strengths and core competencies. What is undeniable is that, during the third generation of family leadership, the company grew from $60 million in annual revenues to $4 billion. And, according to company sources, much of the growth and the lion's share of profits came from the new product lines related to insect control, with brand names like Raid® and Off!® Is it any wonder that S. C. Johnson III advocates allowing each generation to bring his or her own vision to the business?

SOME FINAL RULES OF THE ROAD FOR NEXT-GENERATION LEADERS

Analysis of the age data from the Discovery Action Research Project shows a compelling pattern in the respondents' answers. Those 51 years of age and older and those 30 and younger were routinely more positive about the family, the family business, and its management practices than were respondents in the 31–50 age bracket. The research included parents, sons, daughters, nieces, and nephews. This finding is similar to that of Davis and Tagiuri, who suggest in their work on the influence of lifestage on father–son work relationships that the most harmonious relationship occurs when the father is in his 50s and the son is between 23 and 33.[7] The Discovery findings are consistent with, and may help explain, the increased harmony across generations at that stage.

Davis and Tagiuri also suggest that when the father is in his 60s and the son is between 34 and 40, the work relationship is rather problematic. Discovery study findings, too, would suggest a more difficult relationship, based on the perceptual gap between the relatively less positive 31- to 50-year-old and the 51+ CEO. Both studies clearly imply that the next-generation leader should expect difficult conversations, especially those about strategy, to become more problematic as she or he reaches the mid-30s and 40s and the CEO advances to his or her 60s. It is essential, therefore, to create forums for continuing the dialogue and maintaining the relationship—regularly scheduled meetings, fishing/hunting trips, joint vacations, etc. CEOs' initiatives at building institutions of governance are also very important. Boards of directors with independent outsiders, nonfamily managers in top management positions, family meetings, and family councils all create more balanced and rational discourse on subjects that may carry emotional content.

Research by Colette Dumas found that while sons develop their sense of identity by separating from their father and "proving their mettle," daughters do so through continued affiliation with their father as mentor.[8] This difference means that a next-generation daughter or niece could easily display continued caring for the previous-generation CEO and the enterprise, be more interdependent than a son or nephew, and still be quite capable of leading the enterprise. Although style is clearly not the critical criterion for next-generation leadership success, there is an unfortunate tendency to view a daughter's less confrontational style as a weakness in relation to the challenges of leadership. If the next-generation leader is not the eldest male of his generation, this creates special challenges that should be met with caution. Incongruent hierarchies exist in the family and the business when the individual's position within the family is different from his or her position within the business.[9] Incongruent hierarchies have made succession a more difficult process for many deserving next-generation leaders.

Regardless of gender, next-generation leaders have to understand that their mission is to lead, concurrently, the business, the family, and the shareholders. They must recognize that different perceptions about what is and what needs to be are rooted not necessarily in personalities and politics, but in the fact that nonfamily managers, family members not active in the business, and other shareholders may have different needs and goals than family members actively participating in the business.

Like it or not, change is in the job description of next-generation leaders. How effectively and rapidly that change is pursued, how well articulated the need for change is, how much next-generation leaders respect the past, and how clear the vision remains post-change will make all the difference.

When the cause and effect of a particular action or decision are within the control of the family business leader, change is easy. Entrepreneurs with a well-documented large locus of control thrive on this; it makes them and their companies very flexible and highly adaptable. But next-generation leaders tend to find that the causes of many of the actions and decisions that affect them significantly, such as those surrounding succession, are outside their control. Thus, young leaders have to be aware of the need to initiate change in themselves. Then they need to make change happen by enlisting the active collaboration of others—convincing those with different perspectives of the need for change, walking the talk, and being clear and disciplined in the delineation of the vision, or desired state.

The essence of the next-generation leader's mission is to appreciate all that has made the business and the family successful and harmonious thus far and to simultaneously focus on adapting and changing the family-management-ownership system to meet the new competitive environment and opportunities. In this way, continuing success and continuity across generations can be assured.

SUMMARY

1. Members of the next generation of family business owners are taking over from their predecessors in record numbers and are willing to make the sacrifices necessary to be responsible leaders.

2. Early in their career development, many next-generation members work outside the family business, where results are more objectively and exclusively attributable to their personal performance, unbiased by family influences.

3. Ownership education is becoming increasingly important in the successor development process.

4. Coaches and mentors, both inside and outside the family, are an important feature of the developmental journey.

5. The process of deciding whether the potential successor is right for the job, for the company, and for the company's strategic needs involves years of assessment.

6. A board of directors, a committee of that board made up primarily of independent outsiders, or an advisory board can be extremely helpful in the appointment of a successor.

7. Heirs to the family business must learn early in their lives that they will earn a position in the business rather than inherit it. They should also learn to manage their own money at an early age.

8. When a team of siblings or cousins is chosen for the leadership position, the CEO must establish common goals, carefully create different posts with clearly differentiated roles, reflect those roles in an organizational chart, develop processes that support teamwork and disciplined communication, and transfer ownership with full recognition that the next-generation CEO needs to have the ability to lead.

9. Compared to their predecessors, younger members of a business family are often more inclined to accept new technologies and more ready to accept risk. In order to continue to grow the business, it is important for previous-generation leaders to address conflict within the family, to give consideration to the new ideas, and to embrace the new skills being offered.

EXERCISE

CROSS-GENERATIONAL BRIDGE-BUILDING

Addressing these questions to a current CEO and to next-generation family members is a standard practice among family business advisors who are leading discussions about preserving the past and promoting the future. Ask your students to compose plausible responses to these questions as if they were the CEO and/or a member of the next generation.

1. *(Ask CEO)* What has been key to the business's success and deserves to be preserved? (What does the CEO know about the customers, technology, competitors, suppliers, and business operations that is essential to preserve?)

2. *(Ask Next Generation)* What changes in the competitive environment are of significant concern? (For the business to remain healthy and competitively fit, what growth opportunities need to be promoted in the future?)

3. *(Ask Both)* Empathize with the other generation by imagining what they are likely to answer to question 1 (*Next Generation:* What is key to the business and needs to be preserved?) and question 2 (*CEO:* What growth opportunities should be promoted to ensure the continuing health of the business?).

CASES

CASE 1:
ADELPHIA COMMUNICATIONS

Adelphia Communications' chairman and CEO, John Rigas, resigned on May 15, 2002, after 52 years at the helm of the sixth largest cable system operator in the United States. The following day, his son Timothy Rigas resigned as the company's chief financial officer. Both subsequently also resigned from the board, as a crisis engulfed the company and rumors abounded about its eventual need to file for bankruptcy and carry out asset sales to ensure its survival. John Rigas, 77, was facing an investigation by the SEC; 18 shareholder lawsuits that alleged different forms of fraud, self-dealing, and lack of disclosure; and an 80 percent drop in the value of Adelphia stock when trading on the NASDAQ reopened after being halted.

Adelphia's troubles began on March 27, 2002, when it disclosed that the Rigas family had used company assets as collateral for about $3 billion in off–balance sheet loans to a family-run partnership that had purchased Adelphia stock. Soon thereafter, it appeared that the company was being pushed into a breakup by its other investors. While family-managed and family-controlled, Adelphia had taken that important step of going public, in order to have greater access to equity and capital markets that would help fund its growth.

In 2002, the Rigas family owned about 20 percent of Adelphia's outstanding stock but had 60 percent voting control. The single largest individual shareholder was not a Rigas family member but Leonard Tow, chairman of Citizens Communications, the cable operator from which Adelphia had acquired Century Communications in 1999.[1]

Back in 1999, with valuations of cable systems at historic highs of 20 to 22 times annual cash flow, or $3,000 to $4,500 per subscriber, Adelphia Communications seemed a likely acquisition target. Any transaction would have represented a financial bonanza for the Rigas family, which had acquired many of the cable systems it now operated at much lower values. But, instead of selling, the Rigas family acquired additional cable systems representing about 3 million subscribers, nearly doubling the company's size in one year. In 2002, Adelphia Communications had about 6 billion subscribers and close to $4 billion in annual revenues.

The company, founded by John Rigas in 1952 with a compelling vision and $300 (used to acquire the first movie theater on Main Street, in Coudersport, Pennsylvania), grew tremendously throughout the 1980s and 1990s. Highly leveraged acquisitions of cable systems were the source of much of the growth. "John,

62

like a lot of entrepreneurs, has a huge capacity for risk," said Charles Updegraff, Jr., chief executive officer of Citizens Trust Company and a boyhood friend of Rigas.[2] John Rigas was not about to become a target of the consolidation going on in the industry. His own opinion was "If it wasn't for the children—they've had a lot of experience, they do the job exceptionally well, they know the business and they're committed—then I would probably have been a candidate [to sell] and do what others did."[3]

John Rigas dreamed of continuity for the family business. He expected next-generation family members to continue to participate in both ownership and management of the firm. The son of Greek immigrants, John had founded Adelphia with his brother Gus. The company's name is derived from the Greek word *delphi*, meaning brother. Three of John Rigas's sons worked at Adelphia: Timothy, a Wharton graduate, joined the firm in 1979 and eventually became CFO; Michael joined in 1981; and James, the only married son, joined in 1986. John, Timothy, Michael, James, and Peter Venetis, who was John Rigas's son-in-law, were all on the board of directors; four outside directors made up the rest of the nine-member board.

The company, headquartered in Coudersport, Pennsylvania, exhibited a strong family culture in other ways. Town–company relationships were the source of legends. The Rigas family umbrella covered employees and their family members in times of need, when they required special medical attention or financial assistance. The family also demonstrated significant altruism toward Coudersport. The Rigas family insisted on keeping the company's headquarters there instead of moving it to a larger metropolitan area, helped fund the local hospital, helped get roads plowed in the winter, and refurbished buildings and public spaces to enhance the town's image. This caring attitude toward employees and the community was reciprocated with a special loyalty. For instance, an employee loaned John Rigas money from her inheritance to keep him from defaulting on a $25,000 loan he had used to acquire another cable operator in the 1960s.[4]

The Rigas dynasty was an empire with humble beginnings—the ownership of one movie theatre in Coudersport, Pennsylvania. Clouds gathered around the family when auditors, forensic accountants, and investors discovered evidence of company payments to fund Rigas family interests, including timber rights purchases, a golf course, and cash advances to the Rigas family–controlled Buffalo Sabres hockey team, as well as to bail out family members who faced margin calls on their investments in Adelphia stock.

To the surprise of the four outside directors on Adelphia's board—who, along with the five family members on the board, had oversight responsibility for the company and its management—Adelphia had also guaranteed loans to Rigas family members. The largest shareholder outside of the Rigas family, Leonard Tow, owned 12 percent of Adelphia's outstanding stock. As the company moved closer to a crisis and a bankruptcy filing, Tow insisted on having a seat on the board and being a factor in turning things around. But barely two weeks after joining the board, Leonard Tow resigned, saying "Subsequent revelations of the unreliability of corporate data, as well as the on-going serial disclosures of wrongdoing have made it impossible to contribute meaningfully to the process."[5]

CASE QUESTIONS

1. Using the systems theory, agency theory, or resource-based view, discuss what is happening in this family-controlled company.

2. Do you suspect that John Rigas knew just how bad things were? If not, what could he or others have done to ensure that the office of the CEO had the relevant facts?

3. What governance approaches could have changed the outcome of this case?

NOTES

1. Farrell, Mike, *Multichannel News*, May 23, 2002.

2. Frank, Robert, *Wall Street Journal*, May 26, 2002.

3. Farrell, Mike, *Multichannel News*, May 20, 2002.

4. Frank, Robert, op. cit.

5. Farrell, Mike, *Multichannel News*, June 17, 2002.

CASE 2:
THE *WASHINGTON POST* AND THE GRAHAM FAMILY

I don't think it's an accident that the newspapers best known for quality in this country . . . are, or were until recently, family controlled. It seems that certain attributes essential to quality are more easily provided by families than by public companies. These are the qualities that I think most important: First, deep roots. Families offer longevity—and thus a knowledge of, and commitment to, the local community that's hard to get from professional managers who come and go. . . . Second, a perspective that extends beyond the next quarter's earnings per share. . . . Finally, family ownership provides the independence that is sometimes required to withstand governmental pressure and preserve freedom of the press.

—Katharine Graham, *Wall Street Journal*, March 20, 2000

In 2002, the Washington Post Company was a diversified media organization with 10,700 employees, annual revenues of $2.4 billion, and profits of $229.6 million. In addition to publishing the *Washington Post*, the company owned *Newsweek* magazine, six network-affiliated TV stations, a cable network with more than 600,000 subscribers, education-related businesses (e.g., Kaplan), and interests in other media-related companies.[1] The Post's nonvoting B stock was publicly traded at about $600 a share. Voting control, however, rested in the A stock owned by Katharine Graham and her four children. Publisher and CEO Donald E. Graham, 56, was the fourth member of the family in three generations to hold that post. Don had joined the paper in 1971, after graduating from college, serving in the U.S. Army, and working as a Washington, D.C., policeman.

KATHARINE GRAHAM'S LEADERSHIP

On September 20, 1963, Katharine Graham, 46, was elected president of the *Washington Post*.[2] According to her, neither her qualifications nor her confidence level were at all impressive. She assumed the post after her husband's death, having had little managerial experience. Graham set out to learn the business. She sought the advice and counsel of experienced nonfamily executives and eventually concluded that the *Post* was not yet the paper she wanted it to be. So she increased the editorial staff by 20 percent, doubled the number of foreign bureaus, and brought in Ben Bradlee, then head of *Newsweek*'s Washington bureau, as deputy managing editor of the *Post*. Bradlee hired a cadre of talented reporters and writers and began to promote a new energy and new ideas.

In 1971, Katharine Graham took the Washington Post Company public, though she had never sought public visibility, in order to raise money for expansion. One large investor, Warren Buffett, bought about 10 percent of the non-voting B shares (he continued to invest in the company over the years; by 2002, he owned approximately 20 percent of the B shares) and was eventually invited to sit on the company board. He often acted as an advisor, teacher, and sounding board for Katharine. Among other things, Buffett convinced the Washington Post Company that it was a good policy to begin buying company stock, as so many other companies do today.

In the 1970s, the decision to publish first the highly visible Pentagon Papers and later the Watergate scandal made the *Washington Post* itself news, not just a reporter of news. Both stories made it clear to reporters, journalists, *Post* employees, and many others that the *Washington Post* was independent, determined, and confident of its purpose. A sense of mission and agreement on goals and how to achieve them, in the public interest, were forged into the DNA of the Washington Post Company and the Graham family in this decade.

This clarity of purpose was tested with a pressmen's union strike in 1975. The bitter strike lasted over three months. Profits at the *Post* declined, and a new owner promised to rejuvenate a competitor, the *Washington Star*. One *Post* employee who remained at work throughout the strike remembers it this way:

> What did Ms. Graham learn during the strike? She was the leader from the beginning, sort of a force that carried it through with determination, and people followed it through. I mean Don was there at the time too, but it was a group of people that were just so driven with a dedication that it was going to work out. . . . And it was a leadership that you wanted to be a part of. There was also an outrage over what the pressmen

had done, but even more than that, people were totally dedicated to this family. It's a great feeling within the company—of a family.[3]

DON GRAHAM'S LEADERSHIP

At a staff meeting in early January 1979, Katharine Graham announced that her son Donald, then 33 years old, would be the new publisher of the *Washington Post*. She would remain the chairman and CEO of the Washington Post Company. Described as a more hands-on manager than Katherine was, Don had the reputation of knowing the name and history of every *Post* employee. As Don became "Mr. Inside," Katharine became more active in industry-wide, national, and international roles.

In 1988, *Business Month* selected the Washington Post Company as one of its "Five Best-Managed Companies," and a few years later, *Fortune* gave Katharine Graham its Business Hall of Fame award. In 1991, Don Graham became the CEO, and in 1993, he was named the chairman of the Washington Post Company. The company continued to achieve its goals of quality and profitability. Katharine Graham died, as the result of an accident, in the summer of 2001. Because the family's culture and practices allowed the Grahams to avoid the problems that beset so many family business owners, Don was able to devote most of his time to the Post Company's business problems and its employees.

CASE QUESTIONS

1. To what do you attribute the late Katharine Graham's success as a leader of the Washington Post Company?
2. Katharine Graham transitioned from being a CEO spouse to being the CEO herself. Using a few facts from the case, speculate on what leadership functions she performed in both roles to support family business continuity.
3. What actions did Katharine Graham take to support the leadership transition to Don Graham? What did Don Graham do to accommodate the succession process and complement, rather than compete with, his mother and CEO?

NOTES

1. From *Hoover's* and *Dun and Bradstreet* Company Profiles.

2. Background information for parts of this case comes from Barnes, Louis B., "The Graham Family and the Washington Post Co.," Harvard Business School Case 9-498-031; and Graham, Katharine; *Personal History*, New York: Random House, 1997.

3. Barnes, op. cit., p. 8.

CASE 3:
SIGMA MOTION, INC.

After founding Sigma Motion and overseeing its growth for the past 25 years, Ron Burton was planning to pass the reins over to his two sons, Bob and Michael. Sigma Motion was well positioned in the market and on its way to planning for family business succession; the company had a board of advisors, a strategic plan, and next-generation members who had been active in the management of the business. The question in everyone's mind was "When will the torch be passed, and how?" Ron Burton was now 70, and both sons were in their 30s. The youngest, Michael, wrote this letter to the CEO soon after returning from a European sales trip.

March 30, 2001

Mr. Ron Burton, CEO/Chairman
Sigma Motion, Inc.
4950 E. 49th Street
Pittsburgh, PA 15201

Dear Ron,

It saddens me to be writing you this letter because my love for this business grew out of our shared excitement and vision for Sigma. Without getting into great detail, I feel that it would be in the best interest of the business for me to redirect my efforts elsewhere. At points over the last several months I considered the possibility of staying and fighting for the leadership position of the company, but I have now realized that a battle of that sort would do more damage than just simply leaving the company.

My commitments to customers, reps, trade shows and training extend through May 24th. The scheduled travel with reps will be completed May 8th. My experience with John, whom I recommend as my replacement, tells me that he will rise to this occasion and will carry the Sigma Motion flag proudly. He will certainly need your support as he works with manufacturing.

I have not talked about my plans to leave the business with anyone. I will let you choose the appropriate time to share the news. While I realize that this will certainly disrupt the operation internally and throughout the market, it is my feeling that the effects will be

---

Research associates Charlie Braun, Jeff Chaney, Chris Hetz, and Todd Silverman assisted in the preparation of this case, under the supervision of Professor Ernesto Poza, to provide a basis for class discussion rather than to illustrate either effective or ineffective handling of a family business situation. Note that while the case is factually and historically accurate, the names have been changed to protect the privacy of the family. For permission to publish this case, grateful acknowledgment is made to the chairman of the company.

minimized by my departure at this time rather than years from now. Please let me know what I can do to ensure that this is a smooth transition. I expect that you will not share this letter with anyone.

Sincerely,

Michael Burton
Vice President, Sales & Marketing

THE EARLY YEARS

Ron Burton became interested in sales and distribution while growing up, watching his father run a wholesale automotive parts distributorship. After high school, he attended college and then returned to Pittsburgh to work at an auto dealership. His hopes were to someday run his own business, as his father did. Ron spent two years at that dealership. He left when he realized that there was little chance of buying out the current owner. His next stop was his father's business, which he felt could be expanded significantly. When his father refused to agree to his growth plans, Ron, with his father's encouragement, became a manufacturing representative. He decided this was not a bad way to get closer to his dream of someday working for himself.

For the next 10 years, he represented a variety of product lines for several industrial products manufacturers. At the time he started his business, he had little money, a strong work ethic, a great deal of credit, and a lot of ideas. By 1967, Ron Burton was one of the top salespeople in the country for Erie Products Corporation.

Two years later, Erie Products was sold, and Ron founded The Screw Supply Company, a distributorship for Erie Products. He soon realized that he could add more value by getting into the final stages of manufacturing. In 1970, he added "end machining" capabilities to his company.

The close relationship with Erie Products enabled Ron and his organization to acquire a level of expertise in the linear motion field. Linear motion is responsible for producing movement along one dimension. Products that accomplish such motion include conveyor belts and "screws," which are actually rods with threads that fix the dimension of the movement and a nut that travels back and forth along the threaded rod; Ron focused on the screw technology.

In 1975, he decided to expand product offerings into Acme screws. Adopting a new company name, Sigma Motion, Inc., he trademarked product names and began to add manufacturing capabilities. In 1978, a new division was established to tap the jack/worm gear screw market. Jacks produce vertical movement, lifting or lowering platforms.

The company continued to grow throughout the late 1970s and early 1980s with Ron at the helm. Sales came from a wide variety of sources, but the focus was always on precision motion and superior engineering. In 1982, the company secured orders from television networks for satellite dish actuators—the first of a number of television network contracts. When "the best" was needed, Ron wanted customers to know that Sigma Motion was the answer.

Throughout the 1980s, Sigma Motion continued to expand its product line. Gradually previously contracted operations were brought in-house in order to ensure quality and more quickly respond to customer needs for prototypes and quick delivery.

By 1987, the company had 55 employees and two physical locations. Over the next 10 years, great change took place in the organization. Bob Burton, Ron's eldest son, joined the company in 1989 and began work at the gear division in the manufacturing department. That same year, the company opened another manufacturing facility. In 1994, the company again expanded, opening a West Coast manufacturing facility.

This growth came at a price, and by 1994, the company was in serious financial trouble. The gear company acquisition never generated the synergies that Ron had hoped for, and the debt assumed for the acquisition of expensive gear grinding equipment became a serious burden to the company. An old friend agreed to invest in the company and helped save the business.

By 1997, the company was back on its feet again and had consolidated operations in a 120,000-square-foot facility located in Pittsburgh, Pennsylvania. This was also the year that Michael, Ron's younger son, joined the company in the sales department. The movement to centralize brought with it a change in the organizational structure. Bob, who was operations manager at the gear division, became vice president of manufacturing and operations for all of Sigma Motion, Inc. The two plant managers who were running the Acme and Ball screw facilities both left the organization and were replaced internally by promoting group managers.

To help propel Sigma Motion into the 21st century, Ron Burton put together a professional top management team, developed a strategic plan, and launched an advisory board.

PRODUCT LINES

Sigma Motion produced four distinct product lines, all based on linear motion. The company's focus turned to expanding these existing product lines and increasing sales within each, as opposed to developing entirely new products. One of the initiatives was to develop metric versions of existing product lines, thereby opening up the large European and Asian markets.

Each of the products was positioned at the high end of the segment, with heavy emphasis put on quality and precision. The company's products competed primarily with hydraulic and/or pneumatic systems, as well as other manufacturers' screw-based systems. In general, the advantage of a screw system over hydraulic or pneumatic solutions is that the drive motor can be much smaller and multiple screws can be driven off one motor much more easily.

Sigma Motion products were used by the medical, airline, timber, transportation, and communications industries. They also constituted component parts for

EXHIBIT 1   ACME SCREWS

innumerable types of manufacturing and machine tool equipment. Descriptions of its four product lines follow.

- *Acme screws:* Acme screws are very similar to the nuts and bolts available in hardware stores. Sigma Motion focused on applications where very precise positioning is required, such as in the device that adjusts an electric car seat (see Exhibit 1).

- *Ball screws:* Ball screws differ from Acme screws in both the shape of the groove in the screw and the fact that the nut rides on ball bearings (see Exhibit 2). The advantages of this type of screw over Acme screws are a much longer life and exponentially less friction and heat (i.e., less energy loss and heat distortion). A typical application for a Ball screw would be in the wing flaps of an airplane.

- *Jacks/Worm gear screws:* These days, the most promising product line at Sigma Motion is a jack. Rotational motion from a drive motor is translated 90 degrees through an interlocking gear to a rotating screw; the translation gear is called worm gear (see Exhibit 3). Uses for this unique jack design include leveling tables, airport jetways, and raising Billy Joel and his band out of a pit and up through the bottom of the custom-made concert stage. Sigma Motion has one of the best designed jacks on the market and

EXHIBIT 2   BALL SCREWS

recently introduced a five-year guarantee on the product, something that was unheard of in the industry.

- *Linear bearings and shafting:* The closest thing that Sigma Motion had to a commodity product was their line of linear bearings and shafting, which are cylindrical rods of steel on which sleeves full of ball bearings move back and forth (see Exhibit 4).

MANUFACTURING

Sigma Motion's mission statement is as follows:

> Sigma Motion's mission is to be an innovative and responsive organization whose linear motion products are engineered, manufactured, and delivered to meet or exceed our customers' specifications and expectations.

Manufacturing was central to the success of Sigma Motion. Since the company's reputation was built on quality and precision, the company had taken the road of continuously upgrading its manufacturing equipment and demanding more and more from its suppliers.

BALL SCREW JACK (LEFT) AND MACHINE SCREW JACK (RIGHT)

Sigma Motion bought raw steel, bearings, and roughly cast housings and worm gears for jacks. Then the company took over the process and did everything from engineering components and complete systems to machining the dies necessary to form grooves in the bar and using computer-aided machines to finish the housings and gears. Sigma Motion controlled anywhere from 70 to 90 percent of the manufacturing process, more than any of its competitors. Although this resulted in significant overhead costs, the company felt that the advantages in quality control and turnaround time were worth the price. Sigma Motion could provide a customer a prototype product within two weeks of the request, a feat unmatched by any of its competitors.

One particular technology that set Sigma apart from some of its competitors was its expertise in "rolling," or cold-forming, grooves onto a bar to make the screws. In cold-forming, the rolling dies (cylindrical shapes about 16 inches in diameter with the mirror groove cut in them) actually displace the steel through brute force from the round rod shape into a grooved screw. The result is a very strong, very precise grooved rod with minimal waste—in one pass through the equipment. The machinery required to do this is very specialized, and Sigma Motion owns the largest rolling machine in the world, which can roll bars up to 15 inches in diameter.

Sigma Motion had also been improving its internal documentation for processes and procedures. Some customers had requested that Sigma Motion become ISO 9001-certified, and so the company began work on certification in 1998.

EXHIBIT 4 LINEAR BEARINGS (LEFT) AND SHAFTING (RIGHT)

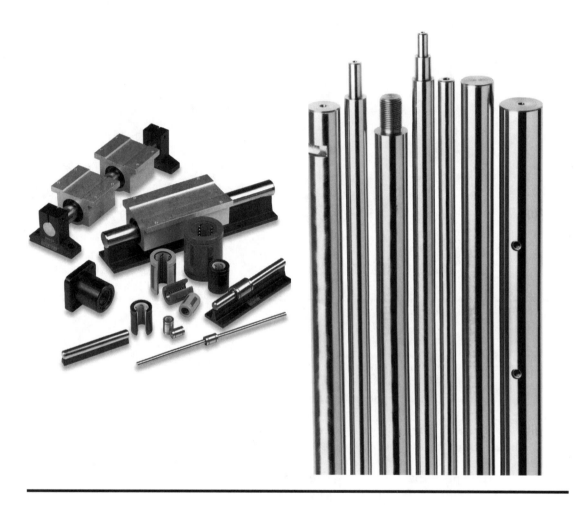

SALES AND DISTRIBUTION

Sigma Motion sold through six in-house sales representatives. They were employees of Sigma Motion and serviced corporate accounts with which they had developed relationships over time. They sold Sigma Motion's products in addition to other related manufactured goods.

Michael, who was vice president of sales, wanted to gradually move away from the manufacturer representative channel because of the questionable amount of value these reps added to Sigma's products in the eyes of its customers. Still, some of the manufacturer reps derived 25 percent of their total commissions from Sigma. Sigma Motion also solicited direct sales from manufacturers that needed linear motion solutions. This was a growing part of the business and included customers like the U.S. government and some automotive component suppliers.

Sigma Motion also worked with a number of large manufacturing distributors. Although most products were highly customized, there were a few standard products in the lineup. The company had a paper catalog and an Internet catalog.

When Michael joined the company in 1997, one of the first things he did was to buy a few of the competitors' jacks and have the engineers take them apart. Compared to Sigma's, the competitors' products used inferior materials across the board and also had design weaknesses. It took some time to come up with a way to exploit this favorable difference; ultimately, the company began drafting a five-year guarantee. In the fourth quarter of 1999, most company advertising was focused on the five-year guarantee.

CORE COMPETENCY AND COMPETITIVE ADVANTAGES

Sigma Motion's core competency was designing and manufacturing linear motion components and linear motion systems, which were used in a wide range of applications where straight-line, controlled movement was required. Sigma Motion had several key competitive advantages that allowed it to excel in its core business:

1. **Small size:** The fact that Sigma Motion was a small company (approximately $20 million in annual revenues) gave it the ability to rapidly adjust to changing market conditions and changing customer needs. Its primary competitor was a company with over $100 million in annual revenues.

2. **Customization:** Sigma Motion was unique in that it controlled 90 percent of the processes required in bringing its products to market. In conjunction with its small size, the vertical integration gave Sigma the ability to customize or change a product quickly to meet a customer's need.

3. **Strong applications engineering team:** Sigma Motion's strong engineering team gave it a competitive advantage in two areas: (1) It helped the company accomplish its mission of introducing new and innovative products in the linear motion marketplace, and (2) it gave Sigma the ability to answer tough technical questions much faster than the competition could, and this translated into increased sales.

4. **High quality:** Sigma Motion was perceived by its customers as the "Rolls Royce" of linear motion products. The company's products consistently outlasted those of the competition. The company offered a five-year warranty on some of its products because of this competitive advantage.

5. **Depth of product line:** Sigma Motion had a product portfolio that covered all linear motion products and most sizes. Many of its competitors could compete only in the small sizes or the large sizes, while Sigma Motion owned equipment that allowed it to manufacture both, giving Sigma an advantage when taking on complicated and integrated products.

6. **Management team:** Ron Burton had put in place a senior management team that was extremely competent and forward thinking. Evidence of this forward thinking was found in the financial control systems that had been implemented and the company's Internet strategy.

FINANCE

Financially speaking, Sigma Motion had its share of ups and downs. Over the course of 30 years, it nearly went out of business entirely because of the lack of financial controls. At the time of this writing, Sigma Motion, a C corporation, had about $20 million in annual revenues and enjoyed a healthy net profit margin after tax. As a manufacturing company with approximately 10,000 products, Sigma Motion invested heavily in assets, including equipment, inventory, and accounts receivable.

"Flash Reports" sent red flags concerning overtime, waste/scrap, and other month-to-date numbers to help management keep its finger on the pulse of the operation. Other reports on daily shipments and orders were posted in the employee lunchroom for all to see.

The following financial goals were part of the company's strategic plan:

1. Achieve 10 percent growth in volume each year for the next five years.

2. Install an electronic labor-collecting barcode system. This will save time running payroll for 160 employees and will provide valuable management information by allocating each employee's time by job function every day.

3. Implement a shop-floor reporting system that will tie into an ERP program accounting for all costs, direct and indirect, and measure variances against standards in time, setup, overhead, efficiency, scrap, etc.

4. Develop product line–specific income statements, using activity-based costing.

5. Become debt-free. Ron Burton wanted to turn the company over to his sons with zero debt.

Ron Burton wanted to make sure that the business was endowed with the capacity to continue to grow and succeed, regardless of the decision his two sons would ultimately make about running the business. Both Bob and Michael were well known by the advisory board members and were considered capable successors, even though they were both still growing into leadership positions.

FAMILY, OWNERSHIP, AND MANAGEMENT

FAMILY. The Burton family consisted of Ron Burton, age 70; his wife, Mary; Bob, age 34; and Michael, age 32. The Burtons all lived in the Pittsburgh area. Family gatherings were fairly regular for holidays, birthdays, and family weddings. In addition to the more formal events, they saw each other informally at least once a month for dinner or casual gatherings.

Mary married Ron in 1966, and shortly afterwards she married Sigma Motion. Mary said, "Sigma Motion is Ron's baby, life, and livelihood, all in one. I don't think he'll ever retire completely."

On the whole, communication was good between family members, although the spouses were generally spared conversations regarding the business. Even during Sigma Motion's darkest hour several years ago, Ron did not tell outside family members about the financial problems. However, one spouse recently complained, "I wish I knew what my husband does all day and what kinds of problems or issues the business is facing."

In the absence of formal family meetings to discuss the business, everyone seemed to confide in Mary. Ron would discuss issues regarding their sons, and each son or daughter-in-law confided in Mary when sibling rivalry reared its head at the office. Mary's job as a mediator, listener, and sounding board was an informal one, and she was more than happy to play this role.

OWNERSHIP. Ron Burton had lived in the Pittsburgh area for a long time and was a well-known civic leader. His connections outside the linear motion industry enabled him to tap other CEOs to serve on the company's advisory board. This commitment to community, family, and friends was obvious to all and influenced the culture at Sigma Motion. Ron began working on his advisory board in 1998. The board was launched and chartered with overseeing the financial, strategic, and management succession issues of the company. He had gifted a large number of non-voting shares to each of his children over the years; the rest of the non-voting and all voting stock belonged to him.

MANAGEMENT. Only Ron, Bob, and Michael from the Burton family were involved in the business. Ron was the CEO and chairman, Bob was the vice president of operations, and Michael was the vice president of sales. Ron had placed the two sons in separate functional areas on purpose, to best utilize their unique skills in ways that added value to the company. Michael and Bob generally worked well together, but each frustrated the other at times. Mary was often called on to facilitate and mediate the differences between the two siblings.

In addition to the family members in management, there were a number of key nonfamily managers, including Chuck Briscoe, president; June Goldberg, chief financial officer; Jim Collins, marketing manager; and Ron Bates, chief engineer.

The nonfamily managers' perspective was that Sigma Motion was one company that was all business. June Goldberg said, "Even though Sigma Motion is a small family business, Mr. Burton runs it as if it were a large corporation." But other non-family managers talked about the Burtons owning the place: "Sometimes things are done simply because the owners said so." Last year, though, Ron Burton started to delegate more and more of the responsibility to his management team. While still the ultimate decision maker on some things, he passed day-to-day decision-making authority to his management team. Rarely did he overturn top management decisions made in his absence.

The outside managers were at Sigma Motion because they wanted to be. June Goldberg left the *Fortune 500* culture because she "wanted something different in her everyday work life." Jim Collins said, "I wanted to make a difference in a smaller organization as opposed to being a cog in the wheel of a larger organization." They felt strongly about the close-knit family culture. They also preferred the flexibility afforded by Sigma Motion. Employees at all levels were willing to offer their assistance, even when a task was outside their area of responsibility. It was this culture, and the competitive compensation given to nonfamily managers, that had enabled Sigma Motion to retain such managers.

Bob, the eldest son, had 8 years of experience on the operations side of things. He knew how to operate every piece of equipment in the company and did an excellent job relating to the employees. However, key managers had some concerns regarding Bob's lack of engineering education or outside experience. Nonfamily managers thought it would be very helpful for Bob to have an engineering degree or a technical background—some considered it necessary. Bob had shown both maturity and business acumen in the past. In January of 1999, Ron Burton offered Bob the job of president with Briscoe remaining as a senior consultant. Bob calmly declined the offer, stating that he did not think that he was ready nor did he think the company could afford hiring another key-level manager to replace him as vice president of operations.

Michael had no more formal technical training than Bob did. And he had not spent time on the manufacturing floor like his brother. Michael did receive his MBA from Case Western Reserve University and had worked outside the family business for 3 years. He had had investment banking and asset-based lending positions with an important regional commercial bank. When he joined the business at a high level—vice president of sales—many in management, including his brother Bob, had difficulty accepting him initially. Over time, he seemed to have garnered much respect.

The company did use titles (see Exhibit 5), but Ron Burton did not care much about formal organizational charts or exact job descriptions; he had always focused on getting results. As long as goals were being met, he thought, the rest took care of itself. The informality of the organization included no formal compensation packages. The lack of red tape seemed to lead to a gentler form of politics and a much closer working relationship among coworkers, according to managers. It is this culture, career opportunities, and competitive compensation that were credited with key nonfamily management retention.

Both Michael and Bob reported to Chuck Briscoe, the nonfamily president. Occasionally, Briscoe was left out of the loop when one of the sons would go

| EXHIBIT 5 | TOP MANAGEMENT TEAM AT SIGMA MOTION |

Ron Burton, CEO

Chuck Briscoe, President

Bob Burton, Vice President of Operations

June Goldberg, Chief Financial Officer

Jim Collins, Marketing Manager

Ron Bates, Chief Engineer

Michael Burton, Vice President of Sales

Tom Hubler, Quality Control Manager

straight to Ron Burton with ideas, issues, or problems. Briscoe served as a bridging president, between the two generations of Burtons. In March of 2000, Ron began to develop the first strategic plan for Sigma Motion. Late that year, the team completed the strategic plan, which highlighted the core competencies of the company and stated an overall objective of becoming a $50 million company by 2009.

SUCCESSION PLANNING

Sigma Motion did not have a succession plan in place. Since both sons had increased their responsibility in the business, Ron had decided to charge ahead with some estate planning work. Transfer or sale of the shares that he currently held had not been planned, although it had been discussed with Mary, Bob, and Michael. Verbal agreements existed, and the parties involved had made assumptions. Ron's plans included transferring the voting shares equally to his two sons.

Ron Burton did not want to pick a single next-generation CEO of Sigma Motion. He felt Bob and Michael would be able to run the company as a sibling team. Bob, with a background in operations, and Michael, with a background in finance and sales, complemented each other and could make a great team (see Exhibit 6). But Michael and Bob were not as confident that it would all work out. They felt that they were always competing with each other for voice, for influence, for the limelight. Their goals also appeared to be quite different. Luckily, their roles were very different, and therefore day-to-day conflict was minimized. Still, when it came to leadership style, business strategy, and the company's financial structure and risk propensity, they had very different perceptions of what the future ought to look like.

Sigma Motion had an excellent customer base, a solid balance sheet, and some talented outside management on the team. Succession was inevitable, despite the fact that Ron would never completely "retire" from the business. Given Michael's apparent decision to leave, how could Ron Burton ever fulfill his dream of having both sons work as a sibling team at Sigma Motion?

EXHIBIT 6	SUCCESSOR DEVELOPMENT

Positions held by Michael Burton at Sigma Motion:

• Vice President of Sales

Positions held by Bob Burton at Sigma Motion:

• Vice President of Operations

• Plant Manager

• Sales Manager

• Quote Estimator

• Inspection Manager

• Gear Cutter

• Thread Mill Operator

CASE QUESTIONS

1. State the facts of this case as they relate to the state of the business. How sound do you think Sigma's strategy is? What about its financial results? Does the business appear capable of competing effectively in the next generation?

2. Why do you think Michael has changed from performing at a high level and being committed to the business to writing a letter about leaving Sigma Motion immediately?

3. What other options does Michael have? What actions should Michael take to support the viability of some of these other options?

4. What do you think will ultimately happen in this case?

CASE 4:
THE COUSINS TOURNAMENT

At the Blanchard family's 1993 New Year's Eve party, Al Blanchard talks for the first time about retiring as president of Grandview Industries. Al, 67, is standing on the back porch of his rambling Southern California home, sharing brandy and cigars with his younger brother, Morris, with whom he has worked for 27 years. "I only want to do this for one more year, Morris," he confides. "I've had enough." Then he asks: "Do you want to run the company, or should we turn it over to one of the kids?"

Gersick, Kelin E., "The Cousins Tournament," *Family Business* (Winter 1995). Reprinted with permission of the author.

Morris has been asking himself the same question for several months. It has not been easy being in his older brother's shadow for so many years. However, Morris suffered a heart attack in 1989, and he, too, is looking forward to more leisure, and devoting more time to the small travel business in which he is an investor. Always a realist, Morris knows it is too late for him to take over a $200 million company with 2,000 employees. "I would be willing to manage things for a short time if you want to leave right away," Morris tells his older brother. "But I think we need to turn things over to one of the boys."

[Al and Morris's] father, George Blanchard, founded Grandview Industries with a partner in 1934. The original company, called Grandview Electric, made small motors for windshield wipers and other automobile components. Under Al's leadership, the company has grown into a diversified manufacturer of a variety of electrical systems for vehicles and small aircraft, with five divisions in California as well as distribution outlets abroad.

George Blanchard and his wife, Molly, had five children—including two daughters, Sarah and Germaine, and a third son, Arnold—but only Al and Morris have had careers in the business. Al joined Grandview before his brother and was quickly viewed as his father's natural successor. A hefty, former high school football player, he was not as dynamic as his father, but he was solid and hard-working, with a certain inner toughness and affability. Morris, five years younger, was a wiry bundle of energy, always filled with new ideas and schemes for reorganizing divisions, creating alliances with suppliers, and taking Grandview Industries into new markets.

Morris never got along with his father and that may be one reason his career took him to the far reaches of the company. He lived abroad for years, developing new customers in Europe. Privately, Morris often expressed impatience and frustration with Al's conservative leadership, but never publicly. Fortunately—or perhaps by George Blanchard's design—their separate responsibilities kept them apart.

In more recent years, the two brothers had developed a greater appreciation of each other's contributions and roles; they had drawn closer. Morris is now at headquarters, as vice president of marketing, and he and Al meet almost every day to discuss company policy. Although Al respects his brother's opinions, he remains the undisputed leader. His fraternal affection for Morris does not mean he believes in shared decision making.

Their New Year's Eve conversation has stirred up a lot of buried feelings. George Blanchard died at age 73, a year after his wife, Molly. The founder left equal amounts of Grandview stock to their five offspring. By then, Al was already running the company. Besides Morris, the only other family member with a position in the business was Sam Chafee, Sarah's husband.

A staunch Methodist family, the Blanchards were a model of togetherness and public respectability. Sister Sarah, a voluble personality, now 61, was for a time a local talk show host. But by and large the family kept a low profile in the affluent community.

The only real threat to family harmony occurred in 1977 when Sarah's husband, Sam Chafee, angrily left the company. An accountant by training, Sam was the company controller, but he had larger ambitions and claimed that Al and Morris were sidetracking his career. Al used his contacts to help Sam get another job, and tried to smooth over Sarah's ruffled feelings, but the incident strained her relationship with her brothers.

Al saw himself as the custodian of the family's wealth. He wanted to keep stockholders committed to the family legacy, but at a distance from operations—a delicate balancing act. George Blanchard gave his oldest son one piece of advice that he has never forgotten: "You will keep the family happy," he said, "if you keep putting dividends in their pockets. As long as you support their lifestyles, you will be the best executive in the world. Begin to lose money, and you will become an ignoramus overnight."

Grandview's gradual expansion reflected Al's determination to protect dividends. Nevertheless, the company grew steadily, tripling total sales during the 1960s and 1970s. Al had brought four outsiders onto the board, which originally consisted of all five siblings and the company's primary banker, now retired. In the early 1980s, he restructured the company, taking it public but keeping family control by creating classes of stock and a holding company. The strategy was a financial success, fueling further expansion while continuing to provide a good income to family members. Each of the five siblings retained equal voting control of the holding company, in keeping with the wishes of the parents.

Family stockholders were comfortable and had few complaints. No one raised questions about what would happen if Al were no longer around.

Meanwhile, the family was growing rapidly, with many early marriages in the third generation and already eight children in the fourth. By 1990, there were six third-generation members in the business. Al and Morris each have two sons in management. Germaine and Arnold each have one, but both are young and in junior roles. Sam and Sarah's two sons and daughter have made careers elsewhere, as their parents urged them to do after Sam's bitter experience.

At a subsequent engagement party for Sarah's daughter in the spring of 1993, Al announces his decision to retire to the family, gathered on the patio of the Chafees' beachfront home. There are expressions of good wishes and a little kidding about Al's age. But Al's brief remarks have stirred up anxieties about the future. His brother Arnold argues that Al should stay on as CEO for another 8 or 10 years, since things at the company are going so well. Germaine jokes about calling her lawyer and selling her stock before morning.

The following weeks are filled with anxious phone conversations between family members. If Al has had any kind of plan for succession in mind, he has never divulged it to other family members, including Morris.

Al reflects on his relationships with each of his siblings, and how he has managed this complex family over the years. He asks Morris whether he thinks they should have a family meeting or form a family council. Morris feels the two of them should manage the succession choice themselves. "We don't want a lot of extraneous factors brought in," he says. "There are only a few people who might be chosen anyway. Why open it up to the fantasies of our sisters about their sons and daughters?"

Al is tempted to go along, but he feels the cat is too far out of the bag to resolve the issue unilaterally. Instead, he decides to create a succession committee to lay out a process for selecting the next CEO and determine the timing of the transition. Seeing that Al has made up his mind, Morris suggests that Peter Franklin be asked to serve as chairman. Peter, the owner of a large freight shipping company, has been a friend of Morris's since college and was the first nonfamily member added to the Grandview board in 1980.

Peter agrees to serve. He has great respect for both Al and Morris as businessmen. He also knows that Al is tired and the company has been slowing down as a result. He thinks Grandview is in excellent condition and ready to make a major jump in size, diversification, and market reach. For those reasons, the choice of successor will be critical.

Al and Morris agree that the committee should have two other nonfamily board members besides Peter. Al argues that the family appointees ought to be members of the next generation not working in the business. Morris argues that because both of his children have jobs at Grandview that would cut out his branch. In the end the brothers appoint Sarah's younger son, Andy, and Morris's daughter, Mary.

The committee is formed, but Peter is already having second thoughts about serving as chairman. All the Blanchard siblings take a passionate interest in their father's legacy and, he realizes, each will push for his or her offspring. He also knows Grandview is way behind in preparing the next generation for leadership. There is no succession plan, and Peter wonders why. Is it Al's personality, or Morris's? Or do both fear that talking about issues might dredge up bitter feelings and cause a rift in the family?

Faced with what is shaping up as a thankless task, Peter nevertheless begins formulating a mental scorecard of the leading candidates' strengths and weaknesses. Of the cousins working in the business, he figures, two stand out as contenders for the top job:

1. Al's oldest son, Joe, who at 42 is also the oldest member of the third generation. Trained as an engineer, Joe has worked in production for most of his career at Grandview. But in recent years he has become more of a manager. Quiet, calm, and thoughtful like his father, Joe led the company's efforts to introduce team methods of work under its TQM program. His greatest plus is that he gets along well with all branches of the family. He is well liked and steady; he has performed well in every sector he has managed. But he is not regarded as charismatic or a strategic thinker.

2. Morris's oldest son, Bill, 41, a trouble-shooter who enjoys his reputation as a hard-nosed manager. A business school graduate, Bill is performance-focused and demanding. His father brought him to Europe to turn around one of Grandview's subsidiaries there, and he did an outstanding job of reorganizing the business and cutting payroll. Bill is also the only cousin in the business with significant international experience, which Peter knows

will be important in developing the company's future markets. He has made money for Grandview in businesses that looked marginal to family stockholders. But his abrasive style is not appreciated by his cousins—especially Joe. A few have confided to Peter that they would be uncomfortable trusting their assets to Bill.

The other cousins in the company are either too young to be considered or have not yet demonstrated exceptional ability. Only Mary, 32, Morris's daughter, appears to have the talent for a leadership position. Mary is a chemist and metallurgist who holds a middle-management position in R&D. Although bright and exceptionally good at her job, Mary has never expressed any ambition to do anything beyond research. In any case, women in the family have always been subtly excluded from management. It is the company's loss, Peter feels, but he sees no indication that the family is yet ready to accept a woman as CEO.

As he runs down his list, Peter realizes that the cousin he admires most is not on it. Edward Chafee, 40, Sam and Sarah's oldest son, isn't in the company. By leveraging the stock he had received as a young man, Ed has built a very successful electronic hardware business in Silicon Valley. Starting out as a computer whiz, he has in recent years shown a flair for deal making as well as for motivating his employees. Ed was the youngest president ever of the State Manufacturers' Association; he has even been mentioned in *Inc.* magazine's "Young Presidents to Watch" column. As far as Peter can tell, he is also popular with his cousins, although he does not socialize with them very often.

Al and Morris, however, are clearly not considering Edward. When Peter accepted the job as committee chair, Morris had said: "We have several children who have been working hard and doing a fine job in the company. Help us pick the right one." Peter has to keep reminding himself that his friends are not only business owners, they are fathers.

At the first meeting of the succession committee, the members agree there is no one individual who stands out as the obvious choice, and that all the cousins now working in the company can use more experience in general management. Following this discussion, the tension in the room rises when Peter Franklin reports: "Al and Morris have come to the same conclusion about the readiness of any of the potential candidates. But Al does not want to continue as president after the end of the year. Therefore, Morris has agreed to take over the CEO role for an interim period, until a successor has been chosen and is ready."

The silence that follows is deafening. Andy Chafee, Sarah and Sam's son, argues that the business will do better if Al hangs on longer. The issue is debated, but no clear consensus emerges. Finally, Morris's daughter, Mary, speaks up: "None of you trust my father. You believe he will interfere in this process in the interest of my brother, Bill. I don't want my father to take on this job either. His heart is not strong enough, and he should be resting instead. But I resent your assumptions about him. He would have been better for the company than Uncle Al all along. We should be glad to have him."

Now there is another embarrassed silence, followed by many statements of support for Morris. But a long-festering issue is now on the table. The committee goes home with a lot that is troubling to think about.

At the next meetings of the committee, the members cannot agree on a process, let alone a list of candidates. Meanwhile, pressures from other family members are beginning to build. Peter reads a letter from Sarah, in which she writes: "I am pleased that the family has persuaded you to chair such an important committee. Having someone not in the family run this committee is the only way we can have objective decisions. I would like to add one other point: There are many members of the younger group who might be the best choice to head this company, who are not in the company now. Are they disqualified? Some of them were discouraged from making a career in the company before. I would like to see them have a chance."

Peter has already gotten an earful on the same issue from Al and Morris's other sister, Germaine, a friend. "If you could convince Edward to give up his business or bring it into the company," she says, "he's clearly the best of the bunch. But I don't think you could offer him enough to do it. Once you've been a success as your own boss, why would you want to work for the family?"

A short time later, Peter talks with Ed Chafee at a YPO lunch in San Cupertino. Ed is curious about how the committee is progressing and, when Peter makes a few oblique references to Ed's own career, he suddenly says: "If you're considering inviting me into this tournament, I think you don't know my family. Al is a nice man; he is truly interested in keeping the family together and finding the best successor. But Morris is out to accomplish his own agenda—which is getting Bill into the president's office."

Peter likes Ed's directness. "All right," he says, "let's leave Morris out of this for a minute. What do you want? What's your agenda?"

"I like my own business," Ed replies. "We've grown to $25 million this year. The future looks good. We have some deals pending that could help us sustain growth for several years to come. It would take a very generous salary, freedom to run Grandview my way, and some financial buyout of my own company for me to take this job."

"Let's be clear," Peter says. "Nobody is offering you a job. We're talking about whether you are interested in becoming a candidate." Then, after a pause, Peter says: "I understand your position, but you are only presenting one side. You are successful, but your company will never be anything but small potatoes compared with Grandview. With strong management and strategic leadership, Grandview can become a major player on an international scale. The facilities are modern and highly productive, there is a good mix of mature and young products, and the balance sheet is in excellent shape. Are you ambitious enough for that opportunity?"

"You make an interesting case," Ed says, smiling. "Captain of my own yacht or the family's hireling on an ocean liner. I honestly don't know. Let's keep talking about it."

What Ed does not share with Peter is his feeling—which has been popping into his head lately—of how much it would mean to his mother, Sarah, if he became the next leader of Grandview.

The following week, Peter has lunch with Al. "I need more guidance from you," Peter says. He tells Al that he feels trapped by conflicting loyalties and responsibilities. "For example, do you want the committee to consider only family members inside the company?"

"My friend," Al replies, "I see that my sisters have been talking to you about their boys. Let me put your mind at ease. There is no solution that will please all of this family. The five of us have kept all our eggs in one basket, the way our parents wanted it to be, for a long time now. I thought it would be relatively simple to continue that for another generation. Morris still thinks so—probably because he thinks that the eggs will fall gently into the hands of his own son. But I'm not so sure. I don't know what's the best choice for the business. My son Joe has solid potential. Morris's boy, Bill, is stronger in some areas, weaker in others. Both of them are dedicated to this company and deserve to be rewarded for that commitment. That's where you come in. Do the right thing for the business. I will try to make it fly with the family."

Peter is beginning to appreciate what a strong-willed and complicated group the Blanchards really are. On the ride home, he reminds himself that Grandview Industries is not a small operation. Hundreds of employees depend on its continued vitality. What everyone needs now is a process that the whole family will support, leading ultimately to the choice of the best possible leader for the company's future. Is that a reachable goal?

When the committee reconvenes, Peter immediately lays it on the line. "We cannot continue to just discuss issues as we have been," he warns. "We have a deadline for a plan: two months. We have to focus on resolving three issues by the end of our next meeting." The three issues to be decided are (1) What should be the process for choosing the next president? Does the committee's present composition ensure maximum acceptance and support of whatever plan is proposed? Should the committee be changed or a new one created? Should Al and Morris be involved? (2) Does the interim CEO plan, with Morris serving until a new leader is chosen, make sense? Or will it only exacerbate tensions between the siblings? (3) Should Ed Chafee be considered? Or should only cousins who have experience in the company be considered?

CASE QUESTIONS

1. What is the central challenge facing Al Blanchard, Grandview Industries, and the Blanchard family?

2. What does your answer to question 1 say about what is truly unique about family-owned businesses?

3. What would you recommend Al Blanchard do, in his leadership capacity, on behalf of Grandview Industries and its shareholders?

MANAGING THE
FAMILY BUSINESS: BEST PRACTICES

5

ESTATE AND OWNERSHIP
TRANSFER PLANNING

Estate planning is to the family business owner like a set of construction plans is to a home builder; without one you are unlikely to achieve a lasting and solid structure.

—Philip Dawson, Family Business Legal Advisor

Estate planning is a family business owner's favorite target of procrastination. Planning the estate has the potential to save a business-owning family hundreds of thousands (or millions) of dollars and allow for continuity of the business, both of which are important to most entrepreneurs and business owners. Still, carrying out the planning is seldom deemed urgent enough to be made a priority. The absence of estate planning puts at risk what has taken a generation or two to build, often doing irreparable damage to family relationships.

Given the importance of the subject, why is estate and ownership transfer planning often avoided, delayed, or done without comprehensive outside professional help? When it is finally done, why is it often done without consulting those most affected by the plan and its implications?

While time pressures, the cost of professional advisors, and aversion to insurance products and agents are often blamed, irrational optimism is more fundamentally responsible for the failure to plan one's estate. The likelihood of illness and inevitability of death loom large late in an owner's life. Not wanting to discuss illness and death—and their implications for the family and the business—is an understandable reason to procrastinate. Woody Allen once quipped that he didn't mind dying; he just didn't want to be there when it happened.

Loss of control is another reason people delay planning. Research on entrepreneurs and successful CEOs has found that they have a wide locus of control, which few look forward to giving up. Letting go of the very control that has been a source of advantage, success, autonomy, and personal freedom is not a simple matter. In addition, although successful business builders seem to have no trouble focusing on things they know well, they are quite averse to committing time and energy to a subject with which they are completely unfamiliar. And if these inherent sources of resistance were not enough, many CEOs fear family conflict. They may be concerned that this kind of planning will require such difficult conversations among family members that open warfare will erupt among them.

Some may worry that the outcomes of these difficult discussions will be too uncertain and/or unpleasant to carry out.

A family business is often a family's principal asset or at least a significant portion of a family's net worth. The Arthur Andersen/Mass Mutual Family Business Survey, most recently conducted in 1997, found a majority of respondents saying that approximately 60 percent of the family's wealth was locked up in the business. One-fifth of all respondents said that 80 percent of the family's wealth was in the business.[1] Similarly, the 1993 Family Business Survey found a majority of respondents saying that over one-half of the family's net worth was tied up in the business. Twenty-six percent of respondents reported that 75 percent or more of the family's net worth was in the business, and only 18 percent reported that under one-quarter of the family's net worth was in the business.[2]

Because of the importance of the business to the family's economic well-being, the owner's estate plan must treat the business as an ongoing concern and not just a collection of assets. The continued successful management of the business is a priority both for the business to survive and for economic returns to the owning family to continue. Estate and ownership planning thus constitutes a strategic decision. The transfer of equity represents not only the transfer of financial resources but also the transfer of corporate control from one generation to the next.

ESTATE TAXES

On June 7, 2001, President George W. Bush signed into law the Economic Growth and Tax Relief Reconciliation Act, which changed federal gift and estate tax provisions. This act is likely to be changed again in the near future, as there have been nearly 100 tax code changes affecting gift and estate taxes in the last 20 years. In any case, it has a sunset provision that makes it applicable only through December 31, 2010. In 2010 and that year only (as of this writing, anyway), there will be no estate tax liability, and therefore business owners will have the freedom to transfer ownership without regard for tax consequences to heirs or to the continuity of the family business. Between now and then, federal estate tax rates will fall gradually. In 2003, the maximum estate tax rate fell to 49 percent. It will continue to decline by 1 percent every year, until the minimum rate of 45 percent is reached in 2007. The 45 percent estate tax rate will also apply in 2008 and 2009 and then will vanish in 2010, for one year only.

The unified credit exemption—which, until 2001, was set at $675,000—was increased to $1 million for 2002 and 2003 and will grow to $3.5 million by 2009 (see Exhibit 5-1). This means that, by 2009, a married couple could transfer up to $7 million of their estate free of estate taxes.

State inheritance taxes are another factor that family business owners must consider in estate planning. Until the 2001 law was passed, 100 percent of state

EXHIBIT 5-1   ESTATE TAX EXEMPTIONS

Year(s)	Unified Credit
2002–2003	$1.0 million
2004–2005	$1.5 million
2006–2008	$2.0 million
2009	$3.5 million

inheritance tax liabilities, up to a certain limit, could be credited against federal taxes. The percentage is being gradually reduced until 2005, when inheritance taxes paid at the state level will be allowed only as a deduction and not as a credit. This change, which is not widely known, means that some estates will face an increase rather than a decrease in their total tax liability (combined federal and state estate taxes) through 2005. Because the specific implications for individual firms and families vary by state and by the size and particulars of the estate, there is no substitute for consulting professional advisors who know the details of the situation.

THE ESTATE PLAN

The very progressive and substantial nature of the estate tax has driven many family business owners to focus on tax minimization as the essential element of their estate planning. Certainly, the estate plan needs to ensure sufficient liquidity so that, upon the death of the current generation, the estate taxes and any outstanding debts can be paid without selling or unfavorably mortgaging the business or selling its assets at distressed prices. Estate taxes are generally due within nine months of the owner's death. Because equity in a closely held family business is both highly illiquid and unmarketable,[3] and because the U.S. Treasury expects the tax bill to be paid in cash and on time, high estate tax liabilities pose a significant threat to family businesses whose owners have procrastinated.

Given the complexity of the tax laws and the tendency of business owners to be pressed for time and prone to control and secrecy, it is no wonder that tax reduction is the primary subject addressed in estate planning. This limited focus in the estate plan represents a terrible but frequent turn of events for family businesses facing generational transitions. And it is estimated that approximately 43 percent of family businesses will change leadership across generations in the next five years.[4]

Many owners consider their estate planning completed when they have selected some transfer-of-wealth approach with their accountant or tax attorney. They fail to address other important aspects of generational transfers, including the following:

- Financial and retirement needs of the CEO and the CEO spouse
- Strategic needs of the business versus financial needs of the estate
- Ownership successor development
- Relationships among family members
- Day-to-day management of the business
- Corporate governance and voting control in the next generation
- Next-generation expectations for the business
- Needs and dreams of individual heirs
- Stewardship capacity of next-generation members as either owners or managers
- Willingness of family members not active in the management of the firm to be loyal shareholders and represent patient capital
- Economic value of the business to family members who do not participate as employees of the enterprise
- Liquidity needs of inactive or minority shareholders
- Retention of nonfamily top managers and their commitment to the enterprise

Estate plans must also consider the possible need for restructuring of corporate forms and assets in order to maximize wealth retention for heirs and for charitable giving, if the owner is philanthropically inclined. Some corporate forms and estate planning techniques will be reviewed later in this chapter.

Because of the appreciation in the value of shareholder equity over time, estate taxes make a compelling argument for an earlier rather than a later transfer of accumulated value to heirs. Over 10 years, a rather modest 6 percent annual growth rate in the value of a family business produces an asset with almost double (1.8 times) its former taxable value. Similarly, a business growing at a healthy, but not extraordinary, 12 percent rate will triple in value in a decade. The dilemma is that, during those 10 years over which the value of the estate is growing, the current generation is probably well served by retaining voting control. That way, the current generation can provide oversight ("nose in, fingers out") while learning more about the next generation—how they perform when tested by competition, recession, periods of fast growth, union negotiations, and in some cases even challenges to their leadership by other family members.

A successful entrepreneur in the product identification industry efficiently transferred his Pacific Northwest firm to one son precisely as it was about to significantly grow in revenues, profits, and value. He pursued this transfer of ownership with tremendous expediency, convinced that his son had tested positively for ability to lead the company. He was concerned that gift and estate taxes would make the accomplishment of his dream much harder in a couple of years. So he commissioned a third-party business valuation, gifted almost all of his stock (freezing the value of his estate before equity growth wreaked havoc on it), and paid the appropriate gift taxes, all at the age of 54. He kept the company building and other properties as income-producing assets (leased at market rates to what was now his son's company) and then proceeded to start work in a nearby office suite turned laboratory. He had a new product he wanted to develop and a new business he wanted to grow—he set out to be an entrepreneur all over again. Seldom are transfers of equity ownership, income sources, and control as serendipitous and straightforward as this one was.

An estate plan that encompasses a family business has to address the appropriate allocation of income sources to the founder, his or her spouse, and non-active family shareholders, as well as the inheritance or beneficial equity interest of the heirs. It also has to address financial control of the corporation via buy–sell agreements, the transfer of voting and non-voting stock, and the allocation of stock to the appropriately qualified heirs (and, in some cases, employees).

As discussed in previous chapters, family business leaders wear many hats—those of father, mother, spouse, CEO, chairman of the board, principal shareholder, and philanthropist, to name just a few. Succession and continuity planning is the most intellectually and emotionally challenging facet of balancing these multiple hats.

PRESERVING SPEED AND AGILITY

Speed and agility are a must for ongoing concerns. Jack Welch, during his tenure as CEO of General Electric, established as a primary mission getting the multi-billion-dollar, multi-million-employee conglomerate to behave like a much smaller firm. He championed organizational innovations like the Work-Out, six sigma processes, and a high performance culture, to make speed and agility core features of GE.

Many family businesses begin as entrepreneurial firms that exploit the speed and agility advantage. These companies are capable of turning on a dime. When faced with competition from a large multi-national company that needs 16 levels of approval for a new product, system, or approach to the market, family businesses consistently win. Unfortunately, a number of these entrepreneurial companies discover the costs of losing this speed and agility advantage. The departure of the CEO/entrepreneur may create a power vacuum, leading to inaction or paralysis. Or a cumbersome trust arrangement or consensus-dependent co-presidency, often referred to as an office of the president, may leave a company unable to make strategic or operating decisions promptly.

Ownership transfer policies motivated by a desire to love and treat all heirs equally or expectations of equality by family members are likely to promote an impasse, much to the detriment of continued competitiveness.

GIVING SUCCESSORS THE CAPACITY TO LEAD

Leaders of enterprises find that distributing voting shares equally among shareholders often erodes their ability to lead. Stock ownership by complicated trusts can also be a problem, unless ownership and management have been sufficiently differentiated through the presence of nonfamily managers with influence in the top team, boards of directors that include independent outsiders, and employment policies that spell out the prerequisites for family members working in the business. By about age 40 or so, even the more patient successors begin to chafe at not having sufficient voting stock in a business that they have presumably shown they can run effectively on a day-to-day basis. To successors in this situation, it seldom matters whether the stock was purchased or received as a gift from the current-generation CEO.

Unlike ownership, authority is earned rather than inherited. However, transferring ownership without an eye toward corporate control makes it more difficult to acquire the authority to lead, which has to be earned slowly and in the trenches. As discussed in earlier chapters, next-generation leaders need to be able to lead, whether through direct control or through the creation of alliances, as if they had 51 percent of the vote.[5]

Consider the following true story. A 48-year-old president (but not CEO or controlling owner) of a heavy-equipment refurbishing company was at wits' end. He had tried to have conversations with his father about succession and about his getting the authority to truly lead the business. He had already run the business in six-month increments while his father wintered in Florida. The father, who was 70 years old at the time, did not consider his son ready to run the business yet and would not transfer any voting stock. As is often the case, both parties had sound arguments for their position, but the son's inability to get full authority to lead, with management and ownership structure support, resulted in his deciding to retire early. He moved with his spouse and kids to their favorite vacation spot in the Caribbean. And Dad, who was not having as much fun in semi-retirement as he had hoped, went back to work full-time. The continuity of this business was now in jeopardy.

Withholding the authority to lead—either by not transferring voting stock at the appropriate time or by requiring that a variety of next-generation shareholders with equal amounts of stock reach a consensus on important decisions—is likely to limit the lifespan of the corporation to the lifespan of the current-generation CEO. Another possibility is a veto by an upset minority. Neither the business nor the family is well served in either case.

CORPORATE STRUCTURES AND CLASSES OF STOCK

As businesses pass to succeeding generations, it naturally becomes more difficult for family members active in the business to efficiently manage because of the ever-expanding number of owners. This is an unavoidable consequence of having a family-owned company in which there are both active and inactive shareholders. Both the health of the company and family relationships may suffer if this potentially explosive issue is not addressed.

One technique that is frequently employed is to rearrange the governance structure of the company by recapitalizing its stock. For example, recapitalizing the common stock into two classes (voting and non-voting) allows the senior generation to divide their estate equally among their heirs in terms of value, but differently in terms of corporate governance. Then inheritors of non-voting stock can be given a way to make their inheritance liquid through buy–sell provisions. This effective method of using corporate governance to deal with active and inactive next-generation inheritors is available to both C corporations and S corporations. If the family business assets are owned by a limited liability company or a family limited partnership, variations on this method can be used to achieve the same result.

Another stock governance technique used successfully to transfer ownership down a generation is preferred stock recapitalization. This technique is available to both C corporations and family limited partnerships where significant growth is expected. The value of the senior generation's ownership is frozen, and all succeeding growth in the enterprise is realized by the heirs.

BUY–SELL AGREEMENTS. Buy–sell agreements are contractual arrangements between shareholders. They are typically used by family business owners to facilitate an orderly exchange of stock in the corporation for cash. To prevent the stock from ending up in unfriendly hands—or even the hands of friendly in-laws—such agreements typically include a provision that the stock will be first tendered to the company or to family members through a right of first refusal.

The most obvious benefit of a buy–sell agreement is that it allows some family members to remain patient shareholders while providing liquidity to family members with other interests or goals. In this way, families can prune the corporate family tree across generations. A buy–sell agreement is often the primary vehicle through which family shareholders can realize value from their highly illiquid and unmarketable wealth—company stock. The ability to sell, whether exercised or not, often makes the difference between feeling fortunate to be able to participate in a family enterprise and feeling enslaved and controlled by it.

While most buy–sell agreements are written so that only death or discord triggers their use, some are created to provide liquidity windows for younger family members. A 30-year-old facing the prospect of purchasing her or his first home, for instance, could convert shares to cash at a predetermined value.

VALUATION OF THE BUSINESS. Determining the value of a business is as much art as science. The outcome of any valuation is frequently influenced by the purpose of the valuation. For example, tax valuations tend to be more conservative than valuations for sale or public offering purposes. When stocks are closely owned, values in general will be lower. Minority blocks of stock especially will have a discounted value, reflecting their lack of marketability. Lack of marketability and illiquidity discounts will be about 20 percent for majority blocks; 35 to 45 percent discounts are common for minority interests. On the purchase side, a premium of up to 30 percent is often applied for controlling shares. Conversely, smaller size and lack of managerial depth often result in a discount of about 15 percent when the benchmark firms used in market approaches to valuation are publicly traded. Although the tax law changes in 1990 were designed to make valuations more market-sensitive and less dependent on arbitrary formulas, deep discounts are allowed in recognition of the lack of marketability of family-owned firms. Exhibit 5-2 shows several approaches to valuation.

EXHIBIT 5-2	VALUATION APPROACHES

Accounting Approach
- Book value

Market Approaches
- Multiple of equity
- Multiple of earnings
- Multiple of sales
- Comparison with publicly owned or privately held companies in the same industry to determine at what multiple of total adjusted earnings (EBITDA), cash flow, and/or return on adjusted invested capital they have traded, adjusted for real estate and other assets.

Income Approaches
- Net present value of future benefits
- Net present value of cash flows or capitalization of earning capacity
- Net present value of expected dividends

Cost Approach
- Appraisal of tangible and intangible assets (particularly suited to appraising the value of holding companies)

Other considerations in arriving at a final valuation include past transactions involving the company and the nature of shareholders' agreements. While shareholders in a family business often agree on a valuation formula, it is important to note that formulas that do not follow one of the approaches listed in Exhibit 5-2 and/or are not regularly reviewed and updated have been successfully challenged by the IRS.

TRUSTS

Trust designations constitute an alphabet soup of names, including GST, GRAT, and IDGT. The real challenge with trusts is ensuring that the right one is used—the one that fulfills the intentions and needs of the owning family.

Trusts are a double-edged sword. In the past, many trusts—particularly the generation-skipping trust (GST)—were used to gain a tax advantage. But the control retained by the gifting generation generally created such difficulties, both for next-generation members and trustees and for the generation of grandchildren, that appreciating the transfer as a gift was the last thing on anybody's mind. Although they comprise only a small subset of the trusts available, GRAT and IDGT are discussed below because they are considered by tax attorneys and estate tax specialists to be particularly beneficial in today's environment. Both have been upheld thus far by the tax courts and so do not represent uncharted or untested legal territory. However, history has shown that the IRS likes to challenge clever estate planning methods, so always check with tax advisors before choosing a trust as a means of reducing estate taxes.

GRANTOR-RETAINED ANNUITY TRUST. A grantor-retained annuity trust, or GRAT, allows one to transfer property to heirs without incurring a gift tax or using up the lifetime unified credit allowance. The annuity formula used to repay the grantor of the trust is IRS-approved. Let's assume that an S corporation (which can now have two classes of stock) recapitalizes, splitting its stock into 10 percent voting and 90 percent non-voting shares. (Why 10 percent? Mortgages provide a precedent for transferring property on the basis of a 10 percent down payment.) The grantor then transfers the non-voting stock to the GRAT, and the GRAT pays the grantor an annuity from cash flow for a fixed term. Shorter-term GRATs (which may be layered over the years) reduce both the risk of poor business performance during the term of the trust and the risk of the grantor's dying before the end of the term. Death by the grantor prior to the end of the annuity would result in the property's being included in the grantor's taxable estate. The heirs then receive the remainder of the trust when the annuity is fully paid off.

INTENTIONAL DEFECTIVE GRANTOR TRUST. The intentional defective grantor trust, or IDGT, enables one to transfer non-voting stock to heirs without gift or estate tax liability. Using this type of trust, an S corporation might recapitalize the corporation so that 10 percent of its stock represented voting shares and the other 90 percent represented non-voting shares. The grantor would then fund the trust with a gift of 10 percent of the sale price, or value, and sell the non-voting stock to the trust. The trust would pay the grantor with an installment note pledging the stock as collateral; the grantor would not have to pay income tax on the interest received on the note but would assume an income tax liability on the income from the trust. To fit the particular needs of the grantor and heirs, the various terms of the note can be varied, including the number of years the note will be held and the exclusion/inclusion of prepayment penalties.

EQUITY AND NONFAMILY EMPLOYEES

Most family businesses prefer not to grant shares of stock to nonfamily members, even if they are key executives. Those nonfamily employees who do hold stock in a family business suffer the same plight as family shareholders. The stock is illiquid and unmarketable. So, unless the family plans to sell the business, these shares constitute little more than a provision for retirement and seldom provide the incentive that the grantors aspire to create.

A few businesses have developed phantom stock plans with the aim of creating performance-based incentives for key management without actually distributing company stock. Under such plans, company stock is valued periodically, and the phantom stock reflects any shareholder value created. Whenever title to the phantom stock vests—whether it is annually or several years in the future—the company redeems the stock from the key nonfamily employees.

EMPLOYEE STOCK OWNERSHIP PLANS. The outright sale of a family-owned company may result in capital gain, income, gift, and/or estate taxes, depending on how the sale is structured. In general, traditional sales, whether to family members or people outside the family, are tax-inefficient; they give rise to a capital gains tax liability that reduces the net after-tax wealth that can be passed on to the next generation. On the other hand, next-generation members may not be interested in or capable of running the business. Because of the illiquid and unmarketable nature of family business stock, family members may realize more current value from an outright sale of the business than from a transfer of ownership within the family, even with the significant tax liability.

Employee stock ownership plans, or ESOPs, represent a tax-advantaged exit strategy for family business owners who want to create liquidity, diversify their portfolio of assets, and/or reward employees for years of hard work. The financing costs of this kind of transaction are generally low, as a result of government policy that encourages ESOPs through incentives and guarantees to banks, which are then able to pass along their reduced lending costs to the seller. In effect, the employer finances the purchase by borrowing from the bank and lending the funds to the ESOP to purchase company stock. As the employer repays the loan, employees' accounts are credited with shares. ESOPs are akin to a qualified retirement plan for employees, with individual employee accounts invested in company stock. ESOPs require frequent appraisals of the company's value, as well as maintenance and oversight of the individual accounts within the plan. Consequently, annual administrative costs can be high. Under certain conditions, ESOP members must also be given the right to vote their shares.

PITFALLS TO AVOID IN ESTATE AND OWNERSHIP TRANSFER PLANNING

The following list summarizes the mistakes that business owners should make every effort to avoid in estate and ownership transfer planning.

- *Procrastinating in planning the estate and ignoring the inevitability of the owner's eventual death.* The emotional barriers to estate planning and ownership transfer are formidable. However, it is the ultimate responsibility of business owners to lead their families and their businesses into the future by actively planning for the continuity of their businesses and the happiness and financial security of their families. Early planning—so that there is sufficient time to test the plan and its assumptions—should be every family business owner's goal. It does not make sense to leave the final decisions regarding the family business for the IRS or consensus-seeking next-generation members to make in the owner's absence, when the owner has dedicated a lifetime to building that business.

- *Single-mindedly pursuing tax minimization to the detriment of the continuity of the business.* Business owners who doggedly pursue tax minimization in estate planning often get what they planned for—a lower tax bill and a business that will not survive beyond their generation. It is important to remember that the family business legacy is about much more than money; it's about a work ethic, a customer orientation, product/service quality, integrity, freedom, continuity, family harmony, and charitably giving to the communities in which the family business has lived.[6]

- *Failing to use estate planning as an opportunity to teach the next generation and to pass on a legacy, not just financial assets.* Greed may step into the vacuum created when goodwill and love are not articulated and acted upon by the business leader. Family meetings should be held to discuss family principles and philosophies. Through personal storytelling and the use of communication media, the family's history, the company's culture, and the business's successful strategy can be captured and passed along to the next generation.

- *Confusing fairness with love and a desire to treat all heirs equally.* Parents are expected—and want—to love their children equally. But individual children have different needs; throughout their children's lives, parents learn that loving equally does not mean treating equally. The estate and ownership transfer plan needs to reflect this reality. Equality in ownership and/or managerial responsibility often leads to paralysis of business operations and undermines the speed and agility advantage naturally enjoyed by most family-owned businesses. Establishing the survival of the business as the primary goal in estate planning will almost always create the best overall result for the family as a whole.

- *Failing to communicate and consult with heirs in order to understand what individual family members most value, desire, and need.* People tend to better support that which they have helped create. Communication and consultation will make the people affected by estate planning decisions more willing and better able to carry out the spirit, as well as the legal text, of the plan. To be effective in achieving goals beyond tax minimization, estate plans need to be tailored to the unique needs, values, and goals of the heirs and the business. If the difficult conversations are held early and often enough, the changes and accommodations necessary to include those things individual family members most value and want can be built into a flexible model of estate and ownership transfer planning acceptable to many different individuals and the company.

- *Insufficiently preparing successors and/or failing to acknowledge the specific strengths and weaknesses of next-generation members.* Wishful thinking about the capabilities of successors or, in the name of consensus, giving an angry minority veto power over what next-generation leaders consider to be in the best interest of the family and the business is a recipe for disaster. (A perfect example of this mistake, by the Bingham family and the Louisville *Courier-Journal*, will be discussed in Chapter 9.) Expecting immediate readiness from successors rather than instituting a multi-year learning and testing period is equally foolish. Accountability for profit and loss on the business side and the capacity to lead the family are abilities developed only over time. Differentiating the economic value of the stock from the controlling interest is an effective tool for estate planning. Another important tool is differentiating the forms of participation by family members in the business by developing policies that establish different prerequisites for working in top management, becoming a lower-level employee, and qualifying for board service (see Chapter 9).

■ *Failing to submit the estate and ownership transfer plan to a professional advisor or board of directors for review.* Professional advice on estate planning and ownership transfer is not an area in which family business owners should be thrifty. Advice from top-notch professionals on gift and estate tax can result in millions of dollars in savings. More importantly, such advice often allows heirs to receive more personal value for the money, family unity to be preserved, and the business to continue, either under family control or under new management and ownership. Advisory or statutory boards can also do much to provide oversight of the multi-year planning process, and they can be invaluable in the event of the untimely death of the company leader. Because tax codes are changing constantly, both professional advisors and a board that includes outsiders can be helpful in staying on top of the changes and promoting periodic reviews that update estate and ownership transfer plans to reflect current realities.

THE ROLE OF THE BOARD OF DIRECTORS

In July 2001, the 70-year-old owner of a $65 million construction materials company died unexpectedly. He had been, up until that point, in relatively good health. Two years earlier, this owner had initiated an advisory board with independent outsiders. His death, while a great tragedy to the family, did not become a tragedy for the business, primarily for three reasons. First, the advisory board had, in its oversight capacity, made the owner accountable for progress in the leadership development of the next generation, and both a son and a daughter were being groomed for general management through jobs with profit and loss responsibilities. Second, the board had repeatedly put on its meeting agenda the subject of estate planning and ownership transfer and had held conversations with the owner's professional advisors to ensure follow-through. Third, the spouse and co-owner of the company had attended the advisory board meetings and had championed its work with the tax and estate planning consultants.

Board members had also facilitated discussions with the potential successors and other members of the family. The board asked probing questions to help family members develop a sense of the goals, principles, and philosophies that should guide the development of the estate plan. In so doing, they improved the probability that the decisions made would be fair and create value and that family relationships would be maintained or improved.

Statutory boards of directors have a certain leverage with owners in regard to topics (such as estate and ownership transfer planning) that are prone to evoke denial, fear, and procrastination on the part of the owners. A board composed of family members is generally not much help in getting an owner to do what is so much more easily avoided. Therefore, a family business capable of assembling a board, whether statutory or advisory, that includes independent outsiders is much more likely to successfully plan the estate and ownership transfer in a timely manner.

Individual members of family business boards are often selected on the basis of their abilities as street-smart peers; that is, they are business owners who have already been where this company's CEO is headed. By design, then, many of the advisors and directors have already had the succession experience and may have a network of resources they can recommend to the CEO for assistance in planning the estate and implementing the transfer of ownership.

SUMMARY

1. Business owners often delay estate planning for the following reasons:
   - They do not want to discuss their death and its implications for the family and the business.
   - They do not want to give up control of the business.
   - They are trying to avoid potential family conflicts.

2. Federal and state gift and estate taxes are progressive, expensive, and capable of decimating a family business whose primary asset is illiquid and unmarketable company stock. Implications of tax laws for individual families and businesses are best understood by professional advisors.

3. An estate plan must address the appropriate allocation of income sources to the founder, his or her spouse, and non-active family members, as well as the inheritance of the heirs. It must also address corporate control issues.

4. The speed and agility that help family businesses gain competitive advantages in the marketplace must not be hampered by an inability to make decisions promptly, whether caused by a cumbersome trust arrangement, a consensus-dependent co-presidency, or the desire to treat all heirs equally.

5. Withholding the authority to lead—either by not transferring voting stock at the appropriate time or by requiring that important decisions be based on a consensus of next-generation shareholders with equal amounts of stock—is likely to limit the lifespan of the corporation to the lifespan of the current-generation CEO or subject progress to a veto by an upset minority.

6. Recapitalizing common stock into two classes (voting and non-voting) allows the senior generation to divide their estate equally among their heirs

in terms of value, but differently in terms of corporate governance. In preferred stock recapitalization , the value of ownership by the senior generation is frozen, and all succeeding growth in the enterprise is realized by the heirs.

7. A buy–sell agreement is often the primary vehicle for family shareholders to have their highly illiquid and unmarketable wealth—the company stock—realize value.

8. Valuation approaches include the accounting approach (book value); market approaches (multiple of equity, multiple of earnings, multiple of sales, comparison of companies within the same industry); income approaches (net present value of future benefits, net present value of cash flows or capitalization of earning capacity, net present value of expected dividends); and cost approach (appraisal of tangible and intangible assets).

9. Two types of trusts particularly beneficial to family businesses in today's environment are the grantor-retained annuity trust (GRAT) and the intentional defective grantor trust (IDGT).

10. Employee stock ownership plans (ESOPs) represent a tax-advantaged exit strategy for family business owners who want to create liquidity, diversify their portfolio of assets, and/or reward employees for years of hard work.

11. Professional advisors and a board of directors that includes independent outsiders can help a family business successfully plan the estate and ownership transfer in a timely manner.

EXERCISE

OWNERSHIP TRANSFER AND ESTATE PLANNING INVENTORY

The following Family Business Estate Planning and Ownership Transfer Inventory has been used in a variety of family business situations.[7] It has often been assigned as pre-work and then analyzed by a third-party consultant in preparation for a family council or family business retreat. The survey has consistently promoted candid conversations about what the owning family wants and what its priorities are regarding the estate and the transfer of ownership in a family business. Anonymity is essential to promoting a high level of candor about what is typically a very hard subject for family members to discuss. Having multiple generations and multiple branches (including in-laws) of the family partici-pate in discussions of the results at the same time can be a very effective way to promote communication. A third-party facilitator is sometimes advisable, depending on the family's history and communication skills. The inventory, as presented here, assumes that a family business is being transferred from a second (G2) to a third (G3) generation, hence the G2 and G3 designations in questions 6, 7, and 8. These questions could just as easily read G1 and G2 or G3 and G4, as the case may be.

Invite your students to complete the survey as a check on their particular priorities.

THE FAMILY BUSINESS ESTATE PLANNING
AND OWNERSHIP TRANSFER INVENTORY

Individual responses will be kept confidential. Feedback will be in aggregate scores. It will take 10 minutes to fill out.

EXERCISE

1. What should be our family's primary motivation for estate and continuity planning? (Please select only one.)

   a. To increase inheritance for the next generation(s)

   b. To reduce estate taxes

   c. To provide continuity for the family-owned enterprise

   d. To make charitable contributions

   e. To preserve jobs and remain a source of employment for the many families that depend on the business for their livelihood

   f. To increase shareholder value today

   g. To increase long-term shareholder value

   h. Other

2. Which statement more closely reflects your views regarding estate and continuity planning? (Please select only one.)

   a. I feel no particular responsibility to conserve assets for the next generation(s) and would prefer to spend the assets during my lifetime.

   b. I feel no particular responsibility to conserve assets for the next generation(s); however, I am happy to have whatever is left pass on to them upon death.

   c. I feel no particular responsibility to conserve assets for the next generation(s); however, I feel responsible for the continuity of the family-owned business.

   d. I feel no particular responsibility to conserve assets for the next generation(s); however, I intend to plan the estate in a manner that will maximize their inheritance.

   e. I feel a responsibility to conserve assets for the next generation(s) and to do what is possible to promote continuity of the business from generation to generation.

   f. Other _____

3. Regarding the investment objectives of shareholders, which of the following are most important to you? (Select only one in each paired choice, a or b.)

   a. To build value for future generations

   b. To maximize value for current owners

   a. To reinvest profits for maximum growth

   b. To maximize distributions to owners for increased liquidity

   a. To focus more on growth than on minimizing risk

   b. To focus more on minimizing risk than on growth

   a. To use leverage (debt) to fund growth

   b. To use current cash flow to fund growth

4. Do you have a total return on equity or return on investment objective in mind?

   a. 10%

   b. 15%

   c. 20%

   d. Other _____

5. Regarding returns on your investment, which would you prefer?

   a. Growth in equity appreciation, or value of the business

   b. Dividends, distributions, or cash payouts

6. G2 family members may be concerned that next-generation members lack the skills to manage the assets they inherit. Which statement most closely reflects G2's view? (Please select only one.)

(continued)

(continued)

a. G2 believes the next generation does not possess the necessary skills to manage the wealth and ownership responsibilities involved and does not feel a responsibility to help it acquire these skills or coach them in the interim.

b. G2 believes the next generation does not possess the necessary skills to manage the wealth and the ownership responsibilities involved and does feel a responsibility to help it acquire these skills or coach next-generation members in the interim.

c. G2 believes the next generation does possess the necessary skills to manage the wealth and the ownership responsibilities involved, but G2 still prefers to pass assets on through a trust or through some other vehicle that requires professional management.

d. G2 believes the next generation does possess the necessary skills to manage the wealth involved but not necessarily the ownership responsibilities involved in a family-owned business.

e. G2 believes the next generation does possess the necessary skills to manage the wealth and the company ownership responsibilities involved. And G2 feels comfortable that the next generation will manage its wealth and ownership responsibilities effectively.

f. G2 is unsure about the skills and interest of the next generation to manage the assets and to be a responsible owner of a family-owned business.

Please discuss any skills or qualities that the next generation could benefit from having in terms of being seen as more ready and qualified for the management of wealth and/or family business ownership.

_____
_____
_____
_____
_____

(In questions 7 and 8, we are interested in both G2's *and* G3's perspectives and their assessment of how the other generation perceives the issues.)

7. Which statement more closely reflects G2's perspective? (Please select only one.)

a. Regardless of their needs, parents should always leave the maximum inheritance to their children.

b. Parents should leave their children the minimum inheritance required to meet the children's individual lifestyle needs.

c. When the inheritance is in family company stock, parents should make family business continuity priority number one.

d. If the inheritance is in family company stock, parents should make sure that equal distribution is priority number one.

e. When the inheritance is in family company stock, parents should make sure that a fair distribution meets the continuity needs of the business, the inheritance preferences of the parents, and the financial needs of the children.

If you selected statement e, rank the three issues in order of priority:

___ continuity of the business
___ inheritance preferences of the parents
___ financial needs of the next generation

8. Which statement more closely reflects G3's perspective? (Please select only one.)

a. Parents should always leave the maximum inheritance to their children.

b. Parents should leave their children the minimum inheritance required to meet the children's individual lifestyle needs.

c. When the inheritance is in family company stock, parents should make family business continuity priority number one.

EXERCISE

d. When the inheritance is in family company stock, parents should make sure that equal distribution is priority number one.

e. When the inheritance is in family company stock, parents should make sure that a fair distribution meets the continuity needs of the business, the inheritance preferences of the parents, and the financial needs of the children.

If you selected statement e, rank the three issues in order of priority:

___ continuity of the business

___ inheritance preferences of the parents

___ financial needs of the next generation

9. Have next-generation members been able to learn sufficiently about the business?

___ Yes   ___ No

Please explain your answer:

_____
_____
_____
_____
_____
_____

10. Do next-generation members have the opportunity to influence the planning for the future ownership of the business?

___ Yes   ___ No

Please explain your answer:

_____
_____
_____
_____
_____
_____

6

PROMOTING STRATEGIC GROWTH

I don't think it's an accident that the newspapers best known for quality in this
country . . . are, or were until recently, family controlled. It seems that certain attributes
essential to quality are more easily provided by families than by public companies. These
are the qualities that I think most important: First, deep roots. Families offer longevity—and
thus a knowledge of, and commitment to, the local community that's hard to get from professional managers who come and go. . . . Second, a perspective that extends beyond the next
quarter's earnings per share. . . . Finally, family ownership provides the independence that is
sometimes required to withstand governmental pressure and preserve freedom of the press.

—Katharine Graham, Late Chairman of the Washington Post Company[1]

Strategic planning is done differently in family-controlled corporations, where
both management and the family shareholder group must be engaged in thinking
about the future. The family shareholder group needs to establish its own goals
and define the nature of its relationship with the business. If family members
intend to continue to own the business in the next generation, will they manage it
themselves or would they prefer to have professional nonfamily managers run it
for them?

Given their unique role in the strategic planning of family-controlled companies, family shareholders must be careful not to usurp top management's responsibility for thinking strategically on behalf of the business and its shareholders. In
addition, the ownership group must not lose sight of the primary objective of any
company—creating value for its customers. Only in this way can a business create
value for itself. This ongoing process of creating customer value will generally
result in healthy profit margins and cash flows, which will then lead to an increase
in value for shareholders.

While it may sound simple, value creation for the customer in a constantly
changing competitive environment is a difficult thing indeed for an organization
that for the most part prefers to maintain the status quo. And most organizations,
whether family-controlled or not, engage in some resistance to change. From a
strategic perspective, family-owned enterprises are most susceptible to accelerated decline and failure precisely because of their heavy reliance on an individual
entrepreneur or next-generation CEO. Founders often display a natural disdain
for organizational architecture, such as establishing systems, professional managerial practices, and governance mechanisms. Next-generation leaders may also

---

EXHIBIT 6-1 FROM SPRINT TO CRAWL

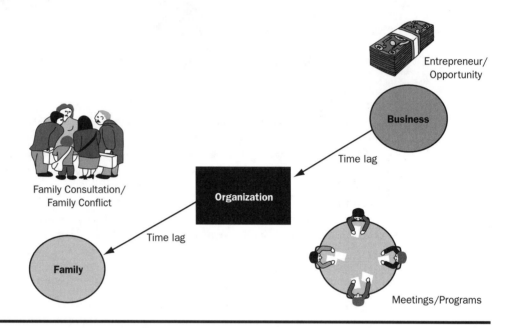

---

exhibit disdain for managerial discipline as they engage in the strategic regeneration and growth of the business. After all, professional managerial practices have bureaucratic roots, and the desire to flee from the bureaucracy of a publicly owned global behemoth was frequently the entrepreneur's reason for starting his or her own company.

When multiple members of a family become active in management and/or engaged as shareholders in thinking about the future of the enterprise, disagreements often arise and paralysis may set in. The varying perspectives of active and inactive shareholders on conflict and tolerance for different opinions make strategic planning a task likely to be avoided.

The speed and agility that once gave a competitive advantage to the family business are often sacrificed across generations. The timeliness with which decisions are made and executed suffers tremendously, robbing a firm of its ability to "turn on a dime."

Time lags are likely to be created as the business grows from being run by an entrepreneur (who knew that the cash from a potential sale would either stay in the customer's pocket or move to his or her pocket) to being family- or management-run. The firm may rely on management meetings and six sigma process improvement objectives to achieve quality and may have to hold family meetings to educate shareholders on business strategy, finance, estate planning, and estate tax implications (see Exhibit 6-1).

The time lags can be significant, especially when an ownership-first orientation replaces a customer-first orientation in the management ranks. This tendency among family-controlled companies to focus internally is perhaps the strongest rationale for engaging in strategic planning. Strategic thinking represents a breath of fresh air in what could otherwise be a vacuum-sealed system, inhabited by owners and managers oblivious to changes in the competitive environment.

THE ZERO-SUM FAMILY DYNAMIC AND STRATEGIC PLANNING

Another important function that strategic planning performs for family-controlled companies is promoting much-needed communication among shareholders. Engaging in conversations about the corporation's plans for the future creates a predisposition to open additional channels of communication, thereby counteracting the natural propensity for secrecy, found particularly among first and second generations. It also helps define the individual as part of an interdependent network—the extended family—in a way that today's society, with its preference for rugged individualism, seldom does. Few things are as damaging to the long-term survival of family-controlled firms as secrecy and "me-ism" among those who hold shares in the corporation. A zero-sum dynamic exists within a family business when there is no business growth; golden opportunities for some stakeholders are linked to lost opportunities for others, resulting in no net gain at the extended family level. The zero-sum dynamic is a precursor to business failure and disharmony in the family.

In the absence of growth, zero-sum dynamics become a corrosive influence, often overriding the goodwill and best intentions of even the healthiest of families. In a declining business, family conflict can easily get the upper hand. Any centralization of power carried out to address the decline represents a gain of control by some and a reduction in participation by others. This often leads to the erosion of individual responsibility and the desire to blame others. The vicious cycle continues, as the goal becomes protecting individual interests or minimizing personal risk, as opposed to growing the business or maximizing its gains. When this happens, promising alternatives for growth may be rejected as competition and in-fighting for resources—and for right or might—spread.

In the business, employee morale suffers, and turnover increases. In the family, conflict may reach crisis proportions.[2] A study of small private companies showed these businesses to be much more susceptible than larger publicly traded corporations to the effects of decline.[3] It seems that the greater momentum and larger pool of accumulated resources, human and financial, act as buffers against an environment that threatens the firm's survival. In plain language, evidence points to the fact that, when the pie is not getting larger, family shareholders often begin to fight over the size of their slice.

Strategic planning, with its natural bias toward growth, serves a family-controlled company well, because growth is the source of new jobs, increased wealth, developmental opportunities, influence, and greater family unity. Growth, as described here, is not a goal in itself, but rather the outcome of thinking strategically about the future. In other words, efforts to create value for customers also create wealth and career opportunities for shareholders.

After almost 100 years of operation, the McIlhenny Company, makers of the peppery Tabasco® Sauce, formulated a strategic plan for growth. Accustomed to receiving substantial dividends from operations, shareholders had become concerned about dilution of dividends as the next generation grew to 90 members. Leaders of this family-owned company decided that the risk of unhealthy conflict among family members dictated that the company grow in order to avoid the zero-sum family dynamic. New products were created and product lines extended. The Tabasco label now graces not just the little bottle of red hot sauce, but bottles of green pepper sauce and ready-to-add spicy mixes for Cajun home cooking.

CREATING VALUE WITH UNIQUE BUSINESS MODELS

How do family-controlled enterprises create value? Speed and agility have already been mentioned as competitive advantages often inherent to entrepreneurial and small, privately held companies with first-generation leadership. The result of unique organizational capabilities, speed allows the business to stay close to the customer, whether through personal or digitally enabled relationships, and to detect when the customer needs change. Dell, the owner-managed computer and digital services company, is well known for its speed. Michael Dell has been the architect of a company that not only makes customized computers quickly through its innovative choice board on the Internet but also accelerates cash flow and asset turns by collecting on the sale before the company even orders the necessary raw materials and assembles the computer.

There are seven primary sources of value on which family companies can build competitive advantage: (1) financial resources, such as cash and securities; (2) physical assets, such as plant and equipment; (3) the product (sometimes protected by patents) and its price and performance; (4) brand equity, which is the market's perception of a distinction in quality or reputation, a perception created over time; (5) organizational capabilities, which are the competencies residing in employees and unique organizational architectures; (6) customer–supplier integration (once called distribution), which includes new ways of getting the product or service to the customer in any form, at any time, and in any place;[4] and (7) the family–business relationship, a resource that can be leveraged. Combining these seven sources of value in various ways will give rise to a unique business model, one that is rooted in the core competencies of the business and can create value for both the owners and the customers. Competitive advantages created by real assets (such as financial resources and equipment) can be copied or cloned and are often temporary and transient. Competitive advantages created by intangible assets (people, their knowledge and skills, company values, and other organizational capabilities) are often more defensible and longer lasting.

FINANCIAL RESOURCES

Traditionally, family-owned companies have bemoaned the fact that they are at a disadvantage when competing with global publicly traded corporations. The financial and physical assets of public companies dwarf those of all but the largest of 100 percent family-owned companies—like Mars, Inc., with $15 billion in annual revenues. Unlike Mars, many family-controlled companies have addressed this perceived disadvantage by going public, while retaining voting control by the family. The Washington Post Company is a case in point; in its quest to grow in editorial influence and business reach, it went public in 1971.

Financial constraints are clearly a barrier to the healthy growth of family-owned businesses.[5] Unless the business regularly avails itself of the financial markets by issuing debt and equity (or the company is in the insurance or banking business, both of which are great cash generators), financial assets are not likely to be a source of value for a unique business model. The beauty of creating value for customers, shareholders, and employees through a unique business model is that it helps the business stand out from competition in the marketplace. A unique model that has the capacity to deliver value (a capacity that the business models of many of the dot-coms operating in the spring of 2000 did not have) will likely provide a level of differentiation and sustainable competitive advantage that cookie-cutter strategies cannot provide.

PHYSICAL ASSETS

Physical assets are seldom major contributors to value creation. The advantages implicit in the "big get bigger" folklore have been wildly exaggerated. The sales to physical assets ratios of two global behemoths, Microsoft and U.S. Steel, provide a little perspective on the subject. Microsoft's ratio is 12.26, while U.S. Steel's is only 1.96, as a result of its oversized investment in plant and equipment.[6] Which company has greater cash flows and has created more shareholder value? In June of 2002, after a severe decline in the value of technology stocks, Microsoft's market capitalization was still $246 billion, 60 times greater than that of U.S. Steel. Of course, successful competition in the steel industry requires significant assets. But, as mini-mills and other innovators in the industry have shown, these assets need not always be in the quantities held by larger, integrated steel producers.

Most family-controlled enterprises today are better served by explicitly choosing *not* to base value creation on physical assets, recognizing both their own fiscally conservative profile and the potential financial danger that such assets represent. As technology, market requirements, and customer needs and wants change, physical assets have a tremendous ability to become liabilities.

THE PRODUCT: ITS PRICE AND PERFORMANCE

The product itself—sometimes protected by patents—and its price and performance can be sources of value creation. Although these sources of value are often associated with technology firms, engineers, inventors, and tinkerers have created many of today's mainstream businesses in low-tech environments. Honey-Baked Hams of Cincinnati, Ohio, for example, owes much of its current success to the fact that its founder's invention, a spiral-cutting machine, was repeatedly rejected by large meat processors. Desperate, but not prone to give up easily, founder George Kurz decided to take advantage of patent protection on the machine to establish a ham-retailing operation. Instead of building a manufacturing operation to produce ham-cutting equipment, he built a retail empire.

Over three generations, owner-managers turned what began as a product performance advantage (with the design for the slicing machine sketched on the back of a paper napkin) into a brand equity advantage. Customers value the difference that the spiral cut produces in the ham's taste and are willing to pay a premium for it.[7]

BRAND EQUITY

Brand equity is a well-known source of value for family-controlled companies. Casual clothing manufacturers (e.g., Levi Strauss), hotel chains (e.g., Marriott), and brewing companies (e.g., Anheuser-Busch) all have it, as do many fashion houses (e.g., Ralph Lauren), fragrance producers (e.g., Estée Lauder), and wine and spirits companies (e.g., Bacardi).

The Washington Post Company is a family-controlled company that enjoys significant brand equity. The brand equity of this diversified media organization results largely from a commitment to quality journalism and independent thinking, forged during a turbulent period in the 1970s when the company decided to publish both the Pentagon Papers and stories about the Watergate scandal. In her later years, Katharine Graham devoted much of her time to public speaking and writing that enhanced the Post's brand equity. She relied on her son, Don Graham, third-generation publisher and CEO, to run the company with a team of nonfamily managers.

The Post's nonvoting B stock is publicly traded. Voting control, however, rests in the A stock owned by Don Graham and his three siblings. The Post has approximately 10,700 employees, annual revenues of $2.4 billion, and profits of $136.5 million. In addition to publishing the *Washington Post*, the company owns *Newsweek* magazine, six network-affiliated TV stations, a cable network with more than 600,000 subscribers, education-related businesses (e.g., Kaplan), and interests in other media-related companies.[8]

ORGANIZATIONAL CAPABILITIES

Often, the brand equity that firms enjoy is built over time through unique organizational capabilities. What are these organizational capabilities that are responsible for most of the value creation of family-controlled companies? Fisk Johnson, president of SC Johnson: A Family Company, has said that it is the people—who care about the customer and each other—who make his company customer-oriented, flexible, and fast. When asked the meaning of the company theme "Family values . . . World class results," he said that it means "replacing chlorofluorocarbons or CFCs from aerosol products much earlier than the competition and government regulations would have had us do, because we knew our customers cared about the environment and we did too." Without a hint of boasting in his voice, he added, "And we took CFC out of our entire product line in 5 working days, unheard of in our industry." This speed and nimbleness are the result of an organizational capability built on several generations of skilled people who care about their customers and the integrity of their products.[9]

Organizational capabilities also include internal processes in administration or manufacturing—for example, processes that streamline the flow of information, resources, or parts within the firm. Companies with unique organizational capabilities are capable of creating value in ways that others find difficult to replicate, whether through enterprise management systems, electronically enabled global teams, or the simpler but equally significant interdisciplinary project teams and multiple-skilled manufacturing or service teams.

CUSTOMER–SUPPLIER INTEGRATION

Because of the significant influence of PCs and the Internet on sourcing and logistics, the traditional distribution system has changed dramatically and so have relationships and the relative power of firms across the entire value-added chain. During the 1990s, many family-owned distribution and retail companies feared for their survival as their suppliers developed a web presence and threatened to take out the "middlemen." Consolidators, with Wall Street financing, bought out many of these family-owned businesses that feared for their future. While the fears proved greatly exaggerated, profit margins, ways of doing business, and the relative power of firms in their respective distribution chains were forever changed.

The firms that survived know a thing or two about sustainable competitive advantage. Yet they must continually ask themselves: To what extent do we need to deploy a digital strategy that will enhance our relationship with suppliers, customers, and the customers' customers? The changes that the Internet has wrought on the value-added chain in almost every industry—notwithstanding the demise of a significant number of dot-coms—have only begun to be discernible. Just as the Internet did not totally replace television, radio, and newspapers, new customer–supplier integration networks will not totally eradicate more traditional distribution channels and relationships. But it is certain that the Internet and its applications have eroded, and will continue to erode, some of the value of traditional approaches, thereby making it harder to create value for customers without somehow adding digital networking capacity to the mix.

At Madco, a distribution company, two generations of owner-managers argued for months about whether to engage in digitally enabled distribution. While the father/CEO wanted nothing to do with a strategy that could possibly cannibalize their existing business, the son/vice president of information technology was confident that, if Madco did not move into the digital arena, another firm, perhaps from outside their industry, would come in and serve that customer need.

THE NATURE OF THE FAMILY–BUSINESS RELATIONSHIP

The nature of the interaction between the business and the family may well constitute a unique competency and source of value in family-owned and family-controlled businesses. When this interaction is characterized by family unity and forward thinking by family members, companies are more likely to engage in managerial and governance practices that control agency costs and bank on unique resources that produce idiosyncratic organizational capabilities.

To better understand this issue, researchers in the Discovery Action Research Project asked the following question: To what extent may the unique interaction between the family and the business be measured and to what extent is the interaction associated with the behavior of the firm? To answer this question, the researchers calculated an interaction variable called the Family–Business Interaction Variable.

First, three indices of the study scales were created, based on a model of family business system performance.[10] This model hypothesizes that the nature and quality of the interaction between the family and the business lead to a set of best management practices related to the high performance of the firm.

1. The Management and Governance Practices Index, which is the independent variable, deals with the practices required for sustainable high performance by the firm and is the sum of the values earned on the planning, performance feedback, succession disclosure, family meetings, and advisory board scales in the survey instrument.

2. The Family Unity Index relates to the owning family and is the sum of the values earned on the family harmony, tolerance of differences, and nature of participation and succession scales.

3. The Business Opportunity Index concerns the business and is the sum of the values earned on the growth orientation, career opportunity, and communication climate scales.

The Family–Business Interaction Variable, calculated from the Family Unity and Business Opportunity Indices at the firm level, characterizes the interaction between ownership and management.

Difference testing was then conducted to answer the research question. The study firms were divided into two groups according to whether they had above-average or below-average scores on the Family Unity Index. A t-test was then carried out to determine whether the two groups had significantly different scores on the Management and Governance Practices Index. This procedure was repeated for the Business Opportunity Index and the Family–Business Interaction Variable. Results of difference testing between the two groups indicated that firms with significantly different scores on the Family Unity Index, Business Opportunity Index, and Family–Business Interaction Variable also had significantly different scores on the Management and Governance Practices Index.

The Family Unity Index was found to correlate positively with effective management and governance practices, including strategic planning activity, performance feedback, succession planning disclosure, advisory boards, and family meetings. These findings seem to indicate that investing in the family's health and harmony—by establishing guidelines for family participation in the business and the employment of family members, clear standards and processes for succession and ownership transfer, and ways of promoting cooperation and positive relations among family members—pays off for the firm. They further support the idea that family meetings, retreats, and councils can play important roles in promoting the effectiveness and continuity of a family business by creating among family members a new reality characterized by goodwill, team problem-solving, and recognition of business opportunities.[11]

Since laws of economics and competitive dynamics apply equally to family-controlled companies and management-controlled corporations, any competitive advantages gained by family businesses must be the result of strategic thinking and a commitment to value creation for the customer. The aura of a "family effect" will not suspend the demands of a constantly changing competitive environment.[12] But the results of the Discovery study suggest that family unity and effective family–business interaction make certain practices and strategies more likely and sustainable. For example, study results indicate that steps taken to promote family unity also make strategic planning processes more likely. And strategic planning processes have already been linked in several family business studies to family business continuity.[13] The Discovery study results also suggest the converse—that one of the unique goals of family-owned companies, family harmony, is more likely to be achieved by running the business like a business, using the latest management and governance practices including strategic planning.

THE CUSTOMER-ORIENTED COMPANY

The enterprise that creates value for its employees and shareholders (the family) by first creating value for its customers has come to understand that, in today's economy, being successful requires providing customers with the service or product they want in any form, at any time, and in any place. In order to accomplish this, the customer-oriented company relies heavily on unique organizational capabilities and core competencies that have translated into competitive advantage precisely because they respond to what customers value.

Many owners of family-controlled companies eloquently discuss what they consider to be their traditional core competencies: quality products/services, skilled employees, and speed and agility. What is largely missing from both the strategic planning literature and the conventional wisdom of practicing owner-managers is an analysis of whether these competencies add value from the customer's perspective.

What matters to customer-oriented companies is the outcome from the perspective of the customer who is using their product or service. Only if customers see value in what a particular organizational capability does for them can that capability turn into a competitive advantage for the firm (see Exhibit 6-2). Because

---

EXHIBIT 6-2   TURNING CORE COMPETENCIES INTO COMPETITIVE ADVANTAGES

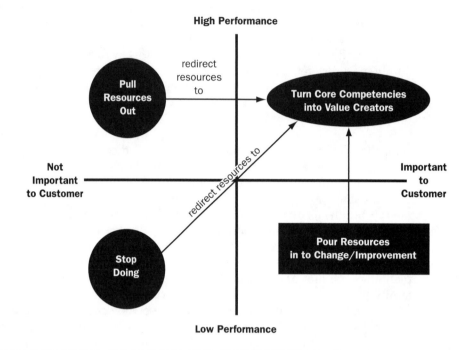

SOURCE: Robert Kauer, professor of banking and finance, Weatherhead School of Management, Case Western Reserve University, 2000.

customer needs are constantly changing, strategic planning may require a reevaluation of these competencies as family-owned and family-controlled companies move from one generation to the next. Even an organizational realignment may be needed to pursue value creation from a customer's perspective.

The practical implication of Exhibit 6-2 for the often internally focused world of the entrepreneur and business owner is that an individual capability or set of capabilities may become unimportant to customers when, for example, lower prices from competitors override qualitative considerations like delivery speed, product or service quality, proprietary technology, customer service, brand equity, and customization capacity. Alternatively, what are thought to be core competencies may be more fiction than fact. For example, the company may have made a premium-quality product once upon a time, but today's product may not be considered superior by customers who also purchase from competitors.

The result of both of these dynamics in a globally competitive marketplace is that business owners have to continuously ask themselves two questions: (1) Is the product or service we are providing the customer still important to the customer? (2) Is what we are producing or supplying still performing at a superior level? Based on the answers to these questions, resources may need to be moved out of some areas and into others to ensure that the current set of core competencies truly results in competitive advantage. Ultimately, only those capabilities valued by the customer provide the family firm with opportunities for gaining differentiation and competitive advantage. And to the extent that the core-competency-turned-competitive-advantage is a resource rooted in the unique family–business interaction, it may be difficult for others to replicate.

STRATEGIC PLANNING AND "JAMMING"

Strategy planning in a family business is not a grand analytical exercise. It is more like playing improvisational jazz, guided by the lead musician's vision for the piece. Strategy making is guided by the owner's vision for the future and a legacy derived from the firm's competencies, both of which insulate the process from chaos and loss of control.

The veteran jazz musician Dave Brubeck and his wife, Iola, have five sons and one daughter. Four of the sons have chosen to pursue musical careers. Dave insisted that the children take piano lessons while they were young, so that they would acquire musical competency, but he had no interest in their launching musical careers. Although they usually work as independent musicians, Dave and his four sons have collaborated on several musical projects, including the 1974 album *Two Generations of Brubeck* and the 1997 album *In Their Own Sweet Way*. In their collaborations, family members tend to welcome exploration and discovery.[14] Dave's oldest son, Darius, commented, "Even though the music is deeply familiar, almost subconsciously so for me, rehearsals take a long time because we all contribute ideas—anything is worth a try—and because Dave keeps astonishing me with the depth and breadth of his creativity. There is probably overall more humor and risk taking. In two words: It's fun."[15]

Among those who contribute to "jam" sessions in a family business may be family members with controlling ownership and key nonfamily managers. Contributors may also include directors of the board or advisory board members who review the strategy developed by management and controlling family members. Crafting a strategy from the accumulated wisdom of the current generation of owners and managers, the dreams and aspirations of the next generation, and the timeless wisdom of loyalty to one's customers leads to innovation and healthy growth for the business across generations.

The need for improvisation has been intensified by the accelerated speed of change in today's competitive markets. There is little time for rehearsal after rehearsal. While both experimentation and practice are useful, strategy making ought to be more a process of active discovery than of divining or dreaming about the future. And discovery is about jamming and learning.

Jamming is creative and playful. Both qualities are needed to develop a strategy for growing or revitalizing a family-owned business. The lone entrepreneur is like the musician who is a skilled improviser but plays solo. Over time, as she grows from playing on street corners to playing in clubs, concert halls, and finally stadiums and arenas, she may hire many helpers—back-up musicians, stagehands, security. But if she never develops a band that she can jam with, she will never benefit from the inspiration of others' innovations. For strategy making to work, allowing the enterprise to evolve and stay healthy over the long haul, owners and managers need to improvise together—as a band.

How does a company build a capacity to jam? Leaders first need to suspend judgment and actively manage themselves so as to avoid second-guessing what the rest of the organization is thinking and doing. This is a prerequisite to developing an organization-wide improvisational capability. Trying out new ways of doing things—whether by taking a different route to the conference room or lunch room in order to talk to employees at their desks or by experimenting with a new approach to customers—may reduce daily efficiency but will likely improve the overall ability to notice, learn, and introduce variety and improvisation into the firm's culture.

General systems theory suggests that as environments become more turbulent or fast changing, the challenge for businesses is to build the requisite ability to deal with variety. As an increasing number of new and unpredictable events occur, companies either develop the ability to deal with that variety or fail to respond appropriately and thus fail to thrive in the new environment. Although the Royal Dutch/Shell Group is not a family-controlled company, it provides a good example of the ability to meet new challenges because it did what seemed at the time to be impossible: It thrived during the oil crisis of the 1970s. Its approach to strategic planning was rooted in creating multiple scenarios of competitive conditions in the world marketplace. In effect, Shell's top management bet on "preparedness," as the military calls it, discussing many alternative scenarios rather than focusing on the most likely scenario and then building a strategy to fit it. Shell used the strategic planning process not as an exercise in predictability, but as a way to increase top management skills in dealing with variety.

Despite Shell's success, not many companies have increased their agility by adding the requisite ability to deal with variety through strategic planning efforts. After all, developing a budget to support the chosen strategy is the next step, and budgets require some degree of certainty and predictability. Indeed, in many corporations, predictability and accountability in the face of changes or variances are what budgets and strategic plans are all about.

For CEOs of family-controlled companies, one of the most essential aspects of preparedness is succession and continuity planning. They will face succession only once in their lifetimes, and they must prepare for it through sound strategic thinking. Succession is not an event. Rather, it is a series of new and unpredictable experiences having to do with the management of the business, the leadership of shareholders, and the promotion of long-term family trust and unity (see Exhibit 6-3). Shell Oil bet on preparedness in the face of unpredictable events by investing in increasing top management's mastery of variety and unpredictability. By doing so, it gave its top management and operating systems the

| EXHIBIT 6-3 | STRATEGIC PLANNING IN THE FAMILY BUSINESS |

Strategic Planning

Financial & Estate Planning

Family

Leadership Succession

Leadership Change

skills necessary to improvise, to be nimble, and to win what has become for all businesses an increasingly unpredictable competitive war for customers. Family-controlled companies must emphasize preparedness in their strategic planning—or be prepared to fail.

BUSINESS DEVELOPMENT AND SURVIVAL

The statistics on the survival of family-controlled enterprises are alarming. Entrepreneurial firms have a dismal record with respect to preserving the spirit of innovation that motivated their founding and propelled them through their early years. In fact, only about 30 percent of these firms survive under the same owning family beyond the first generation. Only about 12 percent survive to the third generation, and only 4 percent survive to the fourth.[16]

Beyond the exciting and exhausting start-up phase and the subsequent growth phase lies organizational maturity. Along with a well-deserved feeling of satisfaction at having finally achieved wealth and influence, maturity brings great risk of protracted decline, leading to the eventual sale or death of the enterprise. At this stage, the business represents a complex set of stakeholders: the banks that have financed the growth, the family members who have worked in the firm since high school or college, the key nonfamily managers who have contributed substantially to the business's success, other family members with financial and/or emotional interests in the enterprise, other investors, lower-level employees, and the government. As discussed at the beginning of this book, each of these stakeholders has a different perspective on the enterprise and feels entitled, for different reasons, to

---

EXHIBIT 6-4 STAGES OF BUSINESS DEVELOPMENT

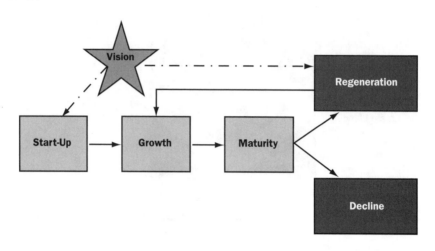

---

certain benefits. Banks want timely debt repayment, profitable new lines of credit, and no surprises. Family members often seek shareholder value creation and high returns on equity, along with employment opportunities. For key nonfamily managers, market-based compensation, career opportunities, and high regard by the owners are essential. Like politicians who run election campaigns by poll results, leaders of family-controlled enterprises, overwhelmed by the complexity of the stakeholder base, may lose the vision that was so much a part of the young organization. This absence of vision often sets the stage for decline (see Exhibit 6-4).

THE UNIQUE VISION OF FAMILY-CONTROLLED COMPANIES

As previously discussed, a unique vision and business model are needed to lead an enterprise to competitive fitness. However, after more than 20 years as an observer and advisor to family-controlled companies around the world, I believe that it is possible to list a set of preferred strategies used by family-controlled companies to create value for customers in differentiated ways. This list is not meant to be a shortcut to creating a unique strategy or an enticement to use cookie-cutter strategies. But it does reinforce the idea that, however fragile family-controlled companies may appear in a fast-changing competitive environment seemingly dominated by global behemoths, regenerating and growing the enterprise in the interest of continuity is doable. It is not easy, nor is it quick, but it is eminently doable. Family-controlled companies have turned the following competencies into value creators for their customers and, thus, into competitive advantages for their firms:

- Rapid speed to market
- Flexibility in response to customers and competitors
- Strategic focus on proprietary products and specialty niches that afford more protected profits
- Concentrated ownership structure that provides more patient capital and commitment to the long term, enabling the company to build brand equity, promote customer loyalty, and sponsor continued reinvestment in family unity and unique organizational capabilities
- Lower total costs derived from reduced agency costs—for example, in administration, supervision, and financial controls
- High quality of product and/or service that builds brand equity, reputation, and higher profitability
- Capacity for customization

Creating value for the customer is at the heart of achieving competitive advantage. Family-owned and family-controlled firms frequently rely on the set of competencies just discussed to gain competitive advantage. Clearly, for a family business, strategic planning that focuses on organizational capabilities rooted in intangible assets, including family unity and the nature of the family–business interaction, plays a critical role in developing a unique vision and business model.

SUMMARY

1. The primary objective of strategic planning in any company is to create value for its customers. Only in this way, can it create value for itself.

2. Time lags can be significant, especially when an ownership-first orientation replaces a customer-first orientation in the business.

3. The zero-sum dynamic is a precursor to business failure and disharmony among family business members. In the absence of growth, family businesses become very vulnerable during the succession process.

4. A steep decline at the end of a successful product line run or the end of a generation's leadership can be the result of the small size of a family business, its propensity for zero-sum family dynamics, limited access to financial assets, and/or the paralysis of business operations.

5. Strategic planning increases owners' and managers' awareness of changes in the competitive environment and promotes much-needed communication among shareholders. With its natural bias toward growth, strategic planning is a great antidote to the challenges of the late maturity and decline stages.

6. The seven primary sources of value for family businesses, giving rise to a unique business model for each family business, are (1) financial resources, (2) physical assets, (3) the product, (4) brand equity, (5) organization capabilities, (6) customer–supplier integration, and (7) the family–business relationship.

7. Competencies that create value for customers and firms include rapid speed to market, flexibility in response to customers and competitors, strategic focus on proprietary products and specialty niches, concentrated ownership structure, reduced agency costs, high quality of product and/or service, and capacity for customization.

THE CRITICAL ROLE OF NONFAMILY MANAGERS

[The Washington Post] is family-oriented—and that makes me nervous as I look around me at other family businesses and what becomes of them. I also see what replaces them when they go downhill. I am trying hard to get strong, able managers around me in an effort to combine the advantages of both.

—Katharine Graham, Late Chairman of the *Washington Post*, in a 1976 Letter to a Friend[1]

The literature on family businesses is overwhelmingly focused on issues of concern to the owning families: family relationships, successor development, estate planning, succession, and wealth transfer. There is little discussion of—or data on—the most productive ways to manage relationships between family and nonfamily managers. Yet family businesses of any significant size depend on the quality and effectiveness of nonfamily managers to ensure their continued success and growth. In a survey of owners of successful 200-year-old and older family businesses, the *Financial Times* of London asked respondents what enabled their companies to continue across so many generations. Beyond quality of product and/or service, business owners credited their firms' continuity to a strong sense of family history, the ability to exclude incompetent family members, and a willingness to employ nonfamily executives whose unique set of skills added value. Their willingness to employ nonfamily executives also more readily enabled these firms to establish hiring practices that were perceived as fair—hiring only *qualified* family managers. Survey respondents said that, by doing so, these firms both ensured business health and maintained family control.

The author wishes to express his appreciation to Theodore Alfred, with whom he first collaborated on this material for the article "What the Silent Majority Thinks—But May Not Tell You," published in *Family Business* magazine in 1996.

THE PERSPECTIVE OF NONFAMILY MANAGERS

The Discovery Action Research Project found that nonfamily managers tended to regard their firms positively; in fact, most would like to see the companies continue as family businesses. Despite the positive attitude, the study identified several problems in the relationships between owners and nonfamily managers that need attention. Specifically the researchers found significant differences between the two groups' perceptions of the efficacy of management and governance practices. Differences also existed in perceptions of the capacity of the firms for innovation and change. The study also revealed some anxiety on the part of nonfamily managers concerning the qualifications of potential successors and the ambiguity of their own positions in the company. To enhance their understanding of questionnaire responses, the researchers personally interviewed key nonfamily managers in the firms participating in the study. The views of one highly regarded nonfamily executive were typical: "I really love working for these people," he told the research team, "but I need more structure. It's nice to be treated like family, but I'd like to know more about where my job begins and ends and how I'm doing."

While both nonfamily and family managers expressed positive feelings overall about their firms, nonfamily managers were generally less positive about management practices and succession issues. Many "love the firm, but . . . ." The differences uncovered in the study represent important challenges, offering significant opportunities for owner-managers to improve the motivation and performance of their top employees (discussed further later in this chapter).

A DELICATE BALANCE

Research by W. Gibb Dyer, Jr., of Brigham Young University, identified serious dilemmas that confront owners of family businesses in their dual roles as family members, on the one hand, and managers, on the other.[2] Balancing the sometimes competing demands of family and business is a challenge for nonfamily managers, too. "Owners have given me much responsibility," one nonfamily manager told the researchers. "Now the delicate balance is between performance in what they hired me to do and keeping the chemistry going with the family."

Obviously, task competence is central to the role of nonfamily managers. Some of the nonfamily managers surveyed were in charge of strategic planning, sales, finance, marketing, manufacturing, or human resources. Some were bridging presidents, who had taken over operations from the older generation until the younger generation was ready. Clearly, key nonfamily managers are expected to keep up to date with professional management practices and be solid contributors in executive, functional, and project areas. Staying current and competent is the best antidote to any concerns that nepotism may influence career opportunities. The complexity of getting the job done, however, is compounded in a family firm

EXHIBIT 7-1   PRIMARY BUSINESS CONCERNS OF THE NONFAMILY MANAGER

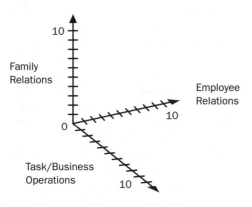

by the need to skillfully manage relationships with family members. One nonfamily manager expressed a common conflict:

> The third generation of owner-managers is in the wings, and my affiliation is with the second generation. In less than 10 years, I may have to let go, if the second generation retires or lessens its role. You see, I am having to "discipline," or be the bad guy, by supervising two of the next-generation family members. And what if I end up having to work for them? I would still need to work; I have two young kids.

Accepting the fact that his or her job includes responsibilities beyond those associated with the position is essential for the nonfamily employee. Management literature has argued over the years that both task and employee relations are important elements of leadership.[3] In the case of family businesses, nonfamily managers would be well served by behaving as if success requires special attention to task, employee relations, and relations with family members (see Exhibit 7-1). Nonfamily managers need to encourage family members to give their comments and feedback directly to other family members, without using the nonfamily employee as the messenger. Talking about family members to other family members invites an "us and them" dynamic that nonfamily managers have little chance of winning.

CONCERNS ABOUT MANAGEMENT AND GOVERNANCE PRACTICES

The ratings provided by nonfamily managers on the performance feedback, succession planning, career opportunity, and advisory board scales were quite different from those of family members in the business. No significant differences were found between the two groups in the business planning, communication climate, and growth orientation scales.

CEOs saw their firms as more innovative than did nonfamily managers. As a group, nonfamily managers tended to be less satisfied with innovation and product development in their companies, and they were consistently less satisfied than CEOs with management practices and systems.

With regard to values and planning assumptions, family members were more likely than nonfamily managers to agree with the statement "People in this organization know what we stand for and how we wish to conduct the business." This difference raises interesting questions about how management conveys its values and business philosophies to staff members and generates strategic initiatives. When business values and philosophies are transmitted primarily through the family, nonfamily managers may be left out of the loop.

Planning for the future is a key management activity. Yet it seems that nonfamily managers are often left behind in this important journey. The nonfamily managers in the Discovery study reported being less involved in "planning the work and working the plan" than did the family managers. As one key nonfamily executive told the research team, "I know more about Bob's grandchildren than I do about where we are headed as a business."

This sense among nonfamily managers may be based on comparisons with previous jobs in other corporations, in which they had a greater role in planning. Alternatively, it may be the result of their perception that they are being kept in the dark regarding succession. Another possibility is that they feel that they have been left out of the loop in some business planning activities.

CONCERNS ABOUT SUCCESSION

Next-generation and other family members were relatively more confident than nonfamily managers that the business would stay in the family. The two groups also differed in the degree to which they believed that the successor to the present leader would be a member of the owning family, with nonfamily managers much more certain that the next CEO would be a family member. So, somewhat counterintuitively, while nonfamily managers were less certain that the company would remain a family company, they were much more convinced that the next CEO would be a family member. There was also a significant difference in the extent to which nonfamily managers and family members agreed with the statement "The successor CEO here will be the best of possible candidates regardless of family relationships." Perhaps not surprisingly, family members were more positive than nonfamily managers that this would be the case.

These findings present a challenge for CEOs of family companies: How can they motivate top-flight executives who realize that the top leadership positions are likely to go to family members who may be less qualified than they are? Some nonfamily managers nurture unrealistic expectations about their future role in the company until the next generation has actually moved into key positions. For this reason, CEOs have to be aware of the thin line between unrealistic expectations and demotivation; they must find ways to prevent their best nonfamily managers from crossing it.

CAREER OPPORTUNITIES FOR NONFAMILY MANAGERS

> I want the next generation of leaders to see Marriott International as being the best at what it does. . . . We're not trying to develop the company and sell our family interest on the open market. We're trying to maintain our long-term family commitment, since whatever wealth our family has is totally caught up in this business. We've devoted our lives to it; I've devoted a lifetime to it; and I hope my kids will. . . . At the same time you watch [other associates] grow and see them develop at work; you see someone enter Marriott as a bellman and become a senior vice president. The opportunity to provide people with that sort of growth experience is very special, special indeed. . . . The foundation of Marriott's success for 75 years has been our enduring belief that our associates are our greatest assets . . . and a focus on growth. —J. W. Marriott, Jr., Chairman and CEO, Marriott International[4]

Family business research shows that career opportunities are unique resources that family companies can turn into a competitive advantage. The Discovery study results highlight the importance of career opportunities for family members to business continuity. It is not much of a stretch, then, to consider career opportunities for nonfamily employees as equally significant, if somewhat invisible, assets. Confidence that future career opportunities will be available to them is important for nonfamily managers, but such confidence is not always easy to maintain in a family business. After all, stories of nepotism in family businesses abound. And the reality is that in many family-controlled companies there is a preference for—if not a commitment to—continued owner management.

Can both family and nonfamily managers enjoy the prospect of career opportunities in the future? For the health of the business, they must. Otherwise, instead of counting the best and brightest nonfamily employees among its resources, the company incurs the costs associated with turnover, low morale, the inability to recruit top-notch managers, and the inability to set benchmarks for family managers. A merit-based and professionally run family business culture is essential. But the surest way to be able to provide career opportunities is to promote business growth.

COMPENSATION AND BENEFITS

Nonfamily managers are generally less satisfied than family managers with their compensation and benefits. Respondents in the Discovery study were asked the extent to which they agreed or disagreed with the statement "Nonfamily managers are compensated fairly and equitably here." On a scale of 1 (disagree) to 5 (agree), CEOs' answers averaged 4.45, answers from the rest of the family averaged 4.36, and nonfamily managers' answers averaged 3.78 ($p < 0.001$). Complaints from nonfamily managers in the study sometimes involved comparisons of the family business with public companies:

- "Owners only look at sales and profitability here. Other corporations would have more criteria to evaluate you against."
- "Bonuses are said to be performance-based, but we have very loose goals. In fact, goal-setting is nonexistent, which means that the bonus is subjective."
- "Career paths to senior positions are not equally available to nonfamily managers."
- "I miss the benefits from a large company, especially vacation policy. We get very little vacation. Owners work very hard, but they also enjoy very flexible schedules—we don't."

Although executive pay varies from industry to industry, nonfamily managers generally seem to be paid less than their counterparts in public corporations. A study comparing compensation policies and practices in large family businesses and publicly held firms found that the average salary in management-controlled (publicly held) firms was 15.4 to 29.5 percent more than the average salary reported for owner-controlled firms.[5] This comparative study indicated no differences in economic performance between these two types of businesses and therefore attributed the pay differential to the agency costs of running a business when management and shareholders are different entities.

Vacation policies were an issue in at least one firm, where nonfamily managers saw family members as enjoying more leisure time than they did. Nonfamily managers craved more flexibility in their schedules. Although nonfamily managers acknowledged that owners work very hard, they pointed out to researchers that owners also tend to have flexible schedules, which give them more freedom and control over how they spend their time. Several research projects have studied the attractiveness of this flexibility to women family members who join a family business. Other employees, including key nonfamily managers, do not always enjoy the same flexibility.[6]

Though they tended to be less satisfied than family members with their financial compensation, some nonfamily managers in the Discovery study nevertheless mentioned the non-monetary rewards and advantages of working for a family-owned business. As one person put it, "The family feeling and accessibility to the top are definite pluses of working in a family business."

Unlike larger publicly held companies, which usually have organization charts and job descriptions that define who does what, entrepreneurial and smaller family businesses often manage their staffs to maximize flexibility and avoid the very costly redundancy of people. For nonfamily managers, this may mean assuming responsibility and taking the initiative and then having to move out of the way when the owner gets involved. On the bright side, the active and flexible role of many family business owners allows employees to see that the owners "work feverishly at making things right, so you know why things are important to them."

Some nonfamily managers described relationships in their firms as relaxed, unstructured, and informal. Others reported that they avoided a lot of social contact with family leaders. One of them noted, "I keep my distance. I'm their friend, but I'm not their friend." Another nonfamily manager described the fine line he walked in his company:

> Sometimes I take an interest in the company that is even larger than the owners', which helps with the chemistry. But then I need to [be able to] let go at the drop of a hat, too. Good chemistry in this case means that I have a common background with the owners, common values. The two owners and I are regular guys, of middle-class origin, with no pretensions. We are about the same age and of similar work ethic; we all work hard, are industrious, and have high energy.

PERFORMANCE FEEDBACK

In only one important category in the Discovery study did nonfamily managers rate their firms' practices consistently higher than did family managers. Nonfamily managers, especially those 51 years old or older, were more satisfied with the performance feedback they received.

Owner-managers who were 51 years old or older were more satisfied with their performance feedback than were 31- to 50-year-old owner-managers. It is possible that older owner-managers get feedback from boards of independent directors and don't really crave it anyway. The fact that younger family managers reported relatively less satisfaction with performance feedback is more significant. While not surprising, this finding points to what may be the Achilles heel of successor development in family companies: CEO parents provide the next generation with little or no feedback on their performance because they find it difficult to stop wearing the "parent hat."

Nonfamily managers, who often serve as mentors, may limit the negative feedback they give to younger family members because of the risks inherent in providing such feedback. As one respondent noted, "[I] could be working for them in a few years." The result of the disinclination to provide even "constructive criticism" is that potential successors are deprived of feedback, and on-the-job learning opportunities are squandered during the most critical development period.

EXTENDING THE FAMILY CULTURE TO NONFAMILY MANAGERS

Despite the need of many family firms to maintain a culture that maximizes the loyalty and performance of nonfamily managers, for too long these managers have been taken for granted by owner-managers (and ignored by family business researchers). Nonfamily managers often feel like outsiders. For this reason, owners must make a diligent effort to demonstrate to them how much their contributions are valued.

Greater openness by CEOs to the perceptions and views of others would clearly be helpful. In addition, CEOs need to close the perception gap that exists between them and both nonfamily and family managers over their firms' management practices and ability to handle future challenges. A CEO must take appropriate actions to avoid imperiling the continuity of the firm by being out of phase with its developmental needs. Potential for improvement on this front is enormous. An ongoing dialogue with top managers may well uncover differing assumptions regarding the firm's future. Boards with independent members seem to be a natural mechanism for aiding CEOs in this discovery process, since outside directors are more neutral observers of the agendas of both family and nonfamily managers. If CEOs are willing to listen, active boards and succession planning committees that involve nonfamily managers and high-influence outsiders can make a distinct contribution to a positive succession process and business continuity. They can also increase the sense of belonging and enhance the performance of nonfamily managers.

MOTIVATING AND RETAINING NONFAMILY MANAGERS

How can owner-managers motivate top executives who realize that the firm's prime leadership positions are likely to go to family members? How can family companies retain such executives, when they could go to another company where they could likely earn more and have a more clearly structured job in which achievement itself was a key motivator? How can family business leaders motivate nonfamily managers without allowing them to participate in setting the direction for the business? How can owner-managers ensure the loyalty of nonfamily employees in the absence of equity participation?

Many owner-managers, blinded by their own success, have difficulty seeing problems in the company's practices and procedures, which they have developed and for which they are primarily responsible. Researchers have found that owners' pride in what has made the business successful so far sometimes supports the status quo and creates a barrier to change, causing a potentially damaging disengagement from key nonfamily managers and next-generation family managers. Increased self-awareness of this propensity for denial of the facts on the part of CEOs can result in significant contributions to future growth for both the family and the business.

It may be up to a nonfamily manager, independent board member, or outside advisor to issue the wakeup call. Given the CEO's role as the primary architect of the firm, a CEO's belief in the validity of the firm's business practices may, implicitly at least, depreciate others' views. Lack of motivation on the part of top management to detect problems can threaten the effectiveness or the very survival of the business. Given the significant differences in perceptions of owner-managers and nonfamily managers, taking action to identify and assess problems could allow the CEO to learn enough about the company's current situation to make more appropriate decisions about the company's future (see Exhibit 7-2).

EXHIBIT 7-2	WAYS TO CREATE A BENEFICIAL ENVIRONMENT FOR NONFAMILY MANAGERS

- Build family/nonfamily management teams that provide complementary skills at the top and set benchmarks for running the family business professionally. Doing so also sends a clear signal to nonfamily managers that career opportunities are available.

- Discuss career advancement opportunities for nonfamily managers—and how the succession process may affect these opportunities—with candor. This is essential and is greatly appreciated by key nonfamily managers. The change and discontinuity that the prospect of succession represents are great stressors and demotivators of ambitious nonfamily employees.

- Involve nonfamily managers in business planning and succession planning. Soliciting their participation in discussions of the strategic direction of the business gives them a much greater sense of inclusion and more focused motivation.

- Offer compensation and benefit plans that are benchmarked to others in the industry, the profession, and the community. Adopting fair pay plans will diminish the risk of losing key contributors. Equity ownership—or, more likely a phantom stock plan that parallels value creation in the common stock and rewards performance over the longer term—is a great motivator.

- Use performance measures—scorecards—to build motivation. Top management derives much motivation from the feedback the job itself provides. Revenues, profit margins, market share, and other financial information all provide significant motivation.

- Periodically hold meetings between key nonfamily managers and shareholders to promote mutual understanding and respect for the different roles and contributions of each group.

- Educate the entire family, whether active or inactive in the company, about business and management in order to create common ground between family and nonfamily managers. For example, a quasi-family MBA curriculum could be part of family business meetings (see Chapter 9).

- Periodically survey nonfamily employees to assess the work climate and determine whether the relationship between management and ownership is healthy or requires attention. Effective nonfamily managers must have high levels of maturity and self-confidence, as well as the ability to self-manage; they must not only perform the task they were hired to do but also nurture their relationships with multiple generations of owners and owner-managers.

- Emphasize nonfamily employees' contributions to the family business. American Greetings, for example, watches its internal communications and press releases to ensure that the balance between family and nonfamily is right. Making nonfamily employees part of a successful family in business builds a culture where people truly are a competitive resource.

- Treat family members like employees when they are at work. Call them by their professional names, require that they follow employee policies and rules, and expect just as much from them as you would from any competent nonfamily manager.

- Use advisory boards or boards of directors with independent outsiders. Such boards help nonfamily managers to feel confident that the family company is being run professionally and objectively, with merit—not blood—as the major determinant of success.

- Develop a family constitution that spells out policy on family employment and family–business relations. This will increase the perception of fairness and mutuality and also reduce the chances of inappropriate family interference in management. (See the sample family constitution in the Exercise section of this chapter.)

- Use high-caliber key nonfamily managers as bridging presidents of the corporation and mentors of the next generation. In some cases, a nonfamily president can serve as a bridge across a generation of owners, as is currently the case at both Anheuser-Busch and L.L. Bean.

Perhaps the most encouraging finding of the research on nonfamily managers in family businesses is that so many have very positive views of their firms and their futures. And most are constantly managing change and opportunity in anticipation of a new, improved, different family firm in the future.

SUMMARY

1. The Discovery Action Research Project found that nonfamily managers tended to regard their firms positively.

2. For nonfamily managers, the complexity of getting their job done is compounded by the need to skillfully manage relationships with family members.

3. When business values and philosophies are transmitted primarily through the family, nonfamily managers may be left out of the loop.

4. Career opportunities for both family and nonfamily managers are unique resources that family companies can turn into a competitive advantage.

5. Nonfamily managers responding to the Discovery study were significantly less satisfied than family managers with the equity of their compensation.

6. Nonfamily managers serving as mentors may limit the negative feedback they give to younger family members because of the risks inherent in providing such feedback.

EXERCISE

MANAGING THE RELATIONSHIP BETWEEN SHAREHOLDERS AND MANAGERS: THE FAMILY CONSTITUTION

To govern the relationship between shareholders and managers, some family-owned and family-controlled companies write family constitutions. The family constitution, or family charter, makes explicit some of the principles and guidelines that shareholders will follow in their relations with company managers. The following example of a family constitution is from a well-known family-controlled corporation. Because the shareholders preferred anonymity, the company and family names are fictitious and the document's content has been slightly edited.

The Kropps Family Constitution

1 Introduction

1.1 Objective

This Family Constitution has been established to serve as a reference point for relationships between family members and the business during the next 10 to 15 years, a period in which we foresee the change from the second to the third generation taking place. We, the members of the Kropps Family, recognize our common bonds and assume the responsibility for carrying on the legacy, through the Kropps Companies, into the next generation.

1.2 Mission

In its introduction and development, it is necessary to bear in mind that the Family Constitution

- Clarifies what the Family Business wants to be and thus outlines the form and content of the main points of the relationships between the business and the family.
- Highlights ways of increasing unity and commitment, which are essential components of the family enterprise.
- Can never be contrary to what is stated in the laws governing the corporation or in the company bylaws.

1.3 Approval and Modification of the Family Constitution

The Family Council is the competent body for the approval and, when necessary, the modification of the present Constitution.

2 Guiding Principles of the Family Constitution

2.1 About the Founders

This company was founded by Albert and Gerald Kropps.

The company has gradually developed and grown to its current size and competitive strength, not only due to its founders' efforts and their founding principles, but just as significantly because of the continued dedication, overwhelming professionalism, and sound judgment of the successors, the second generation.

As members of the second generation, some of whom manage this company, we want to leave written documentation for the members of the third generation of the principles that have guided the conduct of these founders and their day-to-day work and example, because they have served as an ever-present reference point in our business dealings.

2.2 Values to Be Passed On

In the same way, we members of the second generation wish to pass on other values that form the basis of the work done during these years.

2.2.1 *Work ethic and a sense of responsibility.* These are the best vehicles for the continuation of the entrepreneurial idea of the founders.

2.2.2 *Understanding, unity, harmony, and a bond among the shareholders.* These have played fundamental roles in the continuity of the company.

2.2.3 *Stewardship.* As stockholders, we must always keep in mind the consequences that our actions may have for the Company, the rest of the shareholders, and our family's reputation.

2.2.4 *Ethical conduct.* As evidenced by discretion, honesty, and high-mindedness, it works in favor of the common good.

2.2.5 *Dedication and commitment to the attainment of company objectives.*

2.2.6 *Confidence in the governing bodies of the company,* including the people who today carry out the managerial responsibilities and those who may do so in the future.

2.2.7 *Love and concern for family and the family enterprise.* As a result of his/her ownership role, the family shareholder or board member should not enjoy any special treatment in his/her professional career within the businesses of the Group by the mere fact that he/she is a member of the family. In this sense, family members who are active in management will have the same rights and responsibilities that the rest of the nonfamily employees have (salary, working days, promotions, vacations, etc.).

2.3 Other Values

The members of the second generation dedicate themselves to ensuring that the following values become gradually known and appreciated by the third generation.

2.3.1 *A balance between dedication to work and dedication to family,* in order that, over time, unity and an appropriate commitment of service to the company may be maintained.

(continued)

EXERCISE

(continued)

2.3.2 *The hope to form part of an important, socially responsible business* that should be permanently able to compete advantageously. A family member's motivation should be found in the opportunity offered to him/her to be able to collaborate and contribute to the growth and continuity of the family business.

2.3.3 *An understanding of the obligations and responsibilities of the shareholders* of a family business, among which stand out the need to seek out the best for the company and to collaborate positively for the good of the other shareholders.

2.3.4 *An understanding that participation as a shareholder of the family business is a privilege bequeathed by our ancestors,* and as part of our legacy, we must use the capital responsibly to increase it, insofar as it is possible, and to pass it on to the following generation.

2.3.5 *The hope to pass on to future generations a company that stands out in its field.*

2.3.6 *A commitment to search for solutions for liquidity and peaceful separation* (in agreement with the established procedures) with shareholders who don't want to continue participating in the business or who don't share the aforementioned values.

3 The Type of Company We Want to Be

3.1 *A business in which the families,* as represented on the Family Council and the Board of Directors, *retain controlling ownership.*

3.2 *A company that is among the leaders in its field* and among the best in the industry.

3.3 *A business that is a leader in technology,* deeply committed to obtaining the lowest costs available, and with a strong network in the value-added chain in which it operates.

3.4 *A business that continues,* from generation to generation, *to be "A Family-Run Business,"*

with members of the families on the Board of Directors and on the Executive Team. Because of this,

- Job positions cannot be indiscriminately offered to any family member.
- Family members working in the business should do so in leadership positions. Such positions, in order to be executed successfully, demand a person with a vision of unity, the ability to lead people, and advanced technical skills.
- Within the bounds of respect for personal freedom, the development of family members toward positions of company leadership is deemed a priority.

3.5 *A business with an organizational structure designed to offer* both family and nonfamily managers *exciting career opportunities and the ability to act with autonomy,* supported by the latest in professional management.

4 What Can Be Expected from Our Family Business

4.1 *Growth in the size of operations,* notwithstanding existing competition and the evolution of markets.

4.2 *Growth in the value of the estate,* increased shareholder value, by aiming for higher profitability and growth than the average in the industry. This will be accomplished via the following strategic commitments from top management:

- Gaining client loyalty by offering them the best product and/or service value available.
- Developing new products and services.
- Entering promising new segments and markets and abandoning those that are less so.
- Achieving the lowest costs by economies of scale, integration, and continuing vigilance against bureaucracy.

- Procuring and developing subsidiaries and joint ventures.
- Making acquisitions that ramp up the organic growth represented by the above approaches.

4.3 *Growth that is balanced*, without taking undue risks and engaging in speculation.

4.4 *Growth financed primarily out of internal cash flows*. Only in extreme cases, owing to developments in the global markets, should the company rely on external debt and public offerings.

4.5 *A market-sensitive dividend policy* that respects the company's needs for continued reinvestment.

4.6 *Extensive information provided to shareholders* about the status of the business and its markets.

4.7 *First among equals for a top management job whenever a family member is deemed apt and capable* by the President or Board of Directors for a top management position that he/she desires. A qualified family member will be preferred for the job over a similarly qualified nonfamily candidate.

4.8 *Professional advice on ownership transfer and succession*, so that the behavior and actions of individuals do not create problems for the whole.

5 Working in the Family Business: Family Employment Policy

It is important that family members be informed of the unique responsibilities and challenges of employment in The Kropps Companies. They should be advised that in most cases they will be held to a higher standard of conduct and performance than other employees. We support an internship program to introduce future generations to the company.

5.1 General Conditions

5.1.1 Family members must meet the same criteria for hire/fire as nonfamily applicants.

5.1.2 Family members are subject to the same performance review as nonfamily members.

5.1.3 Compensation for family members will be at "fair market value" for the position held, the same as for nonfamily members.

5.1.4 Family members may be eligible for career-launching internships before age 30. This temporary employment will be limited to any one unit of employment not exceeding 12 months. Family members may be encouraged to participate in internship programs with other companies with which The Kropps Companies could reciprocate.

5.1.5 No family member will be employed in a permanent internship or entry-level position; an entry-level position is defined as one requiring no previous experience or training outside The Kropps Companies.

5.1.6 Family members seeking permanent employment must have at least 5 years work experience outside The Kropps Companies. One of those jobs must have been at least 3 years with the same employer, during which time there must have been at least two promotions or similar evidence of rising levels of performance, competence, responsibility, and trust. It is our view that, if a family member is not a valued employee elsewhere first, it is likely that that family member will be neither happy nor productive at The Kropps Companies.

5.1.7 Graduate degrees in management, engineering, and other disciplines related to the knowledge base that is essential to the success of The Kropps Companies are encouraged. A family career development committee will be responsible for interviewing, coaching, and guiding interested family members to

(continued)

(continued)
the Human Resources Department and other appropriate company representatives, where the ultimate employment decisions will be made.

6 Ownership of the Family Business

6.1 Ownership of the Shares

Members of the family should retain ownership of the shares.

6.2 Recommendations for the Owners

While maintaining the most profound respect for their freedom and individual needs and aspirations, the owners should

- Always consider the repercussions that decisions about passing on shares through estate planning will have on the business and the rest of the owners. In this sense, the desirable course of action would be always to look for ways that would most clearly facilitate the unity of the family business and the commitment of the shareholders to its continuity.

- In the most prudent fashion, make it possible for capable members of the third generation to attend, as informed and responsible shareholders, the Annual Shareholders' Meeting.

6.3 Shareholder Liquidity

In order to facilitate liquidity for the shareholders, the company will do everything in its power to pay dividends and also endow a Liquidity Fund. The object of the Fund will be to provide a buyer (namely, the family business) for the shares. The intent is to guarantee liquidity in small quantities, following the spirit of the statutes and the Family Constitution.

Liquidity bylaw's key points:

- *The maximum amount* offered for purchase yearly will be up to 1% of the total shares of the company, depending on the funds available.

- *The value of the family business* will be calculated annually, in agreement with a formula proposed by valuation experts and approved by the Board of Directors. In the aforementioned formula, the different values of the totality of the shares, whether majority or minority, must be kept in mind. The values determined by the valuation process will be made known to the shareholders.

- *Purchase-sale*: In the situation where a shareholder would want to sell and other shareholders would want to buy at a value higher than that offered by the Fund, or in the case that the Fund may not be able to buy, the Board of Directors will authorize the purchase-sale in accordance with what has been indicated in the Buy-Sell Agreement.

7 Governing Bodies

In a family business that has the intent to strengthen the participation of the shareholders in the knowledge of the business, there are two types of governing bodies:

- Those responsible for the management of the company—that is to say, those established in the bylaws, the Annual Shareholders' Meeting, and the Board of Directors. Others may be established by the Board of Directors and the Management Team, as necessary.

- The Family Council, responsible for shareholder education, communication, and developing and implementing the Family Constitution.

7.1 Annual Shareholders' Meeting

During the regular Annual Shareholders' Meeting, extensive information will be offered with the purpose of enabling the shareholders to be very familiar with the family business. Family members agree to refrain from using this information indiscriminately, given its confidential nature.

7.2 The Board of Directors

The Board of Directors is the highest governing body of the company after the Annual Shareholders' Meeting. The Executive Team is supervised and held accountable by the Board of Directors.

The functions of the Board, detailed in the corresponding bylaw, include:

- Reviewing and approving the business's strategy.
- Reviewing the financial performance of the company and holding top management accountable for such performance.
- Ensuring the ethical conduct of management and the corporation.
- Promoting the development of the managerial resources of the company.

7.3 Rules and Regulations for Board of Directors' Operations

- The election of board members is regulated by state laws and company statutes.
- Terms of service of family members on the board should not exceed three three-year periods, encouraging the rotation to other family members most qualified to serve.
- There will always be a minimum of three high-influence independent outsiders serving on the Board of Directors.
- There can be consultants and advisors to the Board of Directors. These consultants will be independent, renowned professionals who can offer insightful information on relevant topics.
- Meetings should take place on a quarterly basis and be scheduled at least one year in advance.

7.4 Family Council

The main purpose of the Family Council is to foster a strong understanding of the business, the family, and the relationship between business and family among the family members/shareholders. Its responsibilities include:

- Informing and educating the family about the business.
- Facilitating the relationships of the families with the business.
- Educating the families about the legacy, disseminating the contents of the Family Constitution and keeping it a living document.
- Proposing to all family members those changes in the Family Constitution that, based on their judgment, can help foster a greater understanding among the family members/stockholders and better relationships between owners and managers of the company.

The Family Council is made up of two members of each of the four branches in the second generation. Representative members are selected by the branches. One family member serving on the Board of Directors will also serve on the Family Council and represent a point of linkage between these two governing bodies. Total membership of the Family Council in the second generation will therefore be limited to 9. Family Council meetings will be facilitated by an outside expert on family business.

7.5 Next-Generation Committee

We want to encourage family participation in the company. We want to raise future generations with a sense of responsibility and commitment and not a sense of entitlement. Because next-generation members may become voting shareholders, company employees, and/or board members, their participation in appropriate family and enterprise activities in advance of this development is essential. The Next-Generation Committee will include nine family members chosen by the Family Council. Membership will rotate throughout the next generation. Its primary functions will include:

(continued)

(continued)

- Defining and guiding the educational and family business involvement opportunities for future-generation members.

- Encouraging a sense of voice and stewardship by providing feedback and ideas to earlier generations about matters affecting family-business relationships.

This Next-Generation Committee will meet on a quarterly basis and in coordination with the Family Council and the Board of Directors.

The members of the Next-Generation Committee will receive information about the state of the business in a way that promotes their education and understanding of the company.

7.6 Family Assembly

The Family Assembly, made up of all the blood members and their spouses, will meet once a year with the purpose of:

- Promoting greater knowledge and understanding of each other.

- Promoting greater knowledge and understanding of the business.

- Having fun and promoting extended family bonds.

1. What is the desired relationship between the Kropps family and Kropps Companies management, according to the family constitution?

2. What benefits might nonfamily managers derive from this family constitution?

3. What are some of the implications of this family constitution for family shareholders of the Kropps Companies?

4. What institutions does this family constitution rely on to effectively govern the relationship between owner-managers, family shareholders not active in management, and nonfamily managers at the Kropps Companies?

8

FAMILY BUSINESS GOVERNANCE

Wemco, Inc. sold an estimated $85 million of neckties in 1992, largely due to the skills of its board of directors. Sounds like an unusual role for a board? Well, conflicts between two brothers had resulted in the loss of business from its two major accounts, May Department Stores and Rich's Department Stores. The brothers could not agree on anything, until they agreed on appointing a board of directors that would help them get the business off dead center and perhaps even help them resolve some of their family conflicts. They appointed 12 directors, 8 of them independent outsiders. The board proceeded to take a very active role in reorganizing the company around well-defined areas of responsibility. The brothers and other key managers with product line and functional responsibility had their own areas now and were individually accountable, not just to the president anymore, but also to the board. The board put strategy and strategy review at the top of its meeting agendas and ultimately helped the company turn itself around and focus outside, on its customers, not inside on turf and family conflict.[1]

Advisors usually suggest that a family business not use its board of directors to deal with emotionally charged subjects, as Wemco did. The risk is that the board will lose its neutrality and become embroiled in the family conflict, thereby becoming unable to serve the business and its shareholders objectively on the larger issues of strategy, financial analysis, and succession and continuity planning. To prevent and manage the kind of family discord described above, firms are usually advised to use family councils, the equivalent of a board of directors for family issues.

Governance is a complicated subject when it comes to family businesses. It can be provided for through classes of voting and non-voting stock, as discussed in Chapter 5. And it can be enhanced by appropriate contributions from boards of directors/advisory boards, family councils, family assemblies, annual shareholders' meetings, and top management teams (see Exhibit 8-1). Given family companies' propensity for blurring boundaries between family and business, these institutions can provide essential help in governing the family-owner-management relationship. The current CEO can hardly leave a finer legacy and contribution to family business continuity than the creation of an effective governance structure.

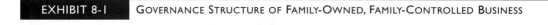

EXHIBIT 8-1 GOVERNANCE STRUCTURE OF FAMILY-OWNED, FAMILY-CONTROLLED BUSINESS

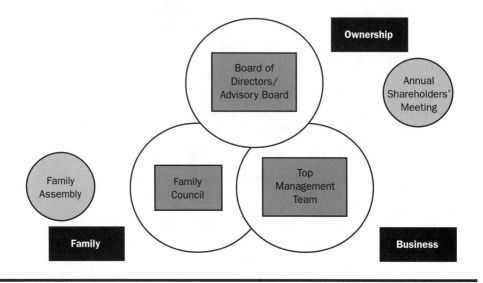

THE BOARD OF DIRECTORS/ADVISORY BOARD

The primary responsibilities of a board of directors include the following:

- Reviewing the financial status of the firm
- Deliberating on the strategy of the company
- Looking out for the interests of shareholders
- Ensuring the ethical management of the business
- Being a respectful critic of management by asking insightful questions
- Holding the CEO and top management team accountable for their actions
- Providing advice to the CEO on a variety of subjects
- Bringing a fresh, outsider perspective to issues
- Assisting in the objective planning and managing of the multi-year succession and continuity process

Unlike many of the governance bodies depicted in Exhibit 8-1, the board of directors is a legal entity, usually prescribed in the articles of incorporation. This status gives the board unique rights and responsibilities, such as reviewing the performance of the CEO and conceivably initiating his or her termination—although these acts are highly unusual in the world of family-owned companies. These rights and responsibilities expose directors to a larger sphere of liability, which may require the company to provide directors with liability insurance and may discourage some peer CEOs from serving as independent outsiders on a board. For this and other reasons, many family-owned businesses prefer to restrict membership on the board of directors to family members and use an advisory board as a complement to the board of directors.

Because the financial performance of firms has been shown to be positively related to the presence of independent outsiders on the governing board,[2] establishing an advisory board with independent outsiders, instead of just relying on an internal board of directors, represents a very healthy development for many family-owned businesses. This change tends to positively influence managerial accountability and succession and continuity planning in the firm. If, as the company grows or moves from one generation to the next, adding independent outsiders to the board of directors becomes more feasible, the advisory board can be folded into the board of directors. Exhibit 8-2 outlines some important points about advisory boards made by outside board members during a panel discussion at Case Western Reserve University.

Throughout this chapter, the terms *board* and *family business board* will be used to refer to both boards of directors and advisory boards. The basic differences between the two types of boards have just been pointed out. Unless the discussion specifically distinguishes between a board of directors and an advisory board, all subsequent references to family business boards should be understood to apply to both governance bodies.

BOARDS VERSUS INDEPENDENT ADVISORS/CONSULTANTS

Advice to the CEO of a family-controlled company can come in a variety of ways. Many smaller family-owned businesses that do not have a board of directors with outsiders and have not convened an advisory board claim that individual advisors—attorneys, accountants, financial planners, business consultants, psychologists—bring enough fresh, independent perspectives to the firm. While individual advisors are generally great contributors to the managerial expertise, strategic planning, and business activities of family-owned firms, many differences exist between fee-for-service advisors and independent outsiders serving on family business boards.

First of all, there is the issue of independence, which is at the heart of the continuing debate about the propriety of accounting firms' auditing and certifying the financial statements of companies for which they also perform lucrative consulting assignments. Individual service providers generally cannot offer a family business the same capacity for independent thinking and respectful disagreement that outside board members can. Then there is the issue of commitment and continuity over the long term. With the exception of some attorneys and accountants who become part of the extended family, most consultants perform their work within the limited time frame (perhaps 6 to 18 months) of a project. A major difference between independent board members and outside consultants is the board members' commitment to a longer-term relationship with the company and its principals.

| EXHIBIT 8-2 | COMMENTS FROM A PANEL DISCUSSION ON ADVISORY BOARDS |

Reasons for Having an Advisory Board

- It's lonely at the top.
- Outsiders with a commitment to the company can add perspective, problem-solving ability, expertise, strategic thinking, and a network of contacts that complement those of an able CEO and top management team.
- Different visions of the future between generations and predictable differences between family members who are active in management and those who are not can be positively influenced by the facilitating, moderating, cajoling, and professionalism of a board.

Conditions Necessary for an Advisory Board to Be Effective

- CEO/family must be willing to share information (e.g., financial information, business plan).
- The CEO must make board members feel welcome, be willing to involve them in the business, be honest with them, and expect them to be loyal critics, not a rubber-stamp board.
- The CEO and board members must do their homework—they must be prepared for meetings and be available for follow-up action and ongoing coaching.

What an Advisory Board Can Do for a Family Business

- Assist in planning for the future
- Provide help with objective financial analysis, its review, and its implications
- Assist with strategy and product/service development
- Help the CEO establish and review goals (but not set or dictate goals itself)
- Suggest ideas on how to make processes, relationships, etc., better
- Assist in networking with other CEOs and partnering with and benchmarking against other companies
- Help in choosing a successor
- Hold CEOs, successors, and top management accountable

SOURCE: Panel conversation during family company program at Case Western Reserve University, March 2001. Participants were William Litzler, CEO and outside board member; Richard Osborne, professor and outside board member; Ernesto Poza, professor, consultant, and outside board member; and Norton Rose, former vice president of human resources for Progressive Insurance, consultant, and outside board member.

Clearly, consultants and other professional service providers offer substantial benefits to family companies. But compelling reasons exist for creating a board so that independent outsiders commit over a long period of time to understanding, influencing, and adding value to the firm. Their unique perspective on what the CEO and other key managers are thinking and doing is invaluable to the family business.

MEMBERS OF THE FAMILY BUSINESS BOARD

The board of a for-profit enterprise is meant to be a working board. Unlike its not-for-profit equivalent, it does not exist to facilitate fund-raising activities and so does not require representation from an exhaustive group of stakeholders who have the capacity to be potential donors. Because the mission of a family business board is to work with and advise the CEO—not represent constituencies—it is better kept small. Most group dynamics research supports the recommendation that

Meeting Schedules and Agendas

- Typically, meetings are scheduled quarterly. The board is convened more frequently during growth or conflict.
- The focus is on planning for the future, not rehashing the past.
- Factual history and financial information are provided in materials prepared for the meeting; they are not rehashed in long discussions or presentations and so play a minimal part in the agenda.

Advisory Board Members

- Members are independent outsiders—people with whom the CEO feels comfortable and who will be supportive but not necessarily agree with the CEO. CEOs should not include on the advisory board those whom they are already paying for professional services (e.g., accountants or attorneys). A minimum of 3 to 4 outside professionals/businesspeople will provide a diversity of opinion and experience and enrich deliberation.
- Suggestions for finding good advisors include networking through professionals and organizations, using relationships established with businesspeople in other situations, and framing a brief statement of the type of person being sought as a board member.
- Board members should have experience in managing, hiring, and firing; have acuity with financial numbers; have a sense of human resource management; be ethical; and be passionate about wanting to make a difference. The first person engaged (when a board is being established for the first time) is critical, as she or he sets the standard for recruiting others. This individual should have experience on advisory boards.
- Family members, especially potential successors, may be invited to attend meetings; however, they should not be members of the board. This eliminates family politics and allows family members to be excused during sensitive parts of meetings.
- Term limits should be clearly established and have staggered end dates. However, the terms of those making a significant contribution to the business should be renewed.
- Compensation for board members will depend on the size of the business. Generally, a retainer fee, along with a per meeting fee, is recommended.

board size be limited to five to nine members. Of those members, independent outsiders should constitute the majority. They could be peer CEOs, business school professors, and/or professional service providers who derive no revenues from their relationship with the company except through board service fees. Ideally, the individuals chosen should not be friends of the family, given the propensity of friends to turn the board into a rubber-stamp board, devoid of independent and respectful but challenging thinking.

It is also important that no manager, except the CEO, be a member. A CEO and four outsiders, for example, would comprise an ideal small company board. In larger, multi-generational family companies, it is often a good idea to include a couple of at-large representatives of the family as board members. In this case, the board could have seven or even nine members. Although the CFO, the vice president of marketing, and potential successors might be asked to attend some meetings or segments of meetings to make presentations to the board, they should not be full members. Indeed, successors should not become full members until their succession is imminent and development of their knowledge of board matters has become a priority.

Invited guests also can bring relevant information to the board and report on matters before it. But the idea is to maximize the independent, objective, and fresh perspectives that the CEO receives from board members, not to promote inclusion in order to make people feel good. If inclusion ends up limiting the contributions of board members (because they are uncomfortable discussing an employee's performance or plans affecting that employee in his or her presence), then it works in opposition to the primary purpose of a board.

RECRUITMENT AND SELECTION. When family members other than the CEO are being selected to serve on the board, as is recommended in the case of large multi-generational firms, it is important that a broad net be cast across family branches to cull the most qualified candidates. The best way to be selective without creating additional issues of fairness for extended families is to have a clearly written board member selection policy, which specifies criteria for selection and a process deemed reasonable by a majority of the family. Crafting such a policy, as well as a family employment policy, is often the responsibility of a family council (discussed later in this chapter).

The best candidates for the board of a family-controlled business are successful peers—CEOs of other private or closely held firms. The fact that they have been in the leadership role, hired and fired, assumed risk, struggled with changing marketplace realities, and still delivered more profits than losses uniquely qualifies them for board duty. An additional consideration should be their ability to work on a team with a diverse group of other successful individuals. Unlike the influence they enjoyed in their own businesses, their ability to add value as a board member will be highly contingent on their effectiveness in a collegial environment. And, of course, their commitment to the enterprise and its mission is essential.

Referrals of candidates may come from other CEOs, business associates, advisors, lawyers, accountants, consultants, bankers, and university professors, particularly those involved in entrepreneurial and family business programs in business schools. Networking through business seminars and university programs can prove very helpful. Selection of the first board candidate is critical, and the standards to be met by this first recruit should be high. This individual's reputation, competence, and willingness to serve on the board will play a significant role in the company's ability to attract other highly qualified candidates. Ideal board members do not serve in pursuit of wealth or glory; they already have both. Good candidates value the company of equally successful peers and the service they can provide to CEOs and their companies. After all, most high-potential candidates are at a stage in life when giving back to the industry and the community is of paramount importance.

Board duty is not exclusively an intellectual exercise. Board members will likely be called on to assist during difficult times and to make difficult choices. This is particularly true if they are going to be involved in succession and continuity planning. In that case, CEOs who have been through the process themselves make excellent board candidates. One of the truisms of owner-manager succession is that it happens only once in a lifetime, which means that most CEOs have a very limited experiential knowledge base from which to draw. And sometimes the experience of a later-generation CEO with his or her own predecessor is not one that he or she particularly wants to emulate. While that experience may cause the current CEO to empathize with the next-generation successor, it likely will not guide the CEO in his or her own process of letting go and transferring power. Somebody who has recently gone through the succession process, on the other hand, can be of tremendous value as a mentor, coach, and confidante.

Criteria must be developed that respond to the company's unique needs, which will depend on the situation the company is facing when the board is assembled. Thus, a company seeking geographic expansion of its market base may want to have on its board the president of a business unit or vice president of global marketing of a *Fortune 500* company. Functional managers—vice presidents of sales, human resources, strategic planning, and engineering, as well as chief financial officers—can be excellent candidates for board service and make special contributions to meeting a company's unique needs.

Staggering terms of board members is a good idea, as is implementing a term length of three to five years. Such a system enables the CEO to bring new, fresh perspectives to the board and at the same time relieve board members who have already contributed most of their thoughts and rich experiences. Those board members who continue to reinvent themselves and show a unique ability to continue to contribute from an accumulated base of intimate knowledge of the company can always be retained beyond their specified term. This system provides the best of both worlds—it allows the CEO to easily make the transition to new directors or advisors, and it permits board members to be offered another term if their contributions continue to be significant.

It is wise to pay attention to the complementarity of potential board members' skills. Having a cross section of board members with a variety of skills, experiences, and capabilities will help to ensure that, as the board responds to the special needs of the business, the CEO receives advice from people who have demonstrated good business judgment in the past.

A specialty apparel company recently contacted the family business center of a local university for assistance in launching an advisory board. A faculty member guided the business in assembling an information book on the company and the owning family to be used to brief prospective board members. This book also contained a mission statement for the board and a succinct job description for board members. In this job description, the company CEO communicated his expectations of board candidates, should they agree to serve. The first recruit was a high-profile third-generation owner of a local supermarket chain with an excellent reputation. Once he joined the board, getting four additional outsiders to say yes to board service was easy.

During the first meeting of the advisory board, the mission statement drafted for the board was reviewed, rewritten with outside board member input, and finalized. Expectations that the second-generation CEO and third-generation president had of board members were discussed. Also discussed at this first meeting were board members' expectations of full disclosure, access to people and information, and periodic reviews of board performance.

COMPENSATION AND MOTIVATION. When it comes to the question of whether to provide compensation to board members, the answer is yes. Attractive compensation is important not because board members need the money but because the money signifies a willingness on the part of a CEO to listen to and be influenced by a group of peers who are forward thinking and well prepared for board meetings. Board members are expected to engage in follow-up conversations and meetings with various members of the firm and/or owning family after the formal board meeting. It seems only fair that such important responsibilities not depend on a sense of volunteerism on the part of generous businesspeople.

Because of the value that board members can add through activities beyond attendance at official board meetings, their compensation often has two components: a per diem fee for attendance at meetings and an annual retainer. Standard total compensation for board service ranges from $7,000 annually per board member (in the case of advisory boards in small family-owned businesses) to about $50,000 in cash and stock options (in larger family-controlled but publicly traded companies). Inflation and changes in the marketplace, among other factors, may affect the appropriate amounts. Thus, it is best to consult the marketplace before making an offer, in order to be sure that it conveys the firm's commitment to the board and high expectations for its members. Trade association guides, annual reports of publicly traded firms in comparable industries, and family business centers in business schools and local universities can all offer guidance on this subject.

More important than their compensation, of course, is board members' continued motivation. Unless the CEO allows the independent outsiders to influence the company with their advice, these board members are likely to exercise their ultimate act of independence and leave the board. Top-notch board members are in demand; they go where their ideas will be listened to and where their contributions will make a difference.

THE BOARD'S ROLE IN SETTING COMPANY STRATEGY

> The contribution of the outside directors of Cadbury Schweppes was to ask the right questions. These questions were sometimes uncomfortable, like whether parts of the business should be sold to put more resources behind those that were to be retained, and they were not questions we would necessarily have raised from within the business. It was up to the executives to provide the answers, but from this board dialogue between insiders and outsiders a bolder and ultimately more successful strategy was hammered out than had we not had the benefit of that external view of the firm and its prospects.
>
> —Sir Adrian Cadbury, Chairman of Cadbury Schweppes[3]

Not long ago, the nonfamily chairman of the board of a family-owned company contacted a family business consultant with an assignment. Over the past several years, the board of directors had been unable to assist the family company in setting direction because the board lacked a clear sense of what the family strategy was. In other words, board members were at a loss as to what the family shareholders wanted of the company. They also did not know what the family wanted its relationship to the company to be in the future and whether continued family control was desirable. The board of directors had just been restructured to add several additional outsiders, and the first nonfamily chairman of the board had been named. Board members believed that the time was right to collect data on shareholders' priorities. The consultant inquired about a variety of possible scenarios, goals, and financial return expectations before asking shareholders to select and prioritize their choices. Aided by surveys and private conversations with shareholders, the consultant summarized the results of the inquiry and reported to shareholders at a family retreat. The results were discussed, checked for accuracy, and validated, with all family members present. Conversations among shareholders were then facilitated, and a third-generation/fourth-generation vision for the family enterprise was drafted. A proposed direction for the company—which shareholders were willing to support—was then presented to the board immediately following the family retreat. The chairman of the board and board members made it a point to express their gratitude to family members for having provided information that would be critical in allowing them to fulfill their responsibilities as directors of the company.

Clearly, outside board members are essential to the strategy-making process in family businesses. However, appointing outsiders to the board means sharing the responsibility for the direction of the business with people beyond the family and the top management team. It means sharing the CEO's dreams. It also means letting outsiders see the company's financial records and get personally acquainted with the members of the next generation, the shareholders, and their dreams. While this may be somewhat uncomfortable for family executives, the board needs to have access to the data and the people involved if it is to help the company plan for the future.

Executives of larger family firms, not unlike executives of management-controlled companies, are generally quite occupied with the daily running of the business. Strategy is often considered important but not urgent. As a result, the company's strategy is in default mode. Periodic adaptations are made in the context of emerging opportunities, but not very often. On the other hand, those family businesses that retain their entrepreneurial tradition make strategy on a daily basis. But the strategy remains locked in the heads of the CEO and a couple of other executives. The board provides a reminder that a disciplined, ongoing approach to strategic planning is needed. It also offers the means to make the plan more substantive, clearer, and easier to communicate to the troops. Questioning and respectful contentiousness on the part of a working board are a source of much wisdom.

Chapter 6 reviewed strategic planning in family companies. The unique advantages enjoyed by family-owned or family-controlled businesses were discussed. It is hard to generalize on the subjects of strategy and competitive advantage, given the population of very different firms with very different products competing in very different markets and market niches. But an important competency, leading to competitive advantage, that has been observed in many entrepreneurial and family companies is their agility in meeting customer needs. Retaining this competency across generations is not always easy. In fact, management experts have argued that computers, sophisticated information and financial systems, process re-engineering, and six sigma efforts, while increasing the speed of business, have turned management attention inward. As a result, these managerial innovations have conspired against a customer orientation. In family companies, this increasing bureaucratization, which may require that employees attend more meetings, be involved in more programs, and have less real-time contact with customers, may be accompanied by a family dynamic that slows decision making. This same family dynamic may lead to a pattern of shelving unresolved issues so as to avoid the conflict and anxiety they produce. Boards can play a critical role in breaking through the logjam and helping family companies retain their competitive fitness.

THE BOARD'S ROLE IN ADAPTATION OVER GENERATIONS

> The job of the board is all about creating momentum, movement, improvement and direction. If the board is not taking the company purposefully into the future, who is? It is because of the failure of boards to create tomorrow's company out of today's that so many famous names in industry continue to disappear.
>
> —Sir John Harvey Jones, Former CEO and Chairman, Imperial Chemical Industries[4]

Customer-oriented businesses are always changing, always adapting to customer-induced changes in competitive dynamics. These businesses recognize the need to change in order to remain competitive. Families, by their very nature, are about stability, consistency, enduring values, love, and caring, all of which support individual development and family harmony. They tend to focus on legacy and continuity, not change. As a result, family companies often have difficulty dealing with conflict rooted in different visions of the future. And yet, quite naturally, the visions of two generations are likely to be very different. Some owning families seek out psychologists and family therapists in the hope of resolving conflict. Others decide to gun the engines of growth so that conflicts may be seen more dispassionately in the context of a company growing in resources and opportunities. Still other families decide to talk and talk and talk across generations, aided by their boards and advisors, until a new direction can be supported by all of the generations involved.

Adaptation is not easy. If it were, the expected tenure of S&P's 500 listed companies would not be a mere 10 years. Nor would 80 percent of all family-owned businesses have failed to survive the 60 years of operation (between 1924 and 1984).[5] The conflict between the old and the new in a family business is more often than not a personal conflict between a parent and his or her child. It cannot get any less objective than that; nothing is thicker than blood. What an opportunity for board members to mediate, facilitate, cajole, illuminate, provoke, and ultimately get the two generations to jointly create something they both can support. After all, it takes two generations to supply the two critical ingredients for sound adaptation in a family business: (1) the wisdom to know what has worked in the past and what has made the company successful and (2) the passion to make a difference, seize today's opportunities, and thrive in the decades ahead.

THE BOARD'S ROLE IN SUCCESSION AND CONTINUITY PLANNING

A formal board was introduced in the Cadbury family business on the death of one of the two brothers who ran the firm from 1861 to 1899. My grandfather recognized that the next generation of family had to be brought into the management of the firm and that a stable structure for the future direction and control of the firm had to be put in place. A board structure of this kind was less dependent on individuals than the previous partnership and it had the authority to decide on such questions as succession and the entry of family members into the firm. The board's authority stemmed from its being formally organized with a clear statement of its responsibilities and from its collegiate nature. The decisions of the board were not those of an individual but those of a team. . . . Although it was more of a management committee than a board of directors in the modern sense, that did not detract from the importance of this move. It brought order into the running of the business, it ensured that issues were dealt with and not shelved and it provided for the future continuity of the business.   —Sir Adrian Cadbury, Chairman of Cadbury Schweppes[6]

A hospitality company with $150 million in annual revenues owns and operates several restaurant and hotel concepts. It has now been working on its succession process for approximately five years. Although the firm is still chaired by the second-generation former owner-manager, it is now being managed and operated by his three sons, who already own a significant portion of the company stock. The owner-managers meet periodically with a family business consultant and have initiated a family council to air and address issues pertaining to the family. This firm and its owners are not short of advisors and consultants, yet they depend heavily on the board when it comes to succession planning.

In fact, while all the other consulting is going on, the issue of how the company is going to be managed—whether by a single owner-manager and CEO to whom his siblings report or by a sibling team operating as an office of the president—is being deliberated by the board. Several recommendations have been made by the consultant, and the board has agreed to an experimental period (not called that, of course) during which all three siblings, running two separate business units and the corporate finance function, will operate as a top team and report directly to the board. The board has a contingency plan, though. It knows that if the sibling team concept does not work, a traditional CEO can be installed. Months of conversations with the siblings, other key nonfamily managers, key customers, partners on some of the properties, and the chairman (Dad) have given the board the information it needs to be able to choose the ideal candidate from among the three brothers.

For a father, the anguish of having to pick one, and just one, of his children to lead the family company is hard to imagine. It is avoidance of this extremely difficult decision that motivates many CEO-parents, who deeply doubt the viability of a sibling partnership, to turn the succession question over to the board. Regardless of how compelling the arguments are in favor of a particular successor, choosing one child over another for that top job is absolute torture for the CEO-parent and his or her spouse.

While a board of directors may have to rely on many others for the facts, it can always consult with independent outsiders who are in an ideal position to review the facts and render objective opinions and recommendations. And a board is in the unique position of being able to enhance the perceived quality and fairness of the succession decision by taking responsibility away from family members. This third-party stamp of approval significantly increases receptivity to the new company boss on the part of both key nonfamily management and family members.

RESEARCH ON THE IMPACT OF BOARDS ON FAMILY-OWNED BUSINESSES

Data from the Discovery Action Research Project suggest that the existence of a board deemed effective by respondents—along with other managerial practices like performance feedback, succession planning, growth orientation, and business planning—was significantly correlated with positive communication processes in the firm. Family business owners who had boards with two or more outsiders acknowledged that these boards had contributed to the effective management of their firms. The following benefits were most often mentioned by these business owners:

1. Outsiders provide unbiased objective views.
2. They bring a fresher and broader perspective to issues of concern to the firm.
3. They bring with them a network of contacts.
4. They make top managers accountable for their actions.[7]

THE FAMILY COUNCIL

The family council is a governance body that focuses on family matters. It is to the family what the board of directors is to the business. Family councils primarily promote communication, provide a safe harbor for the resolution of family conflicts, and support the education of next-generation family members about family dynamics and ownership issues.

Family councils frequently develop family participation policies and deal with issues of liquidity, diversification of the estate, and estate planning. The business/ownership education of family members not active in the management of the business is also an important agenda item for family councils. This body is responsible for ensuring that the non-economic goals and values of the family are articulated (sometimes via a family constitution or family charter) and given the attention they deserve within the family business environment. Family councils seldom vote on issues but instead develop policies to guide decisions made by other governance bodies, such as the board and the annual shareholders' meeting.

A family council is often the vehicle for family philanthropy and the creation of family offices to oversee trusts and other financial matters of the owning family. Because it gives family members a voice in the business, a family council relieves some of the pressure to appoint all family members to the board. Indeed, family councils often select one or two at-large members to sit on the board of directors or advisory board in order to represent the family's interest in board deliberations.

BOUNDARIES BETWEEN THE BOARD AND THE FAMILY COUNCIL

Family-owned businesses tend to have boards that are all family. Family-controlled businesses do not stray far from this tradition, although they may allow an attorney and other service professionals to serve alongside family members. For the most part, these boards remain closed to independent outsiders. As a result, keeping a healthy balance between family and business remains a challenge for most family companies.

As they become multi-generational enterprises, family companies with a tradition of family membership on the board face another challenge: Family members expect that they will automatically become board members because of their family and ownership status. While it is true that families are well served by at-large representation by family members on family business boards, overwhelming the board with family influences is seldom in the short-term or long-term interests of the company, the shareholders, or even the family. A line has to be drawn between family membership and board duty. Family councils derive some of their ability to significantly contribute to family-controlled companies precisely by helping families draw this line and establish a system of governance that both differentiates and integrates family and business agendas. When it is perceived as an entitlement, family membership on the board, unrestrained by the input of family councils or independent outsiders, often leads to a dysfunctional board, paralyzed by the immensity and intensity of family dynamics. As illustrated by the situation at the Louisville *Courier-Journal*, when family members know very little about the business's strategy and finances, their service on the board does little to further the effective functioning of the board as a body of ultimate review and accountability.

Family councils, in the absence of boards with independent outsiders, present their own set of problems. Through the Partnership with Family Business Program at Case Western Reserve University, I have become acquainted with several companies that have launched family councils. A few have family-only statutory boards or majority-family boards and no advisory boards with outsiders. Over time, there appears to be a propensity for family members who are

EXHIBIT 8-3 BOARDS AND FAMILY COUNCILS: HOW THEY WORK TOGETHER

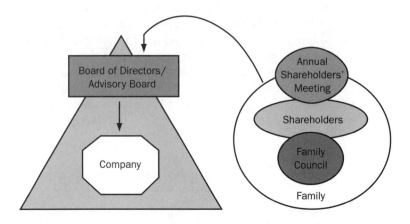

SOURCE: Adapted from Davis, J., "Board of Directors of the Family Firm," Notes 9-800-025, March 28, 2001, Harvard Business School.

not active in the business to become more aggressive in their second-guessing of company management. In the absence of a board with high status and high reputation outsiders, family members who do not truly understand the difference between owning and running a family company may conspire to meddle inappropriately in business matters. It is as if the existence of a family council empowers shareholders to give voice to issues and concerns that lie beyond their level of understanding of company functioning.

Exhibit 8-3 illustrates the boundaries that should exist between family councils and boards of directors or advisory boards. While family councils and boards have different missions, they are also well served by some degree of integration. For example, having two members of the family council serve as at-large representatives of the family on the board will help to ensure that family strategy and family preferences are appropriately considered by the board.

If a company is family-owned or family-controlled, it stands to reason that the family's agenda will, and should, play a part in deliberations on dividend policy, liquidity arrangements, transfer of ownership and control, and even the decision to re-commit to continuity or to sell. The real challenge is paying attention to both the family and the business, thereby jointly optimizing the family–business system. The owning family of the hospitality company mentioned earlier in this chapter drafted a norm, or ground rule, for their family council deliberations that speaks to this issue. In an effort to do well by both family and business, they wrote on easel paper during their first family council meeting, "We will allow the pendulum to swing back and forth between family and business priorities." Family councils will be discussed further in Chapter 9.

THE FAMILY ASSEMBLY

Because of its size, not all members of a large multi-generational family can work together in the policy and education committee format of a family council. As a result, larger families sometimes create an annual family assembly to operate in conjunction with the family council. Family assemblies are another vehicle for education, communication, and the renewal of family bonds. They create participation opportunities for all family members at least once a year. The smaller group that makes up the family council can work on behalf of the assembly during its two or three meetings per year and then report on its progress during the annual family assembly.

THE ANNUAL SHAREHOLDERS' MEETING

The annual shareholders' meeting both meets the legal requirements of corporate law and presents an opportunity for review of company and management financial performance. During this meeting, family members exercise their responsibilities as shareholders and are informed of company performance, returns on shareholders' equity, and dividends to be distributed. The board of directors is elected at this meeting. Shareholders may vote on other matters on the agenda, including the selection of auditors, changes to the articles of incorporation, and dividend policy. Only shareholders may attend, not extended family members or spouses who are not legal holders of stock. The shareholders' meeting usually takes place only once a year. However, special meetings may be called to address important and time-sensitive issues.

THE TOP MANAGEMENT TEAM

Family and nonfamily members of the top management team play a key role in the overall governance of a family-controlled corporation. A top management team that includes nonfamily managers with skills that complement those of the owning family prominently communicates the family firm's commitment to professional management and business continuity.

Key nonfamily managers help set high standards for work ethic, accountability, dedication, and expertise. These competent managers raise the bar for family owner-managers and, in doing so, send a clear message to shareholders who are not active in management. Including skilled nonfamily executives in top management will likely reduce or eliminate second-guessing by these shareholders and ensure that issues requiring deliberation and decision making stay where they belong—whether with the family, in family councils and family assemblies; with the owners, in shareholder meetings and board meetings; or with the top management team, in day-to-day business operations.

SUMMARY

1. Governance can be provided for through classes of voting and non-voting stock. And it can be enhanced by appropriate contributions from boards of directors/advisory boards, family councils, family assemblies, annual shareholders' meetings, and top management teams.

2. The primary responsibilities of a board of directors include reviewing the financial status of the firm, deliberating on company strategy, looking out for shareholders' interests, ensuring the ethical management of the business, being a respectful critic of management, holding top management accountable, advising the CEO on various subjects, bringing a fresh perspective to issues, and assisting in the succession and continuity process.

3. Unlike an advisory board, a board of directors is a legal entity.

4. An advisory board, which consists of independent outsiders, is often used to complement a board of directors.

5. The first recruit to a company's board is critical; his or her reputation, competence, and willingness to serve on the board will play a significant role in the ability to attract other highly qualified candidates.

6. A family council is a governance body that focuses on family matters, frequently developing family participation policies and dealing with liquidity issues and estate planning.

7. A family assembly creates participation opportunities for all members of larger multi-generational families at least once a year.

8. At the annual shareholders' meeting, the board of directors is elected. Family members exercise their responsibilities as shareholders and are informed of company performance, returns on shareholders' equity, and dividends to be distributed.

9. Key nonfamily managers in the top management team help set high standards for work ethic, accountability, dedication, and expertise.

9

THE FAMILY CULTURE

Secrecy, lack of information, and absence of education threaten commitment by family members to the continuity of a family-controlled corporation. They may be the result of a founding culture that supported autocratic leadership and control or a reincarnation of this culture in a later generation. Or they may arise from the family's belief in the many espoused benefits of privacy: flexibility and stealth in relation to competitors, minimization of tax liabilities in relation to the IRS, and management of expectations in relation to relatives, nonfamily employees, and even unionized workers.

Years of not communicating and of editing and/or hiding financial statements, profit margins, cash flows, and market share information erode nonfamily management's ability to substantively assist in the management of the enterprise. Whatever the intent of the CEO, years of requesting signatures with the all too familiar "Just sign here" and being secretive about financial and estate planning information undermine the commitment of the spouse and now-adult children to the dream of having the enterprise continue from generation to generation.

THE STORIES OF TWO FAMILY CULTURES

The following stories of two very different family cultures convey how differently secrecy and open communication can influence the fate of a business.

The Binghams and the Louisville Courier-Journal Companies

On January 9, 1986, Barry Bingham, Sr., chairman of the *Courier-Journal* and *Louisville Times*, abruptly decided that the Bingham family, which had owned the newspapers for nearly 70 years, would sell the business. Barry Sr., about to turn 80, hoped that his decision would bring a measure of family peace. Instead, it brought further blaming, family entropy, chaos, and agony.[1]

In 1918, Judge Bingham, Barry Sr.'s father, had bought a majority interest in the *Courier-Journal* and the *Louisville Times*, Kentucky's pre-eminent newspapers, for $1 million. When Judge Bingham died in 1937, Barry Sr. was 32 and actively involved in the family business, which by then included a radio station and a printing company as well as the newspapers.

The business grew as the Louisville post-war economy prospered. Barry Sr. married Mary Caperton and had five children: Worth, Barry Jr., Sallie, Eleanor, and Jonathan. Jonathan died at the age of 22, when he was electrocuted stringing wires for an outdoor party. Just two years later, Worth, the eldest, who had seemed destined by his charm, smarts, and primogeniture to be the successor, died in a bizarre car accident: A surfboard sticking out of his car's window hit a parked car; as it broke, it ricocheted and severed Worth's neck.

Barry Jr., a year younger than Worth, had always been more interested in the radio business than in the print media, but he agreed to serve as president of the Louisville Courier-Journal Companies in the early 1970s. Sallie, who was five years younger than Barry, had set out on a career as a fiction writer in New York City. She returned to Louisville in 1977, after suffering several major setbacks in her writing career. Eleanor, eight years younger than Sallie, had worked professionally on a series of video documentaries, some financed by Courier-Journal dividends. But her work never landed her a network job, as she had hoped, so in 1978 she returned home from California to work at WHAS, the company radio station. Barry Jr. and his sisters had never been close. In fact, they had barely seen each other in over 20 years, as the difference in their ages and early careers had taken them in separate directions.

Soon after Sallie and Eleanor returned, Barry Sr., perhaps in an attempt to welcome them back into the family and its enterprises, named them to the company's board of directors. They would have both voice and vote in matters of the enterprise. Barry Jr.'s perspective on what happened then reads like a classic tale of sibling rivalry and backroom politics. According to Barry, his sisters knew little about the business. Barry, on the other hand, had been working in the family business for almost 20 years and running it for a decade. But that did not keep them from second-guessing his every move. They did that through memos, through letters to the editor and op-ed pieces published in the company newspapers, and through persistent questioning of Barry Jr. during board meetings. Even Mary Bingham, his mother, on more than one occasion expressed on the editorial page, without warning, opinions contrary to Barry Jr.'s.

To the outside world the family appeared rife with conflict. Seemingly, it was capable of communicating about what ailed it and its businesses only in print, never face to face. In the early 1980s, as broadcast news and other channels of information gained favor, newspaper demand slumped. Evening newspapers in particular—and the *Louisville Times* was an evening daily—began to close their doors. Both the family and the business had problems to address and no way to address them.

The board became paralyzed by the sibling dynamics. Finally, Barry Jr. gave Barry Sr. an ultimatum: Either Sallie and Eleanor had to leave the board or he would resign as president of the enterprises. Eleanor resigned. Sallie, however, would not, and when she was not re-elected by her own family, the war began. Sallie fired the first shot by announcing to the family that she wanted to sell all of her interests in the companies. Lehman Brothers valued Sallie's shares at between $22 million and $26.3 million, but her own appraiser valued her holdings at $80 million. Despite the huge gap, negotiations began. Sallie ultimately lowered her asking price to $32 million, but Barry Jr. would never agree to anything higher than $26.3 million, and the negotiations stalled. In the meantime, Eleanor decided that she, too, wanted to sell or swap her newspaper shares for WHAS shares. In a final attempt to pressure his children into a compromise, Barry Sr. issued an edict that if Barry Jr. and Eleanor could not come to an agreement, the companies would be sold.

This edict put Eleanor, who empathized with Sallie's plight, in the driver's seat and soon led to the announcement by Barry Sr. that the company would be sold. At the age of 80, Barry Sr. still controlled 95 percent of the stock through a voting trust. Unable to communicate and resolve their differences, family members cashed out. All emerged cash-rich, but those who cared about the legacy were heartbroken. The newspapers had won eight Pulitzer prizes and were bastions of quality journalism in the South. Barry Jr. called a company-wide meeting after the announcement to express his disagreement with his father's decision to sell the company and to tell employees how much their collective past meant to him. Employees wept as Barry Jr. spoke; they knew this speech marked the end of an era.

The Bingham papers were taken over by the Gannett Company, which proceeded to close down the evening newspaper, reduce personnel by a third, and cut news staff by 10 percent. Advertising and circulation for the morning paper increased, as did profits. But editorial standards changed, and Pulitzer prizes proved elusive.

Much had gone wrong in the Bingham family's leadership of the Louisville *Courier-Journal* and its other media properties. Absent was visible commitment to continuity on the part of Barry Sr., the chairman and CEO. Also absent was a board with independent outsiders. Also lacking was spousal leadership by Mary Bingham as a chief trust officer; she could have provided the glue that would have kept the Bingham family united and focused on a win–win environment. Relationships in the Bingham family appeared to be characterized by an emotional distance, which created an irreparable gulf between adults of two different generations. Barry Sr. never vested full authority in Barry Jr., as evidenced by several instances of second-guessing on his part and by his retaining voting control. By never communicating plans to transfer voting control to his son and by approving the sale of the company when a consensus could not be reached, he gave the ultimate power to Eleanor, who effectively prohibited the orderly restructuring of the properties in family hands by blocking the transfer of the WHAS shares.

Many of the actions that the Binghams could have taken to reverse course and prevent the disadvantaged sale of their properties would have been in the province of a family council. But without such a governance body, the conflict was taken to the board of directors, composed primarily of family members, which was clearly overwhelmed by the conflict and paralyzed by its membership. Board members Sallie and Eleanor had spent most of their lives away from Louisville, the family, and the family enterprise and had pursued careers that hardly prepared them for leadership of an important media company.

In the absence of a family council, next-generation family members lacked the education, information, and give-and-take communication that would have promoted understanding among the individual heirs. When Barry Sr. named Sallie and Eleanor to the board, he gave them influence far beyond their capacity to understand and plan for the not-too-distant succession and transfer of power. Membership in a family council fosters the understanding needed for such planning, through years of working together in council meetings.

THE BLETHENS AND THE SEATTLE TIMES COMPANY

In the same industry, a decade or so later, an even older media institution planned for the continuity of the business under family control, making the family council a central governance body. In a meeting of the fifth generation of Blethens, Frank Blethen, chairman and publisher, spoke of the commitment of every Blethen generation, which had resulted in 100 years of caring leadership and stewardship of the *Seattle Times* and other newspapers in the corporate group. He emphasized the need to value the extended family over the individual or family branch, and he challenged individuals who participated in the family business to assume stewardship responsibilities. He asserted that, in order for them to be successful as individuals, it was essential that they understand the individual's responsibility toward the group.[2]

More than money, what Blethen family members inherit through their ownership of the Seattle Times Company is a responsibility to others and to stewardship, so that the enterprise they receive from an earlier generation may be successfully passed on to the next. Documents drafted in the mid-1970s by third- and fourth-generation members committed the firm and the family to two basic goals: "To perpetuate Blethen family ownership and to maintain the dominance of The Seattle Times Newspaper." These commitments were tested in April 2000, when a protracted strike created such financial problems for the newspaper that it was on the verge of having to shut down. Frank Blethen calls the period after the strike "Back to the Future." He likens the situation at that time to that of the company when his generation of family owners and senior managers started taking over, in the early 1980s. "He concedes the strike was a tremendous financial hit to the

Times, causing him for the first time in his life to consider the possibility of selling. Fortunately those darkest moments ultimately strengthened the family's resolve. The stewardship they feel toward the newspaper and its place in this community is too important."

So, instead of quitting in the face of serious adversity, the extended family recommitted itself to perpetuating family ownership and building a stronger *Seattle Times*, fully aware of the personal sacrifices that this decision would entail.

Members of the fourth generation were proud to report during their family council, the "Fifth Edition Family Business Meeting," that on their watch both the business and the family had become better off. In the 1990s alone, the company grew from two dailies to six daily newspapers, two weekly newspapers, and two major information web sites. Assets grew 215 percent, and cash flow increased 33 percent during that decade. Dividends paid out by the Blethen Corporation approached $30 million—a significant accomplishment, given that only 20 years earlier no dividends were being paid. The Blethens were also proud to report that the *Seattle Times* had been a finalist for six Pulitzer prizes and had been named the 14th best newspaper in the United States, almost certainly making it the best regional newspaper in the country. At this family council, there was much information shared and much to be proud of. It is precisely this kind of education and information-sharing that keeps patient capital patient.

Unlike the adult Bingham children, the next generation of Blethens was being prepared for stewardship and accommodation. The fifth generation was being coached in the value of subsuming individual agendas for maximum and immediate gain in order to achieve a greater long-term gain for all.

ZERO-SUM DYNAMICS AND FAMILY CULTURE

It is within the rights of ownership to focus on individual gain and retain the right to immediate liquidity. However, multi-generational family-controlled businesses, even those with significant exposure to public markets, are largely illiquid enterprises. This lack of liquidity and need for selfless interest can be a burden for family members operating in a society that tends to focus on the short term, the last quarter, the day trade. They will bear this responsibility willingly only if opportunities to acquire information, education, and engagement with important family values of stewardship are plentiful. Inclusion, affection, and mutual influence across generations and between active and inactive shareholders are a must. Investing sweat equity in disseminating information to family members and encouraging multiple avenues of participation gives rise to trust, a spirit of service, and a sense that everyone is in the same boat on the same long journey.

Because of the myriad ways in which us-and-them behavior can manifest itself, multi-generational families are fertile ground for zero-sum dynamics. Zero-sum dynamics in relationships are characterized by exchanges in which one party's perceived gain is the other party's perceived loss. For example, if one branch of the family uses educational assistance for next-generation members, another branch assumes that less will be available for its members. Or, if family members in top management are to be compensated at a fair market rate, those not active in management assume that they will have to settle for lower dividends to accommodate those higher salaries. Even more critically, if those active in top management agree on a growth strategy, family members employed elsewhere believe that they will have to settle for greater reinvestment in the business and accept reduced distributions to shareholders. This us-and-them zero-sum dynamic can be triggered by any perceived difference: male–female, active–inactive, richer–poorer, better educated–less educated, older–younger, blood relative–in-law. Zero-sum dynamics become rooted in reality when the enterprise or family wealth stops growing or is in decline—that is, when the pie is not getting any larger. Members of multi-generational families may be labeled as jealous or envious when they operate on the assumption that another family member's gain is their loss.

THE BENEFITS OF FAMILY COUNCILS

Beating the odds of having to deal with a zero-sum dynamic in the family environment is perhaps the most compelling reason for holding frequent family meetings and creating a family council. As discussed in Chapter 8, family councils are to shareholding families what boards are to family-controlled businesses. They represent a reliable forum for the education of family members—particularly those not active in the management of the business—about the state of the business, its financial performance, its strategy, and the competitive dynamics it faces. Family councils also offer a safe haven in which to teach family members about the various rights and responsibilities that accompany being a business owner and manager. In the case of older multi-generational families, family councils are where important distinctions between ownership and stewardship are communicated, as at the Blethen Fifth Edition Family Business Meeting. Exhibit 9-1 summarizes the benefits of family councils.

Family councils may educate family members on estate and estate tax issues and guide next-generation members in the management of inherited wealth. They may also allow for policy making on such issues as (1) family member participation in the business, whether through employment, consulting, subcontracting, board service, or the conduct of family philanthropy, (2) family strategy vis-à-vis the business, determining the desired future relationship between the family and the business and between growth/reinvestment and higher dividends/current returns, and (3) liquidity for individuals or family branches that would like to diversify their assets using buy–sell agreements and other internal stock market mechanisms between shareholders.

The very existence of a family council as a forum for family members reduces the likelihood that family concerns will be inappropriately exported to a board of directors or a top management team, as occurred in the Bingham family. Atten-

EXHIBIT 9-1	BENEFITS OF FAMILY COUNCILS

- Understanding the family values and traditions that underlie the business and the family's commitment to the business across generations of owners.

- Appreciating more deeply the history of the family and its role in the business and in the successful competitive strategy pursued over the years.

- Understanding the estate plan, ownership transfer plans, estate tax liability, and the need for corporate control and agility.

- Defining, over time, the nature of family member participation in the business. This is especially important for next-generation members who choose not to work full-time in the business but want to contribute to it in some meaningful way. Opportunities for participation—in family philanthropy, community service, and industry and trade association leadership—may be identified that add value to the enterprise and support the family's role in society.

- Providing support to family members. A family council can be a significant reference and support group—for example, by financially supporting the education of next-generation members and providing emotional backing to family members with special needs.

- Providing ongoing family problem-solving and conflict-resolution mechanisms. These mechanisms allow families to constructively address feelings of alienation and anger over perceived favoritism or unequal distribution of money, love, influence, or opportunity.

- Creating a transparent succession plan and continuity process.

- Reviewing the returns on the family's investment in the business and legitimizing any concerns that shareholders may have about the management of the firm.

- Making the priorities and preferences of family members known to the board of directors, which has the ultimate responsibility to mesh or at least align family priorities with the priorities and strategic imperatives of the business.

- Professionalizing the business by inviting key nonfamily managers to attend family council meetings as resources, teachers, and mentors. By their very skills and abilities, these nonfamily managers convey to shareholders the tremendous value that professional management adds to the family-controlled corporation.

dance at these meetings represents a deposit in the family's emotional bank account—an investment in increasing trust and reducing the family's propensity to become a zero-sum entity.

Renewing the family's commitment to the business also builds a stronger business by improving the chances that shareholders will support the firm over a long period of time, instead of focusing on the most recent quarter in the way the current public company shareholder does. Loyal and patient capitalists in a family business can provide the company with a unique ability to deploy longer term strategies, allowing the business to develop sustainable competitive advantages that public or management-dominated firms can ill afford.

Who should be family council members? It is not unusual to launch a family council with direct descendants only, in the spirit of learning to walk before you run. Ideally, all adults, including spouses, should attend family council meetings. Children over 16 may be invited. Younger children may have parallel activities, such as business games or simulations, Outward-Bound types of experiences, and basic skill sessions in presentation, table manners, communication, dressing for effective image, team participation, etc. Some companies prefer to engage children in the adults' meeting at a young age and are receptive to the idea of having mature 13-year-olds present at the family council.

Do family councils overly formalize something that families do naturally anyway? Certainly, most families have a tradition of getting together for holidays, birthdays, weddings, and anniversaries. Families that own or control businesses often find time during such informal family gatherings to address items that relate to the ownership and management of the enterprise. In most cases, this only results in frustration, both on the part of family members who travel long distances and have little time and on the part of owner-managers or family leaders who fail to get the intended agenda covered.

Overall, family councils are associated with a positive family culture and a well-managed family firm. Specifically, they contribute significantly to strategic planning activity.[3]

FAMILY UNITY AND CONTINUITY

By engaging the family in its responsibilities vis-à-vis the business, a family council often helps the family become stronger. In few multi-generational families that do not share in the ownership/stewardship of an enterprise do the adult members of the extended family remain close and actively involved. The United States is a land of nuclear families, where members of the next generation often move to far-reaching geographic locations and lead separate lives, often disconnected from the family. Seldom are work and love found in the same town in which the extended family is located. A family business can represent a wonderful gift to many families that still care about family.

Studies of family-controlled corporations, including the one conducted at Case Western Reserve University, underscore the importance of family unity in the search for continuity.[4] Family unity is a strong predictor of (not necessarily a cause of, but highly correlated with) the successful use of managerial and family practices by multi-generational family-controlled companies. Many of these best practices are discussed in this book—using boards with independent outsiders, placing nonfamily managers in key positions where their skills complement those of top family managers, holding frequent family meetings, and establishing a family council. Family unity is also a defining element in the relationship between the owning family and the business. Therefore, it affects the firm's ability to capitalize on the unique capabilities and/or resources that family members bring to the company's business model. Thus, it helps the company translate core competencies into a unique set of competitive advantages.

Family companies represent a kaleidoscope of stakeholders, many with very different perspectives on business strategy, succession plans, the need for change in the company, the nature of the change needed, innovation, growth, the managerial capability of top management, the fairness of compensation plans, and career opportunities. These different perspectives are rooted in the stakeholder's

---

EXHIBIT 9-2   CONTINENTAL AIRLINES ADVERTISEMENT

Continental Airlines

- Best Place to Work.
- Best Airline to Fly.
- What a Coincidence.

Ranked among *Fortune 100*'s best places to work for the 3rd year in a row and again named Air Transport World's "Airline of the Year."

SOURCE: Advertisement in the *Wall Street Journal*, January 30, 2001.

role, whether as an owner only, an owner-manager, a family member with no share ownership, a member of the current or next generation, or a key nonfamily manager. Given these diverse views, establishing mechanisms for group-level goal setting, review of performance against goals, and problem solving and conflict resolution seems a particularly relevant practice.

Well-structured processes that involve family members in developing policies and setting direction can increase trust, a sense of unity, and commitment to goals (like continuity) deemed important by family members. After all, organizational behavior research has demonstrated that people support that which they helped create—and when they do, their company often performs better. When his company was the first national family business inducted into the Weatherhead School of Management's Family Business Hall of Fame® in 1996, Fisk Johnson, president of SC Johnson: A Family Company, made the following statement:

> We call our values "Family values . . . World class results." They are not radically different from the values you hear from major *Fortune 500* companies, but I think we are better able to practice those values as a family-owned business. People care about making quality products, really care about the family, each other and the success of the company. I believe this caring attitude translates into the success of the company.

Similarly, when Continental Airlines, a management-controlled company, received the Airline of the Year award for the third consecutive year, it placed full-page ads in the *Wall Street Journal*, promoting the correlation between the quality of its service and the quality of the working environment it provided for its employees (see Exhibit 9-2).

Does it not stand to reason, then, that processes that involve family members in defining the nature of the desired relationship with the business promote family unity and create some of the intangible assets that allow family businesses to achieve competitive advantage? Preliminary research into family companies has not been particularly rigorous. But there is preliminary evidence that the salutary effect of process on family company performance is being recognized. Family unity achieved through family assemblies and family councils is a good predictor of the utilization of a set of best practices that the family business literature has linked to competitive advantage, survival, and continuity.

How Families Add Value

In the Discovery Action Research Project on Family Business, the eight-year-old longitudinal research effort at Case Western Reserve University, several constructs have emerged from the analysis of responses to the Family Survey component. One of these constructs is family harmony. A family business with a high degree of family harmony tends to be more effective in planning for business continuity.[5] Such harmony exists when family members share values of accommodation and cooperation and appropriately handle conflict.

Tolerance of differences is another construct that has emerged from the Discovery study. This construct examines the extent to which a family constructively tolerates differences of opinion and outlook on sensitive issues. It represents the quality and the nature of communication within a family. Family meetings provide the opportunity for non-active family members to share their perspectives and/or concerns, which are often very different from those of family members who are active in the business. Advocates maintain that the positive effects of family meetings derive from different stakeholders' talking to and gaining understanding of each other and thus being more likely to make decisions that are mutually beneficial for all parties. Stakeholders who communicate also tend to be more aware of the likely reactions to and consequences of their decisions.[6]

In the most recent analysis of data from the study, a new composite index—Family Unity—was developed. The Family Unity index characterizes the family system and is the sum of the Family Harmony, Tolerance of Differences, and Participation and Succession scales. Based on scores on the Family Unity index, firms were divided into two groups. Results of difference testing between these groups indicated that firms with significantly different scores on the Family Unity, Business Opportunity, and Family–Business Interaction indices also had significantly different Management Practices scores. The degree of family unity, how the family perceived business opportunities, and how positive the relation was between firm and family all influenced the managerial practices used and the extent of their use.

Family unity, as measured, was correlated with effective management practices, including planning activity, performance feedback, succession planning disclosure, advisory boards, and family meetings. These findings indicate that investing in the family's health and harmony—via guidelines for employment of family members, clear standards for succession and ownership transfer processes, and promotion of cooperation and positive relations among family members—may pay off for the firm. They further support the important role that family meetings and retreats can play in fostering business effectiveness and continuity by creating a new reality for family members.[7] The findings also point to the utility of having advisors and family members work with a principal architect of the family-ownership-management system, such as the CEO or the CEO spouse, on addressing the consequences (both intended and unintended) of his or her policies and practices.[8]

The Discovery study research highlighted a set of idiosyncratic, inimitable, and intangible resources residing in some family businesses, which provide these companies with an opportunity for competitive advantage and superior performance. This resource for the value-creation process of a particular firm is the result of the unique interaction between the family, its individual members, and the business. If a firm's unique family–business interaction is not assessed and managed or if a firm does not recognize this interaction and invest in it as a valuable resource, its relative worth can quickly erode. The family–business interaction can even become an encumbrance to the firm—yielding increased costs and threatening its competitive advantage.

PLANNING AND POLICY MAKING

Having family members rush into uninformed, democratic decision making is one of the biggest fears of current-generation family and business leaders when they embark on the process of holding a family meeting or creating a family council. According to the CEO of a medium-size, family-controlled financial services firm, "Some of my siblings and most of my nieces and nephews have no clue about what is going on in the business or what I have been doing on the estate plan. How am I going to open all of this up for their participation? All I will get is uninformed opinions and passionate second-guessing. And of course they'll want to vote on it." First and foremost, family councils should be about education and communication. Over time, they will become effective planning and policy-making bodies—that is, if the education and communication phases have been properly carried out.

Open and safe processes for sharing information among family members in family council meetings are prerequisites for effective planning and policy making by family groups. Because many family-controlled companies, for understandable reasons, decide to create a family council in order to dismantle the culture of secrecy established by the previous generation, a gradual evolution is best. Decision making should be ruled out as one of the functions of the family council. Voting should be banned, as it is not a relevant tool. The focus should be on conversations, deliberations, and, oftentimes, presentations by experts, including nonfamily managers who might be invited to brief family members on such topics as the latest technology deployed in the field or company finances. The council must strive to come up with plans and policies that, even if not everybody's favorites, most family members are willing to support. Several types of policies that stand out in their usefulness to families in business are listed below:

1. An employment policy that outlines the levels of education and experience required for employment in the business. It should be based on merit and company need, not membership in the business family.

2. A subcontractor policy that offers guidelines for arms-length transactions in an open competitive marketplace. The bidding processes should create a level playing field for relatives and nonfamily alike.

3. A board service policy that includes criteria for the selection of family members to serve as at-large representatives of the owning family on the board. The system should provide a link between family strategy and company strategy without giving undue influence to family members.

4. A family council coordinator and committee service policy that states the criteria for selecting family members to serve as group coordinators of the family council and other committees that may be formed. Among possible goals of other committees are a family newsletter, a family history project, and philanthropic activity.

5. A dividend policy, not to specify the amount of dividends to be paid (which is a company decision), but rather to discuss family needs, balance them against reinvestment in the business for growth needs, and then inform management of the general sentiments of family members.

6. A liquidity policy that includes principles supporting the desired relationship between the controlling family and the company in the future and recognizing that individuals or particular family branches may have cash flow needs. This policy usually differentiates between small transactions and the sale of large blocks of stock within the family or back to the company and references the legal documents in effect (such as buy–sell agreements).

7. A family constitution, used primarily in older and larger multi-generational family businesses. This document is a collection of the established policies and a statement of family history, family commitment, and the desired relationship between the company and the owning family.

Let's consider an example of one of the policies just described—the family employment policy.

THE FAMILY EMPLOYMENT POLICY. Families that appreciate the utility of a family council or other family meeting are, sooner or later, candidates for policies spelling out family participation, particularly the form of participation closest to the heart of a family-controlled business—company employment. By the time a family company is in its second or third generation, the number of potential family candidates can overwhelm prudent employment based on merit, of both family and nonfamily.

Family employment policies, including promotion practices, need to be written down and communicated so as to create greater clarity, transparency, and a sense of fair play. Employment policies speak loudly to the principle of equality of opportunity. While the importance of these policies to family members is obvious, family employment and promotion practices are of great concern to nonfamily managers seeking employment in family-owned and family-controlled companies. Second-, third-, and fourth-generation family firms need highly capable nonfamily managers; they are a critical part of the effective governance of a family business. Communicating anything less than equality in career opportunities to potential and current key nonfamily managers will result in their loss to more egalitarian employers.

The family employment policy shown in Exhibit 9-3 was drafted by 18 cousins, third-generation stakeholders in a $95 million family-owned company. The second-generation siblings, including the current CEO and chairman of the board, reviewed this draft and revised it only slightly. It was then brought for final approval to the family council.

EXHIBIT 9-3   EMPLOYMENT POLICY OF GLOBAL CONSTRUCTION CORPORATION

Our Family Employment Policy

Purpose: The purpose of this policy is to define the criteria, procedures and processes that will govern how lineal descendants and/or their spouses enter and exit from the family-controlled company's employ. This employment policy is intended to remove the ambiguity that currently exists so those interested family members can shape their career paths accordingly. We believe that clear, constructive communication of this policy will contribute to the long-term success of our family and Global Construction Corporation.

Philosophy: We are a family committed to our members being responsible, productive and capable citizens who practice the work ethic and make constructive contributions to society. We believe that for a family member to be employed in this company, there must be a legitimate job, an opening or company need, and a family member with the skills to match. It is the policy of Global Construction Corporation to search out and employ, at all levels, individuals who have managerial abilities and who show evidence of ability and initiative in previous assignments. Furthermore, the company will seek those who exhibit self-confidence and high self-esteem and who are both independent and show evidence of leading responsible lives at work and with their families.

We subscribe to the philosophy that a family member will not automatically be granted a position in the company when seeking employment. That, with the input of the human resources professional on staff, family members will be considered on a par with nonfamily candidates for employment. High-level nonfamily employees are evidence of professionalism, high standards, accountability and commitment to business continuity. They raise the bar for family members and the company as a whole. The company will, however, strive to employ family members when appropriate opportunities arise. After all, it is in the best interest of the company to have committed ownership that understands and supports the future of the corporation.

We also believe in responsible stewardship of the family enterprise. We want to emphasize values like education, a strong work ethic, competence, independence and commitment to the greater good of the corporation and the extended family among family members who are shareholders but choose not to be employed by the corporation.

Employment Conditions:

1. Family members must meet the same criteria for hiring as nonfamily applicants.

2. Family members are expected to meet the same level of performance required of nonfamily employees. Like nonfamily employees, they will be subject to annual performance reviews and to the same rules guiding firing decisions.

3. As a general principle, and whenever feasible, family members will be supervised by nonfamily members to ensure greater objectivity and accountability.

4. Compensation will be appropriate for the position held; this means that salary and benefits will be market-driven and based on recent salary surveys.

5. Family members must have at least 3 years of work experience and an MBA or graduate degree in field related to our business, to be considered for upper management positions. In the absence of an MBA or graduate degree in related field, 5 years of related and/or management experience is expected. The 3 or 5 years of experience should show evidence of high performance, increased responsibility and greater competence that has been recognized by the employer in the form of at least one promotion or high visibility project assignment. Previous successful work experience outside of the family company is considered an important predictor of the contribution potential and fit of family members at Global.

6. Family members interested in company employment must make their interest known, by writing to the President or Chief Executive Officer and initiating the process of mutual self-selection. Family members will not be officially canvassed for particular positions or job openings nor will openings be routinely communicated to family members. The initiative must remain with the individual interested in employment. Only after the written notification and the identification of relevant employment opportunities, will candidates fill the application forms and submit them for appropriate consideration by the director of human resources.

Note: The name of the company has been changed.

GUIDELINES FOR POLICY MAKING.   The following simple set of guidelines can help families that are developing family business policies:

1. Ideally, involve as many family members as are relevant to the particular policy being developed. Relevance is defined by expertise on the subject(s) to be discussed, by the need of family members to feel included, and by the potential effect of the policy on those family members. Still, it may be preferable to start small—for example, in third-generation family firms, involve only direct descendants, not their spouses, in the beginning; welcome spouses at later meetings, once the group has developed a foundation for policy-making activity. Ultimately, this is a judgment call, based on many factors. (Having recently participated in a very successful first family council, attended by 35 direct descendants and their spouses, I got some firsthand evidence of effective group work by a large number of family participants including in-laws. The decision to include spouses in this first meeting was in response to the identified goal of ensuring that second- and third-generation spouses feel they are "in the same boat" as the heirs.)

2. Look at the big picture, and formulate a mission statement or outcome goal that defines what is best for the extended family and the business. Refrain from favoring policies that repeatedly put one individual or family branch above the interests of all.

3. Focus on the future and let go of the past. Self-management (as management literature refers to it) is critical in moving away from repetitive retelling of past incidents and instead breaking new ground that will prevent or minimize the occurrence of similar situations in the future.

4. Use experienced facilitators, who can play a significant role in helping a family business focus on the future, and benchmark your drafts of policies against those of other successful family-owned or family-controlled companies.

5. Agree on the process you will follow to develop, review, edit, re-draft, approve, and ultimately enact policies with the confidence that people will support them because, after all, they helped create them. ■

TRUSTS, LEGAL AGREEMENTS, AND PERSONAL RESPONSIBILITY

Trying to force people you don't trust to do what you want them to do over generations is doomed to failure. No matter what you write into the trust instrument, there are no ironclad guarantees that the company won't be sold. You have to get the people who can make or influence the decision to keep the company to buy into your vision.

—John P. C. Duncan, Attorney[9]

There is now plenty of evidence that generation-skipping restrictive trusts, ostensibly crafted on behalf of family-controlled company continuity and family unity, fail miserably in preventing next-generation members from doing with the company as they see fit. While these instruments often do protect and preserve the asset-based legacy for a period of time, family estrangement and asset sales will result, unless a way is found to rediscover the intangible, value-based legacy of the founder and earlier generations.

Rediscovering this legacy takes time and conversation. It takes family history projects and reviews of the strategies and growth opportunities sought by the different generations and family members acting as chief trust officers. It takes making history come alive again. At a recent start-up of a family council, a second-generation sibling kicked off the meeting not with the usual discussion of goals and expectations for the meeting but rather by reading a fictional letter from her deceased father. Having found out that his widowed spouse, 5 second-generation heirs and their spouses, 18 grandchildren, and 7 of the grandchildren's spouses would be meeting together at a family council, her father had supposedly written this letter in order to convey to all family members in attendance a sense of history, a sense of priorities, his commitment to a few essential principles, and his tremendous appreciation for the job done by his three successors in the management of the business.

This family's first family council meeting was launched with a tremendous sense of history and a personal challenge to the next generation to "do the right thing" as the family and the business moved forward. No amount of legal expertise or foresight in the drafting of legal documents can match the goodwill and personal responsibility that next-generation members begin to assume when the importance and relevance of both family and enterprise are so eloquently stated. If ever there was a compelling reason for family councils in multi-generational family-controlled companies, this is it. Only those shareholders who are engaged by the founder's and successors' shared dreams and vision will choose to be stewards of the legacy. The rest will put their individual interests and agendas before anything else and will most likely exhibit all the behaviors of rich but ungrateful heirs.

CONFLICT MANAGEMENT

Becoming a successful multi-generational family-owned company is evidence of having provided for orderly governance and resolution of problems within the family or in the family's relationship to the business before they overwhelmed the enterprise. Conflict is inevitable in families, and more so in families that live, work, and control assets together. One of the benefits of a family council is its ability to provide a forum for minimizing the potential for conflict and addressing the troublesome problems that confront multi-generational families. Some of the significant problems that can be addressed in family councils include the following:

- Frustration over alienation or lack of inclusion. This source of conflict is widespread as a result of the emotional distance between family members who are active in management and those who are not and between members of the powerful current generation and those of the significantly less powerful next generation. Geographic separation and lack of frequent and consistent communication only heighten this conflict and often lead to mistrust and a propensity for zero-sum dynamics.

■ Anger over the unfairness of hiring practices, promotions, family benefits, and other opportunities enjoyed by some but not by others. In many families, "fair" means "equal." But in multi-generational families, when being fair means being equal, family leaders soon run out of options. The family and, often, the company become paralyzed.

■ Frustration over dividend policies and lack of liquidity. By the time a family-owned company has begun to hire its third generation of family members, the financial needs of the various branches and individuals have become incredibly diverse. A third-generation owner-manager receiving a fair market salary as a manager or corporate officer faces a very different reality than does a cousin pursuing a medical degree and raising two children.

All of these problems must be addressed by family councils and resolved to the best of their ability. Active listening is at the heart of much family council activity. It leads to two-way communication that addresses the sources of feelings and allows plans to be drafted or changed as necessary. Because some of these feelings are based on "perceptions," meaning things that some see and others do not, the education mission of a family council can go a long way in creating common ground and ameliorating conflicts rooted in misinformation or misunderstandings.

THE FAMILY OFFICE

Paradoxically, the less important some established family benefits are, the more trouble they can cause. I was once involved in a dispute in a family firm over the produce from a vegetable garden. The family home, factory and garden were all on the same site and the garden was cultivated for the benefit of those members of the family who lived on the spot. When this apparently modest benefit came to be costed out, it was clear that it was a totally uneconomic way of keeping some members of the family in fresh fruit and vegetables, quite apart from the development value tied up in food production. Any change in the traditional arrangement was, however, seen by those who benefited from it as an attack on the established order and the beginning of the end of the family firm. Eventually, the fate of the vegetable plot was satisfactorily settled. But the sooner a family firm regularizes the relationships between the family and the firm, the less time will have to be spent on matters of allocation between them, which can create trouble out of all proportion to their economic significance.

—Sir Adrian Cadbury, Chairman of Cadbury Schweppes[10]

Larger multi-generational firms often have a family office, whose duties are primarily to provide and organize a series of services for family shareholders. These services include providing legal and financial aid with estate and tax issues; managing the investments and the diversification portfolios of the family; providing information of relevance to shareholders, sometimes by producing a newsletter;

and fairly and equitably distributing family or shareholder benefits, like education funds from family trusts or foundations and even time at the family ranch or Florida beachfront property.

Like family councils, family offices enhance a family's ability to regulate the relationship between the family and the company, enabling more professional management of the firm and fairer handling of shareholder and family issues and requests. A family office may function as a full-time organized arm of the family council, helping the council execute the policies and guidelines it has developed.

SUMMARY

1. Secrecy, lack of information, and absence of education threaten continued commitment by family members to the continuity of a family-controlled corporation.

2. Multi-generational families, because of the myriad ways in which us-and-them behavior can manifest itself, are fertile ground for zero-sum dynamics.

3. Family councils are a reliable forum for the education of family members about the business. In family councils, family members learn about the rights and responsibilities that accompany being an owner-manager and about the important distinctions between ownership and management. They also provide a forum to minimize the potential for conflict within the family.

4. Family unity is a strong predictor of the successful use of best managerial and family practices for continuity by multi-generational family-controlled companies.

5. Policies that are especially useful to family businesses include an employment policy, a subcontractor policy, a board service policy, a family council coordinator and committee service policy, a dividend policy, a liquidity policy, and a family constitution.

CASES

CASE 5:
FASTENERS FOR RETAIL: A QUESTION OF SUCCESSION (PART A)

In December 1999, Gerry Conway faced the toughest decision of his 37 years as an entrepreneur. Something had to be done about the long-term future of Fasteners for Retail (FFr), the business he had founded in 1962. The company had been extremely successful, with sales doubling every five years since the 1980s and the market for the company's point-of-purchase display products still growing. Within the last two years, the company had begun to expand from an enormously successful catalogue company into a full-service provider to global retail chains.

With no dominant players in FFr's niche, Conway saw nothing but opportunity ahead. Still, he was concerned. The company had been debt-free from the start, but feeding its continuing growth would require an infusion of cash. At 69, Conway felt that this was more risk than he wanted to assume. Of even more pressing concern was his son and heir apparent's recent announcement that he did not want to become FFr's next president and instead planned to leave the company. None of his other children were interested in becoming part of the leadership team. Conway mused,

> I am a good entrepreneur, but I am not managerial in nature and I don't like that part of the business. I have a good manager here in Don Kimmel [the nonfamily company president]. It is time to move on. Until a year ago, I couldn't decide what to do because I was ambivalent, but now I have reached a point where I want to make a transition.

This decision would affect the future of his family, his business, and its 95 employees. Should he sell the company, appoint a nonfamily CEO, or persuade another family member to come into the business?

Research associate Tracey Eira Messer prepared this case under the supervision of Professor Ernesto J. Poza as the basis for class discussion rather than to illustrate the effective or ineffective handling of an administrative situation. For permission to publish this case, grateful acknowledgment is made to Gerald Conway, chairman emeritus of Fasteners for Retail.

THE FOUNDER

Gerry Conway was the classic American entrepreneur—visionary, charismatic, driven, impatient, and independent. Born in Cleveland in 1931, Conway was the ninth of thirteen children. His love of the retail environment, his strong independence, and his deep appreciation of people stemmed from his childhood experiences:

> With a little exaggeration, I can say that I've been in retail for 60 years. My Dad managed approximately 200 food stores, and my first jobs were as a stock boy and butcher's assistant. At home, we'd talk about business over the dinner table. With 11 sons and 2 daughters in the family, it was a lively conversation. I already had the entrepreneurial itch, and, from the grocery experience and from having a newspaper delivery route, I learned how to get along with people.

After college, Conway and his wife, Marty, returned to Cleveland. He began working for an industrial firm and quickly learned that, while sales attracted him, working in a large corporation did not. Conway's next job was with a smaller firm:

> I started selling display lithography for a small printer. When that company went belly up, I founded Gerald A. Conway & Associates and became a display-printing broker. I was 31 years old, had $600 in the bank and a wife and six kids counting on me. For the first five years, I had one goal—survival. Even after we were established, the company was a central part of my life.

Conway was an extremely personable man. He made friends and networked with ease. One day, a colleague suggested that he sell the plastic parts that retailers use to display signs (called display and merchandising accessories) as part of his printing broker business. The advantage of selling accessories was that he could sell the same product to many companies simultaneously, which wasn't possible in display printing, where each printing job was customized. An early product idea was the Arrowhead® fastener, which was designed to hold coupons and signs on store shelves (see Exhibit 1). It was a best-seller from the start. For the next decade, Gerald A. Conway & Associates was a printing broker and a supplier of display accessories.

During this time, Conway struggled with alcohol:

> In 1970, alcohol was becoming a problem, but through a self-help program I chose sobriety and regained focus in my life. The following year, my first year sober, my income shot up by about 35 percent—a direct correlation. So, anyway, that was a significant event in the business and for my family.

THE POINT-OF-PURCHASE (P-O-P) INDUSTRY

In the mid-1970s, Gerald Conway & Associates was renamed Fasteners for Retail (FFr) to acknowledge its exclusive focus on display accessories and fasteners within the point-of-purchase (P-O-P) industry.

| EXHIBIT 1 | ARROWHEAD FASTENERS |

110

sign holders
Arrowhead®

our very first fastener for retail

Here's where it all started. Our very first product: the AF-101 Arrowhead® Fastener. Still in widespread use today, holding coupons or signage from shelf channels and a myriad of other flat display surfaces.

AF-101 Arrowhead® Fastener

A cost-effective way to securely hold pads of coupons or single signs in the centered flush position.
- Fits most standard 1 ¼" shelf channels
- 530 78951 02 has permanent adhesive for use on most flat surfaces
- Stem ½" L
- Natural Polypropylene

530 78951 01

Part No.	Style	1-999	1,000	2,500	5,000
530 78951 01	w/o adh	52.00/M	39.00/M	29.00/M	24.00/M
530 78951 02	w/ adh	72.00/M	59.00/M	49.00/M	44.00/M

Custom colors available. (minimum order required)

AF-101F Arrowhead® Fastener

Designed for even easier insertion in shelf channels.
- Easy flex design
- Holds coupon pads or single signs
- Fits most standard 1 ¼" shelf channels
- Stem ½" L
- Natural Polyethylene

530 78951 04

Part No.	Size	1-999	1,000	2,500	5,000
530 78951 04	½" L	52.00/M	39.00/M	29.00/M	24.00/M

Custom colors available. (minimum order required)

AF-102 Arrowhead® Fastener

Securely pin coupon pads or single signs to shelf fronts.
- Fits most standard 1 ¼" shelf channels
- 530 77348 02 has permanent adhesive for use on most flat surfaces
- Stem ⅞" L
- Natural Polypropylene

530 77348 01

Part No.	Size	1-999	1,000	2,500	5,000
530 77348 01	w/o adh	79.00/M	60.00/M	49.00/M	45.00/M
530 77348 02	w/ adh	104.00/M	85.00/M	74.00/M	70.00/M

Custom colors available. (minimum order required)

800.422.CLIP (2547)

Point-of-purchase products include the signs, displays, devices, and structures that are used to merchandise services or products in retail stores. The P-O-P industry was estimated to be a $13.1 billion sector, based on 1997 industry figures (see Exhibit 2). FFr's segment was estimated to be approximately $600 million. While the broader P-O-P market was expected to grow at 4 percent annually, FFr and its competitors experienced much higher growth rates. FFr, for example, had grown 19.6 percent annually since 1984.

The accessory hardware segment (FFr's niche) was highly fragmented. No single supplier had more than 10 percent of the sub-supplier market, and many competed in only a few product categories. FFr was the largest company in this niche, with a market share of approximately 7.5 percent. The company's major product offerings included shelf and non-shelf channel sign holders, display hooks, display construction, and custom products. FFr also offered shelf systems, ceiling display systems, product strips, hang taps, literature holders, and other accessories. Several key contractors manufactured these products for FFr, but no single manufacturer had unique or proprietary capabilities.

FASTENERS FOR RETAIL (FFR): VALUE ADDED FROM THE START

FFr distinguished itself from its competitors in several important ways. The company offered a broad and innovative product line, free samples, quick turnaround on orders, and a liberal sales return policy.

EXHIBIT 2	P-O-P TRENDS

P-O-P products are displays, signs, structures, and devices that are used to identify, advertise, and/or merchandise an outlet, service, or product and that serve as aids to retailing.

2002	$15.5 billion
1997	$13.1 billion
1996	$12.7 billion
1995	$12.0 billion
1994	$11.1 billion

- Almost three-quarters of customer purchase decisions are made in-store, at the point of purchase.
- Product proliferation is on the rise.

Supermarket Assortments:

1992	13,067 skus
2001	30,580 skus

SOURCES: Point of Purchase Advertising Institute; POPAI Consumer Buying Habits Study; and Food Marketing Institute.

FFR PRODUCTS.   The willingness to emphasize new products became a defining characteristic of the business. While the company's early expansion began with imported Swedish design accessories, the product line grew because of Conway's creativity and dissatisfaction with the status quo.

Successful design accessories are functional, fit a specific space, and are inexpensive. New products were developed from scratch, acquired, or adapted from other industries. Conway excelled in all aspects of product development—imagining how new products could meet customer needs and seeing how existing products could be used in or improved for the P-O-P market. Two products in particular, the Shipflat® literature holder (see Exhibit 3) and SuperGrip® sign holders (see Exhibit 4), were critical to FFr's success in the early 1980s. (The complete FFr online catalogue can be found at http://www.ffr.com.)

Shipflat Literature Holder.   At a trade show, Citibank challenged FFr to make a better literature holder. At the time, literature holders were made from rigid plastic. Only four holders could be shipped per box, and they frequently broke in transit. After a year of effort, FFr successfully designed attractive and durable literature holders that were unique in that they shipped flat and were set up at the point of use, eliminating breakage and reducing inventory space and shipping cost. Citibank had exclusive rights to the Shipflat for several years, and it placed the Shipflat at the core of its credit card program. Working with Citibank enhanced FFr's credibility and raised its visibility in the market; Citibank recognized the company as an "Outstanding Merchant" for its product and customer service. The Shipflat became FFr's first proprietary product in the literature holder category and was well received by auto clubs, insurance companies, and pharmaceutical firms, among others. Within two years, the Shipflat became FFr's top seller.

SuperGrip Sign Holders.   In the early 1980s, a new product began appearing in the accessory market. FFr recognized this product's superior holding ability—it was able to hold paper signs in place more securely than existing technology. It represented a threat to FFr's product line, so the company tracked down the patent and began trying to develop its own version of the clip. At almost the same time, the clip's Canadian inventor, unhappy with his distributor, negotiated with FFr to distribute the product. FFr began distributing the clip and eventually purchased the patent with its Canadian partner. FFr renamed the clip and applied the technology to its existing products, thus expanding the product line. SuperGrip products were very successful with both retailers and consumer goods companies and, at one point, accounted for almost 20 percent of sales.

For years, FFr's marketing thrust was proprietary products. More recent efforts focused on developing an increasing number of custom products, designed to meet specific customer needs. New products were introduced as they were designed, without concern for cannibalizing sales of existing products. FFr encouraged the development of both custom and proprietary products, promoting internal competition within the organization.

EXHIBIT 3 | SHIPFLAT LITERATURE HOLDERS

194

Shipflat® Literature Holders

Shipflat® literature holders ship flat, eliminating breakage and reducing your inventory space and shipping costs by up to 50%! A few simple folds turn your Shipflat® into a rigid information holder. The clear material helps present literature in the best possible light, whether freestanding or wall-mounted.

IS Shipflat® Literature Holder

These literature holders ship flat and feature both pop-out and easel mounting holes.

▶ Simple, snap-together design
▶ Wide range of sizes
▶ Also available in custom colors
▶ Color imprinting available (below)
▶ Clear K-Resin

IS-91 (920 76692 01)
▶ Holds literature up to 3 ⁷/₈" W
▶ 3 ⁷/₈" W x 7" H x 1 ⁵/₈" D
▶ Imprint field 3 ³/₁₆" W x 1 ⁹/₁₆" H

IS-2 (920 19821 01)
▶ Holds literature up to 3 ⁷/₈" wide
▶ 3 ⁷/₈" W x 10" H x 1 ⁵/₈" D
▶ Imprint field 3 ³/₈" W x 1 ⁹/₁₆" H at base plus additional imprint area on header

IS-4 (920 80594 01)
▶ Holds literature up to 4 ¹/₈" wide
▶ 4 ¹/₈" W x 7" H x 1 ⁵/₈" D
▶ Imprint field 3 ⁵/₈" W x 1 ¹/₂" H

IS-4H (920 16546 01)
▶ Holds literature up to 4 ¹/₈" wide
▶ 4 ¹/₈" W x 7" H x 1 ⁵/₈" D
▶ Imprint field 3 ⁵/₈" W x 2 ¹/₂" H

IS-6 (920 77745 01)
▶ Holds literature up to 6 ¹/₈" wide
▶ 6 ¹/₈" W x 7" H x 1 ⁵/₈" D
▶ Imprint field 5 ¹/₂" W x 1 ⁹/₁₆" H

IS-8 (920 18977 01)
▶ Holds literature up to 8 ¹/₂" wide
▶ 8 ¹/₂" W x 10" H x 1 ³/₄" D
▶ Imprint field 8" W x 2 ¹/₂" H

new lower prices!

Part No.	Width	1-9	10	25	100	200	500	1000
920 76692 01	3 ⁷/₈"	2.88 ea	2.16 ea	1.80 ea	1.44 ea	1.31 ea	1.19 ea	1.05 ea
920 19821 01	3 ⁷/₈"	3.24 ea	2.48 ea	1.94 ea	1.71 ea	1.55 ea	1.45 ea	1.30 ea
920 80594 01	4 ¹/₈"	2.25 ea	1.95 ea	1.75 ea	1.55 ea	1.40 ea	1.25 ea	1.08 ea
920 16546 01	4 ¹/₈"	3.19 ea	2.43 ea	1.89 ea	1.66 ea	1.52 ea	1.42 ea	1.28 ea
920 77745 01	6 ¹/₈"	3.60 ea	2.88 ea	2.34 ea	1.98 ea	1.85 ea	1.75 ea	1.58 ea
920 18977 01	8 ¹/₂"	5.24 ea	3.24 ea	2.84 ea	2.34 ea	2.24 ea	2.04 ea	1.94 ea

Patented

920 76692 01

920 16546 01

Shipflat® Imprinting

One-color imprinting is available on the front face of all Shipflat® Literature Holders.*

▶ Actual-size camera-ready art required
▶ 2- and 3-color imprinting available with prior art approval (call for details)
▶ Die Charge: $125.00 per color
▶ Minimum order: 100 pieces

*IS-2 model (920 19821 01) can also be imprinted on the header (above)

Part No.	100	200	500	1,000	2,500
IS-IMPRINT	.60 ea	.35 ea	.20 ea	.15 ea	.12 ea

800.422.CLIP (2547)

literature holders *Shipflat*

| EXHIBIT 4 | SUPERGRIP SIGN HOLDERS |

79

Patented

021 33276 00

Clips directly to most Economy Data Strip® Ticket Molding (page 32).
▶ Hinge lets you flip up the sign, revealing information underneath
▶ Holds signs up to .080" thick in the flag position
▶ Clear PVC

DSGE-2H Economy Data Strip® Hinged Flag Sign Holder

Part No.	Size	1-999	1,000	2,500	5,000
021 33276 00	¾" W	234.00/M	175.00/M	156.00/M	140.00/M

Patented

181 88231 01

Clips directly onto most Economy Data Strip® Ticket Molding (page 32).
▶ Hinge lets you flip up the sign, revealing UPC scanning information underneath
▶ Flip sign out of the way when re-stocking shelves
▶ Holds signs up to .080" thick in the flush position
▶ Clear PVC

DSGE1H Economy Data Strip® Hinged Flush Sign Holder

Part No.	Size	1-999	1,000	2,500	5,000
181 88231 01	1" L	181.00/M	136.00/M	121.00/M	109.00/M

Custom lengths and colors available. (minimum order required)

Patented

440 12566 01

Snaps onto all Extra-Duty Data Strip® and Dual Data Strip® Ticket Molding (page 32).
▶ Holds signs up to .080" thick in the flag position
▶ Clear PVC

DSG-2A Extra-Duty Data Strip® Flag Sign Holder

Part No.	Size	1-999	1,000	2,500	5,000
440 12566 01	¾" W	280.00/M	224.00/M	201.00/M	179.00/M

Patented

440 39975 02

Snaps onto Extra-Duty Data Strip® and Dual Data Strip® Ticket Molding (page 32).
▶ Holds signs up to .080" thick in the flush position
▶ Clear PVC

DSG1 Extra-Duty Data Strip® Flush Sign Holder

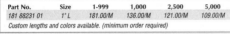

Part No.	Size	1-999	1,000	2,500	5,000
440 39975 02	1" L	132.00/M	99.00/M	82.00/M	70.00/M
440 39975 03	1 ½" L	198.00/M	148.00/M	123.00/M	105.00/M

Custom lengths and colors available. (minimum order required)

sign holders
SuperGrip

www.ffr.com

FFr

FFr typically offered customers more than 100 new products every year. New product ideas came from FFr personnel, from customers, and from the acquisition of new product concepts. New product development statistics were impressive. In a niche known for commodity products, FFr had almost 75 patents and patents pending. Patented products accounted for 20 percent of all products offered and represented a significant competitive advantage. On average, products that had been developed in the last five years accounted for 30 percent of sales. FFr valued and actively protected its designs.

SERVICE. FFr's products and superior service separated it from its competition. Independent audits repeatedly found that customers rated FFr's customer service as superior. An early hire recalled,

> When I began working here, we weren't quite sure who we were or what market we were in, so we looked around at other organizations and emulated what was best about them. Through that process, we became leaders. Following Gerry's lead, we never took things for granted. As a family-owned company, we were able to respond quickly to opportunities and customer needs.

While its competitors maintained limited inventories and dictated shipment terms to customers, FFr offered a complete line of products, kept a well-stocked inventory, bagged products to meet the customer's specifications, and shipped products as requested. Other vendors offered better prices but poorer service. FFr came to dominate its market by offering both service and selection:

> We created our competitors. After a few years, they looked at us and said, "We can do that too." We had a broad product line and did custom work; others began adopting those programs. Our success in branding is evident from the wide-scale copycatting of our colors, style, and product line.

FFr was both a direct sales and a marketing sales company. It relied on its sales force, direct mail catalogue, trade media advertising, trade shows, and sample department to promote its products. The company's unique product catalogue, the FFR Yellow Pages®, set a new standard for the industry and helped establish FFr as a "first-look supplier" within the industry. The sales organization consisted of a direct sales force, international distributors, a customer service group, and a telemarketing staff.

FFR CULTURE

From its first hire on, FFr was a company whose employees, from designer to warehouseman, focused on customer satisfaction (see Exhibit 5). As a 16-year veteran recalled,

> Gerry had the ability to hire people who would work independently, but in a common direction and for a common goal. He was fortunate to have surrounded himself with people who had the sense of urgency and good work ethic to make things happen. This was true even of outsourced services. . . . Employees of our service center treated our clients as if they [the service center employees] were actually FFr.

EXHIBIT 5   FFr's STATEMENT OF VALUES

 Fasteners for Retail

Welcome to FFr!

On behalf of all the employees at FFr, I welcome you to the FFr team and our thriving organization. We realize you may have put significant time and effort into your decision to join FFr, and we are pleased you have made a commitment to further your career with us. It's important we work together to fulfill both your professional goals and our overall company goals.

Since 1962, FFr has been recognized as a leader in custom and stock merchandising systems and accessories, as well as in providing outstanding customer service. We are very proud of this recognition, as well as our long-term customer and employee relationships.

To this end, the following Statement of Values guides our daily operations:

- Commit ourselves to excellence in creativity, quality, and service.
- Treat our customers and each other with respect.
- Seek opportunities for continuous improvement, with our goal being 100 percent customer satisfaction.
- Focus on developing and maintaining customers for life by maximizing the value we provide.
- Work as a team to support each other and achieve our goals.

We realize our continued success rests solely on our ability to recruit and retain the best people, like you.

Again, welcome to FFr. I wish you every success in your career with us.

Sincerely,

Donald F. Kimmel
President & COO

FFr's customer-first focus extended to the company newsletter, which told tales of employees going above and beyond expectations to deliver superior customer service. It offered hints for achieving customer satisfaction, solicited new product ideas, and reported on product development. The newsletter also filled a more traditional communication role, introducing new hires and announcing promotions, company anniversaries, and birthdays.

Maintaining profit margins was also part of the FFr culture. President Don Kimmel recalled,

> When I arrived, the focus on margins was so strong that I occasionally had to take a hammer to break it a bit. We would rather lose an order, if we couldn't beat the hell out of a supplier to get the margin we wanted, than deviate from our margins.

FFR GROWTH IN THE 1980s

FFr grew at a consistent and steady pace. In 1980, the company had five employees and sales of $3 million. Business began to boom in the early 1980s as a result of an expanding product line and a larger sales force. FFr grew steadily, adding employees in accounting, customer service, product design, and marketing. Company offices were moved to accommodate additional warehouse and distribution functions. Paul, one of Conway's sons, observed,

> Dad managed the business like a football halfback, scanning the horizon looking for an opening and then heading for it. He was never afraid to explore new business possibilities and was always looking for opportunities.

This opportunistic philosophy supported FFr's growth. The business was always profitable, there was no debt, and the company never got tied up in long-term commitments. Production and most warehousing were subcontracted, and office space was leased. The company made quick decisions, and arrangements with vendors were frequently based on handshakes.

The flip side of FFr's opportunism and speed was that it lacked a business plan and strategic discipline. When Conway came across an interesting idea, he wanted to implement it. Company lore had it that when Conway sat next to a consultant on an airplane, the consultant would be on-site the following week to redesign something. This approach led to some important innovations and prevented the company from becoming stagnant, but it also created a sense of confusion and the feeling that priorities were constantly changing.

To keep the company growing, Conway realized that he needed to hire a president with managerial expertise. Although he understood the value of management, he was an entrepreneur, not a traditional manager. The company went through several presidents. FFr, for a time, was a company with an organizational chart but not a lot of organization. That changed in the late 1990s.

FFR GROWTH IN THE 1990s AND BEYOND

In the early 1990s, Conway and his wife, Marty, joined Case Western Reserve University's Partnership for Family Business. Through the program and conversation with other business owners, Conway began to see the need for different points of view regarding the business, and he decided to establish an advisory board:

One of the things that sprang from the family business program was that we set up a board of advisors. The board consisted of four independent current and former company CEOs. It included my brother and my son, Stuart, who ran his own non-profit organization. Preparing for these meetings was a great discipline. The Board challenged me through a review process and an implied evaluation of my performance. These men had all managed their own businesses. From their advice, I learned that entrepreneurship alone isn't enough to generate continued growth. Management and systems become essential once a business reaches a sales volume of $10+ million or has 50+ employees.

These advisors helped the family better understand nonfamily management's needs and helped nonfamily managers appreciate the unique aspects of family firms. Most significantly, the board encouraged Conway to professionalize the staff and to build internal controls and an infrastructure (see Exhibit 6). The board had no statutory power but did provide good advice and served as a valuable sounding board.

After several unsuccessful hires, Conway named Don Kimmel as president. Kimmel was the perfect foil to Conway's creative vision and energy. He introduced a financial system and an organizational structure to complement the creative design and sales energy that had propelled the company for many years. Kimmel's strengths as a manager allowed Conway to shift out of the daily management role and focus on sales and product design, his strengths.

Under Kimmel's leadership and with the support of the advisory board, FFr began a rigorous strategic planning process in 1997. An internal analysis recommended that the company upgrade its management talent, consolidate its sales

EXHIBIT 6 ORGANIZATIONAL CHART OF FASTENERS FOR RETAIL, 1999

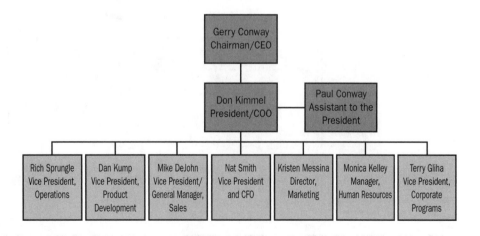

organization, and focus on selling to the major retail chains. These chains were rapidly expanding and represented a potential $600 million market. The needs of these retailers were different from those of FFr's traditional customers, so FFr created a program selling division and made other internal changes to address those needs. The company expanded its engineering, design, and in-house sales team to meet customer expectations. FFr revisited its previously inviolate margins and adjusted them to be price competitive. It began sharing cost and margin information with its suppliers, partnering with them to meet customer needs for design and price. The company made its first significant sale to Wal-Mart in 1998. A few years later, program sales to retailers accounted for over 20 percent of sales.

FAMILY INVOLVEMENT

Family involvement began in the 1970s when the Conway children earned extra money by putting adhesive on the backs of Arrowhead fasteners. They had all done odd jobs for FFr, but of the seven children only three worked in the business as adults (see Exhibit 7).

Initially, the children did not see joining FFr as a career option. During their formative years, the company was pretty much a one-man operation. In the words of one son, "There was nothing to join." As the company grew, several of the children began to consider joining the firm.

Kevin, the eldest, joined in the early 1980s and became an outstanding salesman. Kevin had Gerry's gift for sales and was frequently on the road, visiting cus-

EXHIBIT 7   CONWAY FAMILY TREE

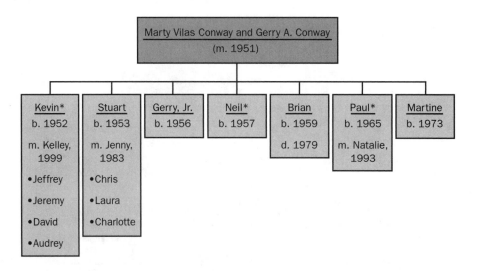

*Family members active in the business

tomers and closing on orders. Kevin worked at FFr for many years until health problems prompted him to resign.

From an early age, the youngest son, Paul, planned to join FFr. At his father's urging, he began his work career with another employer. It was only after he'd been successful there that he joined FFr in 1988; his first job was in the marketing department.

Neil, the fourth son, worked in the warehouse. Neil developed schizophrenia during his first year of college, and the structure of part-time employment in the warehouse worked well for him and for the company. As a result of the positive work experience with Neil, FFr hired other workers with neurobiological disorders.

It wasn't until the early 1990s that Gerry Conway began to focus on succession. His attention was driven by the company's success, his sons' active presence in FFr, and participation in the family business program. Through the program, the Conways were introduced to the components of a well-executed succession process, including strategic planning, communication and accommodation among family members through family meetings, estate planning for business agility, leveraging family skills with those of nonfamily managers, using outside board members as advisors, and promoting the development of the next generation.

Family meetings were a high point for Gerry's wife, Marty:

> From the family business program, we learned about family meetings. We had an outside facilitator at the first meeting, and it was marvelous—he had experiential learning games for us to play and different ways to communicate. By the third meeting, different family members were taking responsibility for planning activities for the meetings. The focus for the meetings shifted to the business of family from family business. Everyone in the family looked forward to the family meetings. They were a chance for us all to be together as a family. We talked about business and caught up with each other as family.

The family meetings were important to Gerry as well:

> Before we had family meetings, I kept pretty much everything to myself. I was not that open. One of the things I learned was the importance of communication. At the first meeting, there was a critical point where I had to remind my family that while this was a family business, I had to make the final operating decisions.

As adults, all seven next-generation members of the Conway family got along well and respected each other and each other's life and career choices. They also respected FFr—"the house that Gerry had built"—and the family values that Marty continued to nurture. Their sense of family unity was balanced by an appreciation for individual differences.

As part of their estate planning, Gerry and Marty created a trust and transferred the majority of their FFr shares to their children. However, Gerry retained voting rights. Family meetings began around this time and proved to be a useful way for the new owners, particularly those not active in managing the business, to learn more about the business and the estate.

ESTATE PLANNING

One of the goals of the Conways' estate plan was to transfer a substantial amount of the value of FFr to their children during their lifetime so as to avoid estate taxes, but to do so without relinquishing control of the company. Gerry and Marty knew that, by transferring sizable value while they were alive, they would avoid the 55 percent estate tax—not only on the value transferred but also on the future growth of the value transferred. In order to transfer value without relinquishing control, the company's stock was split into voting and non-voting shares. Non-voting shares were used for gifting purposes.

In addition, the Conways utilized a grantor-retained annuity trust (GRAT) for each child. In other words, the non-voting shares were transferred into a trust for each child, and the trusts required that Gerry and Marty, as grantors, receive an annuity (income stream) from the trusts for a period of years. The per-share value of the shares transferred was reduced by the present value of the annuity interest Gerry and Marty retained, meaning that they could give more shares away.

After a period of years, the GRATs terminated in accordance with the trust provisions. Children who were over 30 took their shares outright; the shares belonging to those who were not over 30 remained in successor trusts. In order to provide liquidity in the event of the untimely death of a shareholder, the Conways and their children entered into shareholders' agreements for the voting and non-voting shares. They funded the cross-purchase obligations in the agreements with life insurance policies, held in an insurance trust.

SUCCESSION: PAUL AND KEVIN'S STORIES

While Kevin was the first child to join FFr, he was never a candidate for CEO. Like so many excellent salesmen, he did not like managerial activities. As the company grew, his interest in it waned, in part because he disliked the increased number of systems that were implemented to support the company's growth.

Paul Conway joined FFr a few years after Kevin did. Paul's earliest memories were of working for FFr. When he was eight years old, he had put adhesive tape on the backs of 10,000 Arrowhead fasteners and had earned enough money to buy his first bicycle. An entrepreneur was born. Over the next 10 years, he and his friends continued to put adhesive on the backs of fasteners each time they needed spending money.

Paul began seriously imagining his future with FFr while he was in high school. He worked at FFr during college vacations and then joined another business after college graduation to gain additional work experience. After only one year, FFr's nonfamily marketing manager encouraged Paul and Gerry to negotiate Paul's entry into the company. Paul began work as a marketing assistant and sales representative and rotated through FFr's business units. Paul had clear ideas about how he wanted to be perceived:

I admired my Dad's knack for success and was happy to be with him in the business. Still, I wanted to make sure that I was not the typical SOB [son of boss]. I didn't want to take advantage of my family relationship or have people perceive that I was, even though I knew that some people would, no matter what I did.

Paul became the international sales manager and built FFr's international business while also maintaining a position in the marketing department. After 7 years, he became the marketing manager. Two years after that promotion, Paul was asked to become the assistant to the president, Don Kimmel. The timing of the offer was significant. FFr's rapid expansion had left Don without time for long-range planning. Adding Paul to the executive suite provided needed support and allowed Paul to learn the business from a different vantage point:

> I reached the Peter Principle as Marketing Manager. I didn't have formal training and the position was getting a little unwieldy for me. I just didn't have the tools, and Don needed help with management. Either I was going to use this new role as a launching pad or I was going to figure out that I didn't want to work at FFr anymore and would move on to something else.

For the first time in his career at FFr, Paul was working directly with his father on a regular basis. With greater access to management's decisions, he came to a realization about his future with FFr:

> I didn't like my Dad's management style. I'd always tell him about it, and we'd talk it through. We argued at times, but our arguments were always short-lived. It was as healthy an element of communication within our family as I had. But regardless of that, the disagreements were part of why the experience grew sour. I started to think about the reality of working in a larger corporation. When the business was smaller and a little more family-oriented, it was more enjoyable to me.

Paul worked for over a year to clarify his goals, first to understand what leading FFr would mean and then to explore other career opportunities. In his view, Gerry was able to manage the business because he had grown with it. Paul felt that he was less equipped than his Dad to manage the large and growing business (see Exhibit 8). Members of the advisory board felt that Paul could learn the job, if he wanted to, and that having an experienced management team in place would give him time to learn. One board member recalled:

> At the beginning of the succession process, Paul was really the only son who was actively involved in the company. I thought that Paul would become president and believed that he had the capability to do the job well.
>
> At one point, Paul said that he didn't want to be in the position of making some of the tough decisions. Now that is being very honest, but I think he was looking at the responsibilities and the pressures of being the CEO as being more than they needed to be. Gerry was a loner in the way he ran his business. Paul may not have realized that he could do the job differently—probably in a more decentralized and collaborative way. I kept wondering if there was something I might have done with respect to Paul that would have made him feel more comfortable in the potential role.

EXHIBIT 8	ANNUAL REVENUES FOR FASTENERS FOR RETAIL, 1994–2001

Year	Net Sales ($ millions)
1994	$18
1995	23
1996	29
1997	33
1998	41
1999	47
2000	52
2001	62

Gerry's brother, FFr board member Bill Conway, suggested that Paul give himself more time in the business before he made that decision. Paul thought about his choices for about a year and ultimately decided that he wanted to leave the company and become a teacher. The decision to leave FFr was not easy:

> I felt like I was the last of the Mohicans—the last possible guy to run the company. When I decided that I didn't want to do it, I felt guilty. . . . My Dad deserved a lot of credit. He really wanted to pass the business along to one of his children. After I said that I didn't want to stay in the business, he said "ok," and then we met as a family to discuss the implications.

SUCCESSION: MARTY'S POINT OF VIEW

Marty Conway was one of Gerry's chief advisors. While Gerry was the obvious leader of the company, it was Marty who signed the checks and kept an eye on corporate finances. She had a public role at company functions and was a people booster. She played a more significant role behind the scenes, supporting Gerry as he considered important business changes, such as handing over the administrative reins or making personnel changes. Both family members and outsiders described Marty as the glue that worked behind the scenes to hold the family together through the predictable challenges that families who work together face. She summed up Paul's role at FFr as follows:

> When Paul would come over, Gerry and Paul would talk business all the time, which used to drive me crazy. But that was just part of their life together. The only person I really talked to about the business in terms of succession was Paul. When Paul was young, he said, "Someday, I am going to grow up and I am going to run the company."
>
> After he graduated from college he went to work. . . . Gerry's advice to all of them had been if you want to join the company, you have got to go out in the real world first. Paul worked very hard for an insurance company and won salesman of the year during his first year. At that point, FFr was just starting to grow. I said, "If you really want to get involved in this company, now is the time." So Gerry took him in then.

About 10 years later, Paul looked into his heart and said, "I don't want to succeed my Dad." He could see the stress building up in Gerry as the company grew, and he didn't want that for himself. At one of the board meetings, Paul said, "I don't think I want to run the company."

SUCCESSION: GERRY'S DILEMMA

Gerry Conway was a passionate entrepreneur, a business builder. During the early part of his career, he traveled extensively, meeting customers and serving as chief salesman, marketer, and innovator for the company. Whether he was on the road or in the office, his presence was felt throughout the organization.

Conway's life had been organized around his family and his company. For almost four decades, home and work were the center of his life—his passion and his zeal. He had always thought of them as being joined. Suddenly, that didn't seem possible any more:

> Kevin was out of the picture. Stuart had, long ago, decided that he didn't want to work in the business. Paul recently had decided he didn't want the responsibility. None of the other kids were interested. At the same time, I felt frustrated every day as I tried to handle this big company. I thought it was time to move on.

Then, his thoughts shifted to his personal situation, and he said to himself,

> Oh my God, what am I going to do with the rest of my life? I hadn't done a tremendous amount of planning on the retirement side. I had done some, but the demands of running a business didn't leave a lot of time.

As Conway contemplated the future of FFr, his management team put the finishing touches on the company's new strategic plan. The plan made a strong and well-supported case for making a significant capital investment to develop fulfillment capabilities, to consider manufacturing selected items, to expand sales internationally, and to increase the product line through strategic acquisitions.

Conway intuitively knew that the time for the business to aggressively explore these growth opportunities had arrived. Funding the plan would take all the cash out of the business and would also require outside financing. A combined advisory board and family council meeting was scheduled for the following week. It was time for Conway to decide what action to take.

CASE QUESTIONS

1. What was Gerry Conway doing to lead these three key constituencies: (a) nonfamily employees, (b) family members working in the business, and (c) other family shareholders?

2. What managerial and governance best practices was Gerry Conway relying on to promote family business continuity? Please discuss each practice and how it was used.

3. What do you predict will happen in this case? Explain your reasoning.

CASE 6:
THE VEGA FOOD COMPANY

In February 1997, Francisco Valle, Jr., president of Industrias La Vega, organized the first family council meeting in the owning family's history in order to address problems he was having with his youngest sister, Mari, a shareholder in the company. He felt that the problems were not of his making and were interfering with his management of the company. Francisco, 45, had worked closely with his father, Francisco Sr., since 1976 and had become president of the company in March 1994, when his 72 year-old father was killed in an automobile accident. Industrias La Vega was a Spanish meat-processing business that produced hams, sausages, and other delicacies for domestic and export markets. The $104.8 million-a-year business was demanding, of course, but Francisco Jr. felt most challenged by the family conflicts that often overwhelmed him.

The ownership structure of Industrias La Vega had been updated just months before the tragic accident involving Francisco Sr. At the request of Francisco Jr., who was concerned about the possible loss of control of the enterprise he had co-managed with his father for years, Francisco Sr. and his attorneys had created two classes of stock. The voting A shares did not pay dividends. The non-voting but dividend-bearing B shares had a par value 10 times higher than that of the A shares.

Except for brief stints, none of the Valle daughters had worked in the business prior to their father's death. Ana, the second eldest daughter, was an artist, and she had been instrumental in designing the image and logo of a new premium product line. Working alongside her father, she had created the look for the Gold Label line of meats and cold cuts, Francisco Jr. had not been particularly enthusiastic about this new line.

Mari, 27, the youngest of the Valle siblings, was concerned about her future and the security of her own young family after her father's death. She worried about how her interests as a shareholder would be protected. She had trusted her father completely, but she was not sure she had the same faith in Francisco Jr.

She did admit to being a little more optimistic now that Francisco was making an effort to get closer to the lower-level employees and be more of a leader in the company. As it turned out, Francisco was not just his father's successor in the company, but also in politics. His father had won a Senate seat in the last elections before his tragic accident. Francisco campaigned for and won the seat and served what would have been his father's term. Mari and his four other sisters would chide Francisco about being so effective in his political campaigning and yet so unable to instill a team spirit among the company's employees. He was, in fact, still spending three to four days a week on political endeavors.

This case was prepared by Professor Ernesto J. Poza as the basis for a class discussion rather than to illustrate the effective or ineffective handling of a family business management situation. For permission to publish this case, grateful acknowledgment is made to the chairman and the executive vice president of the company. Note that while the case is factually and historically accurate, the names have been changed to protect the privacy of the family.

The farmers and cattle ranchers of whom Francisco Sr. had been a life-long customer trusted him. As a major customer for their products, he had much influence with them. His successful run for the Senate at the age of 72 was evidence of the degree of this influence, even outside of business circles. In the food-processing industry, good relations with the government represented an asset for the Valle family, from which both generations derived competitive advantage.

THE VALLE FAMILY

The Valle family was wealthy by the standards of the small town in which they had most of their production facilities. Francisco Valle, Sr., was a self-made entrepreneur. He married Isabel in 1947 and had five daughters and a son (see Exhibit 1). In 1997, Valle family members included Isabel, 71, Francisco Sr.'s widow; Rosa, 47; Francisco Jr., 45; Ana, 42; María, 38; Tere, 33, and Mari, 27. Of these, only Francisco Jr. and Tere worked in management positions. And Tere had joined the company only three years earlier.

Relations between family members were warm, particularly among the women, though several next-generation members had created very different lives for themselves. Rosa and Maria lived overseas but visited Isabel two or three times a year. The only son, Francisco Jr., had studied agribusiness overseas and then returned to run the family business.

In a traditional display of primogeniture, Francisco seemed pre-ordained to be the successor to his father. He took his responsibilities toward his mother and sisters seriously, although they all complained a little about not being involved enough, not being kept sufficiently informed, and not being treated the same way Francisco

| EXHIBIT 1 | VALLE FAMILY TREE |

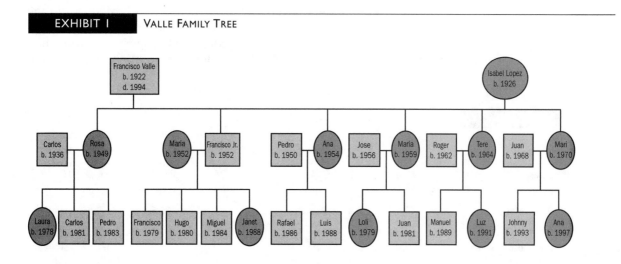

Key: Squares: Male; Ovals: Female

was treated by the company. Francisco received a reasonable CEO salary, bonus, and benefits package. But the sisters' dividends were nowhere close to his take-home pay, and Francisco, with his expensive tastes, seemed to flaunt the difference. A palatial home, luxury car, helicopter, boat, and assorted other "toys" all seemed essential to Francisco in his executive post. A couple of the sisters were divorced and had additional financial responsibilities toward their own children. Even Isabel lived in a more modest house and drove a less expensive car than Francisco did.

Family members characterized themselves as being "hermetically sealed," meaning that they were not great communicators. This was particularly true on the subject of money; the few conversations about finances that took place were one on one and had the quality of family gossip. Tere remembers one of her sisters saying, "Is it true that you receive 1 percent of the company's profits and Francisco gets 10 percent? That is robbery!" Francisco was often the target of the gossip, but mostly he ignored it, except for telling himself and his advisors, "After all, I have been the one working the business for more than 20 years now."

There was plenty of evidence of love, caring, and tenderness in the family. There was less evidence of respect for titles, organizational structure, hard work, reporting relationships, institutions, and formality of any kind. The family seemed ill equipped for financial responsibility. In the past, dividends had been distrib-uted infrequently. Individual family members' needs were brought to the atten-tion of Francisco Sr., who usually granted requests, as a generous father would. For Mari, the youngest daughter, who grew up surrounded by evidence of the family's wealth, and for other siblings who needed money for new houses or trips, asking was often akin to receiving.

FAMILY COUNCIL MEETING, FEBRUARY 1997

Francisco took the initiative in sponsoring this first family council meeting. It fol-lowed a day-long shareholders' meeting, where financial information and the state of the business were discussed with shareholders. The news for shareholders was not great. Although company sales had continued to increase, profits had plummeted in the last couple of years, and dividend distributions had been cut (see Exhibit 2).

EXHIBIT 2	FINANCIAL RESULTS FOR INDUSTRIAS LA VEGA, 1992–1999							
	1992	1993	1994	1995	1996	1997	1998	1999
Sales	42.5	51.7	57.4	69.4	84.1	104.8	112.6	109.7
Cost of Sales	32.1	36.6	41.1	52.6	62.6	78.2	79.6	74.9
Gross Margin	10.4	15.1	16.3	16.8	21.5	26.6	33.0	34.8
Administration Expenses	5.6	10.2	11.9	13.3	19.6	18.8	22.4	22.7
Interest Expenses	0.0	0.0	0.0	0.0	0.0	3.1	4.4	5.6
Net Profit	4.8	4.9	4.4	3.5	1.9	4.7	6.2	6.5

With Tere's help, Francisco had interviewed and selected the family business advisor who facilitated the family council meeting. The consultant had conducted a private meeting with every member of the family. A few days prior to the meeting, Mari told the family business consultant,

> It is important that each of us know what we have, what we don't, and what we can and cannot do as shareholders. We have to speak clearly about these things. Right now, bringing up the subject is taboo. We need more transparency in all of this. We need to recognize that we are all siblings here.

Tere observed, in her meeting with the advisor,

> The reason for these meetings is that we need Industrias La Vega to continue as a family business. In order for that to happen, Francisco needs to be supervised. There has to be more balance between Francisco and the sisters. Those inside the company have to live by corporate rules, manage with transparency, and meet the needs of the inactive shareholders. There has been too much centralization by Francisco. Financial information about the company has to be sent out regularly and explained in such a way that all shareholders understand it. Without this education, there will be no sense of justice. But don't get me wrong; we love each other a lot. We have grown in family unity. My mother is a very strong woman and a very steadying influence.

Isabel expressed her own expectations of the meeting this way:

> In the interests of the family and the business, everything has to come out well defined and organized. Things have to be clear for everybody, after some discussion and reflection, so that there is no second-guessing later.

The meeting started with the setting of meeting goals and behavioral norms for constructive problem solving and conflict resolution. Feedback from the conversations with the family business consultant was provided for family members to discuss, clarify, and then use to build an agenda that responded to the identified needs, problems, and opportunities. Selected as the top two priority items on the agenda were (1) the lack of clarity and organization in the ownership structure, estate plan, and financial reporting mechanisms for shareholders and (2) the lack of a well-organized family forum and board of directors. Board meetings existed only on paper, and only family members were on the board. While a mini–family business presentation made by the consultant early in the meeting may have influenced the selection of topics, both Tere and Francisco had attended a family business course for next-generation members and had been convinced of the need for both of these governance bodies. Obviously, their opinions had significant influence in the larger shareholder group. Other topics selected for discussion included the need to define the responsibilities of shareholders toward the business and of managers toward shareholders, the need to define the rules guiding relations between members of the family acting as suppliers or subcontractors to the company, and the third-generation scholarship fund.

By the end of this first family council meeting, an action plan had been drafted that directed various family members to review the ownership structure and the possession of stock certificates, retain a valuation expert to perform a company valuation, review and account for the family benefits that individual members had been granted in order to make appropriate decisions regarding family bene-fits in the next shareholder meeting, and continue to schedule open conversations about what shareholders wanted from the business—things like higher dividends, more reinvestment for long-term growth, and liquidity of shareholdings via buy–sell agreements. An agreement was reached among family members that the company hierarchy would be respected, and any information required by share-holders regarding the company and its finances would be directed to Francisco, the president, and not to accounting department personnel. Francisco, in return, agreed to respond to such requests in a timely manner. Shareholders also reached other agreements regarding the expectations they had of management and what management could rightfully expect of shareholders.

Finally, a discussion on family business boards produced a consensus on the desirability of a board with independent outsiders and a list of board responsibil-ities. These responsibilities were to promote the continuity of the business, review the strategy of the business, review and approve financial reports and budgets, review the compensation of key executives, and provide oversight on large capital investment decisions. The criteria for selecting board members were to be devel-oped by a task force made up of Francisco, Tere, and Rosa. The selection of inde-pendent board members themselves and the holding of the first board meeting were deemed to be the responsibilities of Francisco, though shareholders wanted to be consulted.

FAMILY COUNCIL MEETING, SEPTEMBER 1997

The next family council meeting was held in September 1997. This meeting addressed three new topics: (1) the family foundation (a study of its various proj-ects in the past five years had been done), (2) college scholarships for members of the third generation, and (3) the possibility of selling a couple of parcels of com-pany farmland. The bulk of the meeting was focused on following up on the action plans drafted at the February meeting. While there had been much progress on many fronts, shareholder information, company valuation, and liquidity con-cerns had not been addressed by the time this second meeting was held. And a new board of directors or advisory board had not been assembled.

MARI BRINGS IN THE ATTORNEYS

The semi-annual family council meeting was scheduled to take place in May 1998. Mari felt sick and checked herself into a hospital for observation. This precluded her from attending the meeting. Instead, she sent two attorneys whom she and her husband had retained to put pressure on Francisco for fuller disclosure of corpo-rate financial information. The family council meeting was canceled after a brief conversation with the attorneys to determine the nature of their involvement.

Francisco was very upset and quite worried that if the company's accounting and financial records were scrutinized, they would be found lacking and this would create more chaos and family disharmony and possibly even result in legal ramifications. The business, as a result of a very strong entrepreneurial culture and unsophisticated financial and administrative systems, had very unsophisticated accounting procedures. Francisco Sr. had never been very concerned about establishing such systems. Now, the responsibility for historical reconstruction of financial information had fallen on Francisco Jr. He said,

> That was the reason that I could not be any clearer with shareholders about the books than I was. I was not hiding anything; they had the same information I had available to me. But I knew how shrewd those two attorneys that Mari hired were, and I was very worried for the family and the business's reputation.

In the aftermath of the family council meeting, Francisco stayed very close to his mother, Isabel, and consulted her often on what to do. But, of course, all of this was very hard on her, as she did not want this to be the legacy of her very successful late husband. Francisco respected Isabel's wisdom and her ability to influence her daughters. Mari had hired the lawyers, but most of her sisters were secretly rooting for her. They too wanted to better understand what they considered to be rightfully theirs. Isabel talked to her daughters on many occasions during that period about the importance of preserving the family and about the need to give Francisco time to run the company, get things in shape, and show them what he could do. But her arguments did not dissuade Mari, who continued her inquiry through her attorneys.

About this time, company and family attorneys finally unraveled the details of the estate plan. It was determined that upon Francisco Sr.'s death, Francisco Jr. held 50 percent of the voting A shares and 20 percent of the non-voting dividend-bearing B shares. Each of his five sisters owned 15 percent of the B shares, and Isabel retained 5 percent of the B shares and the remaining 50 percent of the voting shares. Voting control therefore rested in the hands of the founder's surviving spouse and Francisco Jr., the successor president.

Hurt and disillusioned by Mari's actions, Francisco began the process of negotiating with Mari and her attorneys for a buy-out of her shares. On the advice of her mother-in-law, an influential banker in town, Mari asked for $10 million, but she was offered $4 million instead. During the last round of negotiations, Francisco, concerned about the future of both the family and the business, agreed to $6 million on an installment basis—a price he considered exorbitant but worth the peace of mind and the ability to move on, both of which he so desperately wanted. Mari agreed to this offer and sold all of her shares to Francisco, who, as a result, now owned 35 percent of the B shares.

FAMILY COUNCIL AND SHAREHOLDERS' MEETINGS, OCTOBER 1999

Family council meetings were not held for over a year, while the wrangling and negotiations were going on. In October 1999, family members held their next family council and shareholders' meetings. (Mari, who was no longer a shareholder, decided not to attend either meeting.) The agenda for the one-day shareholders' meeting and the additional day for the family council meeting included discussion of a draft of a shareholder buy–sell agreement, discussion of the new dividend distribution policy, and discussion of a draft of a family constitution. The family constitution included an emergency contingency plan naming Tere, the one sister active in management, as the successor if something should happen to Francisco.

THE PRUNED FAMILY TREE GROWS

All this upheaval and animosity did have several positive side effects. Francisco dedicated himself fully to the business. He fired several members of the top management team who were hurting his efforts to professionalize the business, replacing them with competent key managers. Concurrently, he began to successfully execute a growth strategy that had been in the planning stages for several years. In 1998, revenues and net profit rose to $112.6 and $6.2 million, respectively. Then, in 1999, when revenues went down slightly, to $109.7 million, net profit rose to $6.5 million (see Exhibit 2). Starting in 1998, dividends increased significantly, which gained Francisco much respect with shareholders (see Exhibit 3).

Francisco retained a financial consultant as the CFO and, to his delight, found that this CFO knew as much about business as he did about finance and was a great general manager. Francisco now had key nonfamily managers whose skills complemented those that he and Tere brought to the corporation. Together, they turned things around dramatically and increased company profitability.

While Mari achieved her goal of liquidity and personal oversight over her own inheritance, the other family members re-committed themselves to the business and stayed involved. The work of the family foundation continued. The foundation was successful in getting a highway named in memory of Francisco Sr., and all the family members got together to honor and celebrate the family's proud past. The increased participation by the Valle sisters in committees, task forces, the family council, shareholders' meetings, and the family foundation led to a greater sense of transparency and ownership. As they walked to a shareholders' meeting in the spring of 2000, Ana reflected on the changes:

> A long time ago, my father gave one of my siblings $650,000 to buy a house. Francisco has been adjusting distributions to equalize us all with that gift. After that, we will receive our dividends based on our ownership stake and company profitability. Dividends have increased. We receive company information. There is a great effort to be fair. We've come a long way.

EXHIBIT 3	DIVIDENDS FOR INDUSTRIAS LA VEGA, 1995–1999
1995	$181,000
1996	$322,000
1997	$639,000
1998	$1,256,000
1999	$1,488,000

CASE QUESTIONS

1. What are the key facts of this case? List the factors that, in your opinion, led Mari to sell her shares.

2. Would you have called a family council meeting when Francisco Jr. did? Why, or why not?

3. To what do you attribute the improvement in Valle family–business relationships over the last couple of years?

4. What major issues should Francisco and the rest of the Valle family continue to address in order to ensure the survival of the business? Select one to three issues, and support your selection with the facts of the case.

5. What actions should Francisco take next? What should he do to promote shareholder loyalty and the effective governance of the family–business relationship in the future?

CASE 7:
THE FERRÉ MEDIA GROUP

This is a very successful family corporation. *El Nuevo Día* enjoys the highest circulation of any newspaper in Puerto Rico, and the three-year-old *Primera Hora* is the fastest growing daily. Combined, they dominate the market for news and advertising on the island. Our family name has the highest recognition factor in all of Puerto Rico, according to a recent survey. But as we move the enterprise to members of the next generation, how do we nurture a culture of cooperation and communication vs. sibling and branch rivalries as the extended family grows? How do we integrate their spouses into what they are doing, to what they are working so hard to build? For that matter, what should we be doing to prepare the generation after that, for stewardship and the continuity of this family enterprise?

—Antonio Luis Ferré, Chairman, Grupo Ferré Rangel

These were the questions that Antonio Luis Ferré, chairman of the Grupo Ferré Rangel, was asking himself as he pondered the next phase of the multi-year succession process he had been leading since 1993. At stake were a media and publishing empire and a family that was an icon in Puerto Rico. *El Nuevo Día* and the Ferré family were among the most trusted institutions in the country, and the paper's editorials and news coverage calmed or roiled political life on the island. Its

This case was prepared by Professor Ernesto J. Poza as the basis for a class discussion rather than to illustrate the effective or ineffective handling of a family business management situation. For permission to publish this case, grateful acknowledgment is made to Antonio Luis Ferré, chairman, and María Luisa Ferré Rangel, president, Grupo Ferré Rangel.

investigations made or broke administrations and governors. Five next-generation members were either already successfully running business units or in leadership positions in the editorial departments of the newspapers or in the holding company. The Grupo Ferré Rangel consisted of publishing and other media, printing, recycling, real estate, a family venture capital fund, and, until recently, a controlling stake in Puerto Rican Cement, an NYSE-listed company with $250 million in annual revenues.[1]

AN ENTERPRISING FAMILY TRADITION

Antonio Luis Ferré's grandfather had founded Puerto Rican Cement in 1944. Luis A. Ferré, his successor and Antonio's father, had earned an engineering degree from MIT before joining the growing company, into which he eventually brought his sons. Antonio joined Puerto Rican Cement in 1955, after graduating from Amherst College. He received his M.B.A. from the Harvard Business School in 1957. At Puerto Rican Cement, he worked first in production and labor relations, later becoming general manager and eventually president of the company. But by the mid-1960s, amid tension and sibling rivalry, Antonio and his brothers agreed to divide up the companies and their shares rather than risk further family disharmony.

In 1968, Luis A. Ferré was elected governor of Puerto Rico. That same year, Antonio paid his father $400,000 for the struggling small newspaper *El Día*, located in the southern city of Ponce. Antonio nurtured the dream of turning *El Día* into the largest and most influential newspaper in Puerto Rico. He preferred the news business to the cement business because of its involvement in politics and the world of words and ideas, as well as its deep roots in the community. He nevertheless continued serving as president of Puerto Rican Cement. He led this firm as it became the first Latin American company to be listed on the NYSE, and eventually he became its chairman.

Antonio moved operations of the small *El Día* to the capital city of San Juan, and on May 18, 1970, he published the first edition of *El Nuevo Día* (ENDI). As its name implied, the new daily would be different, modern, and dynamic. It would have a fresh new tabloid look and display its agility with independent and informative news coverage.

ENDI's first editorial, entitled "What We Believe," declared that the publisher did not wish to just create one more newspaper, one more business, but rather express the aspirations of a people. It stated, "We want to be a manifestation of the new Puerto Rico and the new Puerto Rican." The editorial went on to assert that as a public trust, the pages of *El Nuevo Día* would always be open to those who, with respect for the reader and Puerto Rico's well being, wanted to express their thoughts and opinions to others. *El Nuevo Día*, the editorial further declared, would fight crime and corruption and bring to light the social ills that beset the people of Puerto Rico so that, as citizens, they might better understand the social problems they confronted. This first edition consisted of 32 pages, and the printing was outsourced. Competition at the time consisted of two very successful large-circulation Spanish language newspapers—*El Mundo* and *El Imparcial*—and an English language newspaper, the *San Juan Star*.

Only two and a half years after its founding, *El Nuevo Día* had become an important editorial voice. Its circulation grew from 40,000 to about 120,000 in the next five years, as its competitors folded. *El Mundo* and *El Imparcial*, newspapers with afternoon editions, got into financial trouble, and *El Imparcial* ceased publication. In the mid-1970s, when ENDI covered and investigated corruption in the ranks of the police on the western part of the island, it was denounced as irresponsible and sensationalist. Sued in federal district court by the police department, *El Nuevo Día* confronted the first of what would be a series of attacks on its journalistic independence. The continuing coverage of corruption and abuses and excesses by the executive and legislative branches of the government would forge a stronger character and a new journalistic image for the paper. Its growth accelerated, and by 1978 the new daily had surpassed the circulation of its largest rival, *El Mundo*, and become the largest print advertising medium. By the mid-1980s, daily circulation had grown to about 180,000, and by 1990 circulation had surpassed 200,000 copies.

In 1995, when *El Nuevo Día* celebrated its 25th anniversary, it counted among its honors being among the top 10 Spanish-Portuguese language newspapers in Latin America; being ranked among the top 45 dailies, by circulation, in the United States; and being a source of employment for close to 1,000 dedicated people. During the celebration ceremonies, Carlos Cabrera, one of the newspaper's mailroom employees, remembered how in the mid-1980s, after a fire broke out in the old press building, he and others had joined in fighting the blaze before the firemen arrived. After the fire was controlled, Antonio Luis Ferré came and personally thanked him for his efforts. Cabrera remembered saying to his colleagues, "An owner like him is very hard to find. That is why everybody wants to work here—they know it is a great company." Cabrera went on to highlight the strong culture of cooperation and caring that the founder had built. (Exhibit 1 shows the mission statement of *El Nuevo Día*.)

El Nuevo Día had grown to an average of 206 pages an issue, with a circulation of approximately 230,000 issues daily and 245,000 issues on Sunday. New sections and features kept the product young and fresh. It held a 70 percent share of the advertising market and was now being printed in color. Diversification was being pursued, and a series of companies—some related to publishing, others not—had been founded. By the late 1990s, the Grupo Ferré Rangel consisted of two newspapers, including ENDI and the young *Primera Hora*; El Día Directo, a telemarketing company; Virtual, Inc., an Internet portal and electronic version of *El Nuevo Día*; Pronatura, a recycling company; Advanced Graphics Printing; City View Plaza, a real estate development company; and a family venture capital company (that included El Norte Acquisitions, Inc., and El Horizonte Acquisitions, Inc.). Antonio Luis Ferré and his five sons and daughters all worked in the company, holding key positions with profit and loss responsibility in the businesses and editorial responsibilities in the newspapers. (Exhibit 2 provides a chart showing the companies under family control.)

EXHIBIT 1   The Mission Statement of *El Nuevo Día*

Our Mission

El Nuevo Día is a family enterprise, a leader in the communications industry, committed to excellence on behalf of its customers. As a communications medium, with editorial independence, we keep citizens informed, serve as a free forum of ideas, and disseminate democratic and cultural values with the intent of promoting a fairer society.

Our Creed

Integrity, Respect and Humility

Customer Service

Excellence

Leadership

Profitability

Spirit of Enterprise

Open Communications

Teamwork

Socially Responsible and Community Responsive

EXHIBIT 2   Grupo Ferré Rangel Companies

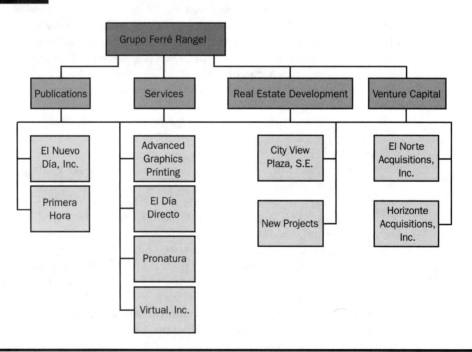

THE FERRÉ RANGEL FAMILY

Antonio Luis Ferré married Luisa Rangel in 1968. She was the daughter of a successful bank president who, in 1960, had migrated to Puerto Rico from Cuba. Antonio considered his marriage to be his most important and best decision. Luisa, he says, influenced him tremendously through her counsel; she placed great emphasis on keeping the family informed and nurturing the participation of the children in the family and the business. Luisa held a variety of positions within *El Nuevo Día* over the years, including book review editor; more recently, she led the Ferré Rangel family foundation. She was also on the board of directors of *El Nuevo Día* and the Grupo Ferré Rangel, the holding company. Their five children—María Luisa, 38; Luis Alberto, 36; his twin brother, Antonio Luis (Toño); María Eugenia (Mañu), 35; and Loren, 32—were all married and had children of their own (see Exhibit 3).

Antonio and Luisa believed that the succession process began before the beginning. In other words, the way they brought up and educated their children had much bearing on the family's ability to both attract to the enterprise and retain in the enterprise the very capable members of the next generation. They lived by the maxim "Plenty of love, equally distributed." They paid attention to the unique needs and potential of each individual child as he or she grew. They communicated frequently with each of them. The women in the family maintained that tradition into adulthood, calling each other daily, while the men reputedly had less frequent contact with each other and the female family members. All next-generation family members considered themselves ambitious and equally capable. They were encouraged not to harbor rivalries but rather to enjoy things as a group. The

| EXHIBIT 3 | FERRÉ RANGEL FAMILY TREE |

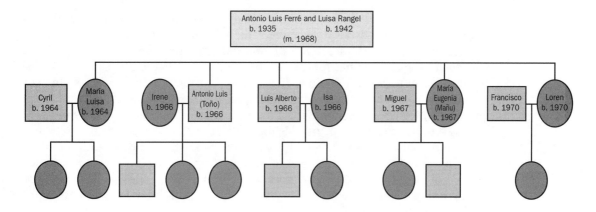

Key: Squares: Male; Ovals: Female
Note: Grandchildren's names are not included to protect the family's privacy.

household they grew up in was disciplined and orderly; respect for every member of the family was a key tenet. Besides working together, they played together— tennis and other sports were part of the family tradition.

At an early age, the Ferré Rangel children were told that their only inheritance would be their education. The rest was up to them, and therefore seeking excellence and doing things well would be important to their future. As they grew into adulthood, they had the advantage of good schools, summer educational experiences, and the careful selection of colleges and graduate schools. Their involvement in the business began while they were still in college, but their jobs in the company after graduation emphasized a ground-up approach. They all worked in lower-level jobs, whether as writers, researchers, reporters, or administrators, and generally reported to nonfamily managers. They were mentored and received feedback on their performance, both from their direct supervisor and from their parents, who oversaw their development. The adult siblings considered it critical that they agree on business goals, since they could all conceivably want to be president of the company.

Antonio Luis Ferré, ENDI's founder, had been president and editor-publisher for 25 years. As he began to transfer his power, he insisted that the next generation pay attention to the details. Antonio felt that the newspaper business lived and died by those details and, over the long term, by its reputation for responsible citizenship and journalistic independence. He considered himself a very good role model for the next generation on this issue and a few others. He believed that the best way to lead was by example: "Luisa and I are good role models of a strong work ethic, compassion and love towards others, integrity and Christian values, respect for others and their ideas, steadfastness, and a good marriage."

FAMILY COUNCIL MEETINGS

In 1993, the Ferré Rangel family began to meet regularly as a family to discuss family and business issues. Collectively, they developed a family constitution, a document that guided succession planning discussions for several years. In it, they established guidelines for the involvement of family members and the eventual transition across generations. The family constitution included a statement of family values; criteria for employing family members and restricting the employment of in-laws; behavioral expectations of next-generation members involved in the company; principles regarding the relations between family and nonfamily managers; guidelines for decision making, including Antonio's tie-breaking role during the next five to seven years; policies for the performance reviews of next-generation members; and a commitment to the professional management of the family-owned enterprise by both family members and key nonfamily executives.

Family council meetings, which were held monthly, were given top priority in the busy schedules of all the owner-managers. These half-day meetings included discussions about the business, investments, the succession process, conflicts between the siblings or between family and nonfamily managers, relationships between family members, and stress management. Any emerging conflicts were addressed. Discussion of individual aspirations was encouraged. According to one in-law, family dynamics improved as a result of the meetings: "I am a lot more confident and optimistic since these family meetings started and the brothers and sisters started communicating more and more regularly. It takes time to express and listen to other opinions and understand the different perspectives. Without it, and without accommodating others' ideas, all you are doing is competing."

Family harmony and family unity were given the utmost priority in these meetings, and through much communication, listening, and compromising, trust was built. These family-only meetings became the family council.

In 1995, the first family weekend retreat was held. It included the spouses of next-generation members. The meeting began with a review of the goals for the meeting and development of behavioral norms for an effective meeting, including timeliness, open and honest communication, not taking things personally, assuming that everyone attending had only the best intentions, the suspension of business hierarchy in the discussions, no interruptions, and 100 percent participation.

Spouses were then briefed on the state of the business (financial results, strategy of the various business units, and new developments) with the intention of leveling the playing field for all participants. Later in the retreat, the family reflected on its legacy and recommitted to several core values that it wanted to pass on to the next generation. Subsequently, the family developed a mission statement for its principal holding, *El Nuevo Día*, and for the Ferré Rangel family. The family mission statement acknowledged the important role of spouses in a supportive role vis-à-vis the family members who worked in the family enterprise. Several spouses had demanding careers of their own in other fields.

In response to the next generation's growing understanding of the challenge that their diversity represented and their growing appreciation of how they complemented each other, a learning exercise on the zero-sum propensities of families in business was carried out. Their interdependence, they concluded, represented strength. Antonio Luis Ferré established a preliminary time frame for the multi-year succession process. Recognizing all the work that needed to be done in order to be ready for the transition, given the complexity of the enterprise, he called for a transition of power by the year 2004. This represented a nine-year focused effort on next-generation development. Future steps were agreed to, including the scheduling of a follow-up family retreat.

Over the next several years, these annual retreats continued to update spouses on the family enterprise, promote analysis and discussion of family business cases with relevance to the family's current situation, nurture candid discussion about the unique skills and career aspirations of various next-generation members, and review the dynamic vision for the family and the firm (see Exhibit 4). Preliminary designs for the holding company, which was to become the Grupo Ferré Rangel, were also drafted at these meetings.

> As he prepared himself for a family retreat, Antonio recalled, I had set 2004 as the target date for the transition because I wanted us to plan and be disciplined about doing what

---

EXHIBIT 4   VISIONS FOR THE GRUPO FERRÉ RANGEL, AS STATED AT FAMILY RETREATS

Grupo Ferré Rangel Vision 2000 (Developed in 1997)

We continue to let larger, more highly capitalized media and communications firms experiment with the new technology. By lagging somewhat in the adoption process, we will be knowledgeable of the latest advances while remaining flexible and more able to capitalize on unique growth opportunities. All new growth opportunities have enjoyed profit margins equal to or better than those obtained by our benchmark company, *El Nuevo Día*. We are being increasingly more strategic in our thinking, which has led to new business units in advertising, communications, entertainment, and information. We have captured the core competence of the newspaper—content (knowledge and information)—and made it available via a variety of media or channels of distribution that we also own.

Grupo Ferré Rangel Vision 2005 (Developed in 1997)

El Nuevo Día dominates the advertising market with a 30 percent market share of the total market and 70 percent of the printed media market. Its reporting is leading edge, utilizing the latest technology to give customers the best and most readable information. Perspective, analysis, and research/investigation are as much a part of the daily newspaper as is reporting. We have maintained net profit levels of 15 percent, thereby protecting our financial and, most importantly, our journalistic independence.

Our Internet site is considered the primary source of information on Puerto Rico by U.S. companies and others interested in doing business on the island.

Our structure is that of business units with different strategic profiles, all reporting to the holding company—the Grupo Ferré Rangel. We realized that running the collection of businesses as an ownership team was impractical, and the holding company allowed us to clearly delineate responsibilities and hold key family and nonfamily managers accountable while nurturing family unity.

As a family, we have been able to advance a series of communication and information technologies through businesses that are as essential to the infrastructure of the Puerto Rico of tomorrow as Puerto Rican Cement was essential to the infrastructure of Puerto Rico's past growth and development.

---

we needed to do to be ready. But I started noticing some impatience with the process, a certain rush to the presidency, that I found quite troubling. I wanted to be able to remain as a mentor and advisor to the leaders of the next generation and not feel pushed out. So I brought it up in a family meeting prior to the retreat, and we discussed and reached agreements on what the 2004 transition point meant and didn't mean. My sons and daughters were actually very relieved by my statement that I wanted to continue to be a supportive advisor after transferring my power to them. One of them, I believe it as María Eugenia, even said, "Dad we want you to continue as our partner."

THE NEXT GENERATION

Between 1997 and 2002, every member of the next generation grew into a position of significant responsibility. Antonio's son Toño joined Puerto Rican Cement. He worked in production and then management and eventually became the fourth-generation president of the company. He reported to a key nonfamily executive, Luis Nazario, then CEO of the company.

Daughter Loren played a key role in the development of City View Plaza, a real estate development that appealed to her artistic and design capabilities. She later became the marketing manager who helped launch *Primera Hora*. María Eugenia became president of *El Nuevo Día*, the flagship newspaper, which is a major employer, an asset-intensive company, and a public trust. The paper requires both visible leadership in the community and administrative acumen in the company—a perfect fit for María Eugenia's capabilities. Luis Alberto became the paper's editor. He changed much of the editorial style and substance, while retaining the respect and loyalty of the independent souls in the newsroom. As president of the holding company, María Luisa led the Grupo in its strategic renewal.

Next-generation members continued their education and leadership development work in academic and seminar settings, but their true education was occurring not in the classroom but in the workplace. They were getting feedback from the work itself, their direct supervisors, and Antonio Luis Ferré. He regularly scheduled meetings with top family managers and acted as their mentor and senior advisor.

Along with developmental opportunities, the new roles of next-generation owner-managers brought visibility and profit and loss implications, both of which increased the amount of work they had to do. There was little time for anything other than work. Workdays were long and arduous. The balance between work and family life was being threatened. According to some, family communications and, thus, investments in family relationships and family unity suffered during this period. Luisa acted as the chief trust officer, keeping the family side on the agenda. She provided help to keep the family together at a time when the speed and intensity of developments appeared likely to throw the family into chaos. Some next-generation members helped her in this role.

THE EXTENDED BUSINESS FAMILY

During this rush to the presidency, the family appeared less united in the eyes of key nonfamily managers. Family members had to come to grips with the fact that differences of opinion or priorities among Ferré Rangel family members were providing opportunities for these nonfamily managers to take sides. Still, family members had much confidence in the level of professionalism of these managers.

A family council meeting produced an action plan to address the gaps in communication and to improve the family's relationships with key nonfamily managers during the entire succession transition period. The frequency of family and nonfamily management meetings was increased. Periodically, key nonfamily managers were invited to attend the family council meeting. Bridges were built to clarify the succession process and its direction for all involved, thereby reducing stress and unnecessary wear and tear on an important part of the fabric of the enterprise.

World-class professional managers had a long history in the Grupo. They had always held responsible positions in Puerto Rican Cement, whose latest CEO, Miguel Nazario, was not a family member. Various entrepreneurs had helped Antonio Luis Ferré launch *El Nuevo Día*. For instance, Carlos Castañeda had had editorial responsibilities at the Associated Press and *Visión* and had been the

Latin American editor for *Life* magazine before setting the framework and editorial style for the first edition. Antonio Arias, Fernando Sánchez, and Adolfo Comas Bacardí were all experienced top managers who had joined the firm and remained with it for the rest of their careers. The Grupo provided advancement opportunities and compensated managers with market-based pay and benefit plans. It also had a history of involving nonfamily managers in top-level decision making and in setting the direction of the company. However, the entry of five next-generation members within a seven-year time frame and all the talk of succession were casting a large shadow over future career prospects for nonfamily employees.

But as the strategic planning process moved into high gear, the holding company structure permitted the promotion of nonfamily managers to the presidency of several business units. Carlos Nido, who assumed the presidency of Virtual, Inc., and Luis González, who moved to the holding company as vice president of corporate sales and marketing, saw their responsibilities increase immediately. Nonfamily managers then began to believe that the succession process could be a real win–win opportunity for the extended business family.

CORPORATE STRATEGY MEETING, FEBRUARY 1999

María Luisa became president of the Grupo Ferré Rangel in late 1998. A year earlier, some next-generation members had observed that there was a significant gap between the planning in which they participated at family council meetings and their ability to then make and execute decisions. Key nonfamily managers, it turned out, had similar difficulties; there was clearly a disconnect between planning the work and working the plan. One of María Luisa's first highly visible acts of leadership of the newly structured holding company was to sponsor a series of strategic planning sessions. With the assistance of a former strategy professor who had become a corporate consultant, she sponsored a series of education and planning meetings that focused the strategy of each of the business units, clarified the roles of the Grupo and central services, and created a stronger culture of execution of plans and accountability. María Luisa reflected on the reason for the renewed strategic planning effort at the holding company level: "We need to guide these various communications companies to the future. I do not believe we can direct all of this as a team, without growth. Growing is very important."

Strategic planning was not new to the company. In fact, while the tremendous success of *El Nuevo Día* might have led many other corporate leaders to rest on their laurels, Antonio Luis Ferré was not one to do so. He had sponsored strategic reviews since the 1980s. In the 1990s, both as a continuation of this discipline and as an extension of it in order to accommodate the entry of the next generation into the business, he had created a new ventures unit, RANFE (Rangel-Ferré). RANFE was charged with giving serious consideration to the appropriate diversification of the company as the next generation of owner-managers took over.

The FCC was in the process of changing regulations affecting the ownership of multiple media companies within particular markets. Given the increased competition already available via cable TV systems and the Internet, the FCC was moving toward allowing the same company to own multiple media channels serving a market. This presented additional growth opportunities, as well as increased financial risk; most of the new media were capital intensive. Which would produce the desired growth, while maintaining profitability—market specialization (concentrating further in the Puerto Rican market with new media) or market diversification (investing in growth opportunities in new markets)?

Primera Hora was a successful example of growth through market specialization. Management saw a need for the product in the local market; researched the product in the United Kingdom, Costa Rica, and Chile; and hired talented top management to help lead the effort. Working with a key nonfamily circulation manager, Hector Olave, and supported by the Grupo's strategic five-year plan, Loren Ferré had managed to grow daily circulation to 120,000 in just three years. The much older competitor in that niche, *El Vocero,* had a circulation of 155,000.

There were concerns about stress, and yet the enterprises were humming with new energy. Next-generation members were re-discovering what they loved about the company and beginning to understand what unique contributions they could make to the Grupo. Next-generation members were also called upon to act as ambassadors on behalf of *El Nuevo Día* and the Ferré Rangel family. The journalistic independence of the flagship newspaper was once again being attacked.

EL NUEVO DÍA VS. THE GOVERNMENT

Directing its always independent journalistic voice at the incumbent governor of Puerto Rico and his administration, *El Nuevo Día* had published a series of articles that revealed incompetence, corruption, self-dealing, and undue process. The governor and his administration responded swiftly; they mounted a campaign to discredit the paper, pulled all government advertising (from tax notices to bond issue announcements) from *El Nuevo Día,* and failed to issue the environmental permits needed to operate the Puerto Rican Cement plants. The government was attempting to shut down the Grupo Ferré Rangel just as the Nixon administration had attempted to silence the *Washington Post* in its investigations of Watergate and the Pentagon Papers.

El Nuevo Día filed suit in federal court to stop the unjust and excessive use of governmental powers. This landmark first amendment rights case was settled out of court in Washington, D.C., in late 2000, but only after exacting a heavy price from the flagship newspaper (circulation dropped by 30,000 during this period) and the cement company. The family did come together and emerged triumphant, with renewed strength of character and commitment to its mission, its legacy, and the journalistic independence of its newspapers. The next generation now understood firsthand that the newspaper business sometimes requires financial and personal sacrifices to uphold the public good and preserve the freedom of the press.

Antonio Luis Ferré Faces New Challenges

The organizational structure of the group had changed with the creation of the Grupo Ferré Rangel as a holding company. Business units were more clearly separated from *El Nuevo Día*, and the presidents of the respective units had more authority in the new structure. A strategy, strategy implementation plan, and budget were developed for each business unit. Individual company boards and María Luisa, president of the holding company, held the business unit presidents accountable. Central services and corporate staff reported to María Luisa, who then reported to a board of directors at the holding company level. Antonio was chairman of the board.

This corporate board had been created on February 11, 1997, before the holding company structure was developed. The fourteen-person board was composed of seven Ferré Rangel family members; five key executives from the various companies, including Miguel Nazario of Puerto Rican Cement; and two independent outsiders, a professor and former industry association president and a general manager of a smaller family-owned corporation. Several next-generation members were now concerned that this board of directors was not holding management accountable to any significant extent. According to the siblings, the large number of family members and key executives on this board made it a great developmental vehicle, but one prone to rubber-stamping.

Next-generation members believed that, as a result of the five-year developmental stretch, they had all found their niches and their unique ways of contributing to the business. But they still harbored concerns about their ability to make the big decisions as siblings and co-owners, without the tie-breaking role of Antonio.

For its philanthropic mission, the Ferré Rangel family had created a family foundation, headed by Luisa Rangel. While the family had a long tradition of community involvement and community service (including sizeable gifts to the arts and charitable organizations), this foundation was meant to direct and govern the relationships between the family's philanthropic intentions and the many needs existing in the community.

Spouses of the next-generation heirs, the in-laws, seemed to be getting pulled into taking sides over the amount of work and the pressures of public service and public relations activities. The estate plan was being developed with the advice of an estate tax attorney. Several of the discussions between the attorney and the individual next-generation couples had generated some controversy.

Once all of the power and responsibility were transferred to the next generation, who would have an oversight role with regard to the relationship between the owning family and the management of the enterprises? Who would have the final word in, say, a $1 million investment in a new press, when significant investment was also required in Virtual, Inc.? Who would decide which of Antonio and Luisa's grandchildren met the criteria for employment at the Grupo? And who would set the employment criteria?

What would happen to a family member who decided to leave the Grupo to pursue her or his own dream—to become a full-time father or mother, retire early, become an entrepreneur, or take a lengthy sabbatical? It was September 2002, and Antonio Luis Ferré was pondering these and other questions. Would each sibling have voting control over the business unit for which she or he had primary responsibility? What about the in-laws? The family constitution precluded them from working for the Grupo Ferré Rangel, but could they provide the corporation with professional services or become suppliers, sub-contractors, or co-investors in some projects? Without their employment in the enterprise, what could be done to keep them informed, involved, caring, and supportive of the demanding lives of their business leader spouses? And what about the 10 grandchildren, ages 1 to 11, who might one day want to be involved with the Grupo Ferré Rangel?

CASE QUESTIONS

1. What are the facts of this case as they relate to
   a. the entire enterprise?
   b. the Ferré Rangel family?
   c. the nature of the relationship between the family and the business?
2. What leadership, management, and governance best practices have the firm and the owning family already implemented? How do they seem to be working?
3. What does the CEO need to do next to ensure continuation of the legacy of the enterprise and its history of innovation?
4. How can corporate governance and control contribute to the continuity of this family-owned business?

NOTES

1. Puerto Rican Cement agreed to be acquired by CEMEX, the multi-national cement company headquartered in Monterrey, Mexico, on June 12, 2002, for approximately $180 million and the assumption of all outstanding debt.

The Evolving and Changing Family Business

10

LEADING THE EVOLUTION

The goal of continuity challenges owners and managers to achieve change while maintaining enough stability to keep the enterprise successful in the short term. The quest for continuity requires that the enterprise adapt, through vision and strategy, to the changing competitive dynamics that will predominate in the next generation. At the same time, there must be a deep understanding and acknowledgment of what has made the enterprise successful so far. Since different generations may support opposing views on continuity, achieving this goal poses a challenge to inter-generational collaboration and accommodation. Resolving this dilemma requires evolution, not revolution, across the multi-year succession process.

Different generations have different leadership tasks when it comes to continuity. The founding generation builds an enterprise from next to nothing and makes every effort to ensure its survival. Building on the foundation created, the next generation must grow the enterprise by rejuvenating and changing it or else face organizational decline precisely when the family is growing, a recipe for family conflict and tragedy. The third and fourth generations are often called on to again adapt the firm to changes in its competitive environment. In addition, they must be active stewards of the enterprise and the owning family's legacy, before the family's collective memory dissipates. In essence, then, next-generation leaders have to be both leaders of change and growth and stewards of culture and values.

I would like to dedicate this chapter to the loving memory of Richard Beckhard, my teacher at MIT—Sloan School of Management and life-long advisor and friend, who dedicated himself to coaching and mentoring the next generation. Many of the ideas on managing change that are discussed in this chapter were his creation. Further utilization of this material by next-generation members of family businesses will serve as a tribute to his wisdom and caring and become part of his tremendous legacy.

CONTINUITY AND CULTURE

The research on organizational culture suggests that businesses that enjoy a high level of performance over a long period of time have a strong culture that fits the strategy of the business. The Marriott Corporation, for instance, has a culture that makes customer satisfaction a priority, and it educates new associates about this culture. Marriott is intimately familiar with the connections that exist among employee satisfaction, systems and structures that allow employees to actively care for customers, and the quality of service provided to guests.

Culture is a collection of beliefs, values, and ground rules that shapes and significantly influences how individuals, groups, and the company as a whole behave or operate when confronted with choices, decisions, opportunities, and threats. Company cultures are often composed of unique values that define the nature of the company's commitment to its major stakeholders: customers, shareholders, employees, suppliers, and the communities in which the business operates.

SC Johnson: A Family Company launched an advertising campaign that highlighted the inherent strengths and advantages of being family-owned and family-operated. Its Chicago-based advertising firm, Foote, Cone & Belding, found in its research that family ownership was a tremendous asset to a business. According to the research, Americans prefer products and/or services from family-owned companies over those from publicly held corporations. More than 80 percent of the people surveyed believed that family companies make products they can trust, in contrast to 43 percent for publicly traded companies. Many perceived family-company products as being of higher quality. Sam Johnson, the third-generation patriarch who grew the enterprise from $171 million in annual sales to four divisions with combined sales of $6 billion, says, "A great family business, no matter its size, has to be more than a financial investment. To survive long term, it has to be a social positive for the employees, a benefit for the community, a passion for future generations of the family, and committed to earning the goodwill of the consumer every day."[1]

Another very successful family-owned business that distributes health care products nationally—Edgepark Surgical—attributes much of its success to its unique culture. Ron Harrington, the company's CEO, has grown the business from $2 million in annual revenues to $160 million in the span of 11 years. He credits others with this success—all those people who embody the culture and values of the company, whether family or not. The company's culture and values statement was presented in Chapter 1, but it bears repeating here:

We are:

■ Family-Owned, Professionally Managed: We are a family acting in the Company's best interest.

We believe in:

■ Integrity: We do what we say we will do.
■ No Walls: We have no barriers to communication.

- Tenacity: We have an unrelenting determination to reach objectives.
- Profitability: We are committed to performance and results.
- Improvement: We are never satisfied.
- Service: We are loyal to our customers and respect them.

CHANGING THE CULTURE

The research on organizational culture suggests that the culture needs to be flexible—adaptive and agile in the face of change. That is, having a strong culture is not sufficient for the long-term effectiveness of a firm. Many companies with strong cultures that fit their strategies have come to realize that the very strength of the culture poses challenges to its adaptation to changing competitive environments.

In 1987, Bill Hewlett and David Packard led what they considered to be a revolution at Hewlett-Packard when, as controlling shareholders retired from the management of the firm, they believed the company was simply resting on its laurels. Back in 1987, Hewlett-Packard primarily produced scientific measurement devices, such as oscilloscopes. It was enjoying very healthy profit margins, but, according to its founders, it was not focusing as it should on emerging competition from Asia in its product lines. Hewlett-Packard needed to return to the "HP Way" in innovation and new product development in order to grow out of its overreliance on measurement systems. The result of this owner-issued wake-up call was the launching of the company's hugely successful printing and imaging business. The architects of the company's renowned strong culture were able to remold it, creating flexibility and a capacity for adaptation. Owner-managers and active owners who hold management accountable are in a unique position to help their companies remain successful over the long haul.

Leaders who have assumed responsibility for making change happen, in order to build a company that lasts, believe that leadership of this kind requires the following:

1. Challenging the status quo by asking fundamental questions and collecting external data, including customer, competitive, social, or demographic data. Leaders need to create dissatisfaction with the status quo.

2. Having an external (customer/competition) perspective. The desire for this type of perspective led IBM to tap as its new CEO Lou Gerstner, who had been running American Express, a major customer of IBM. IBM clearly was in need of fundamental change when he assumed the company's leadership. None of the key managers who had been with IBM for many years seemed capable of leading the change effort with the dispassionate drive that Gerstner demonstrated. This finding has implications for what may constitute appropriate early developmental career opportunities for next-generation members who will be called upon to rejuvenate their family-owned businesses.

3. Having the capacity to forge a new direction—to articulate a vision of where the company should be headed—that is rooted in meeting customer needs and creating value for customers.

4. Being able to generate a sense of urgency. After all, need and speed are friends of change. Jack Welch, reflecting on his fundamental reshaping of GE during the 1990s, said, "If I could begin the fundamental change effort at GE again today, based on what I have learned in the last decade, I would insist on greater speed. I would accelerate the change process and avoid a lot of the resistance, confusion and loss of motivation that was part of a slower process."[2]

The leader of the evolution needs to build the "case for change," the reasons why the company's only option is to change. By setting a deadline for the change to occur, one that is rooted in preserving the loyalty of customers, he or she establishes a sense of urgency. The leader also needs to communicate the customer-based vision and strategies to the entire organization, to repeat the message often, and to engage the rest of the organization in effective ways of determining how the change will be carried out. Cultural change takes time, but the leader must act with speed.

NEW LEADERS OF THE EVOLUTION

For the successor charged with becoming the leader of the evolution, few characteristics are as practical and influential as self-awareness and self-management. To fulfill their responsibilities and roles well, leaders often depend on words, on having a voice that compels others to act. Young leaders who have been charged with changing the firm's culture soon realize that they are the primary instruments of the change—that the nature of their relationships with others and the outcomes resulting from those relationships are very much dependent on their own actions and behaviors. Leaders of change also recognize that they will eventually be judged by whether their words and actions are consistent; that is, "Does she walk the talk?" Clearly, self-awareness and self-management are critical skills for a young leader.

As a "mere mortal," the successor charged with a company's evolution has to transform the foundation for leadership from a belief in the invulnerability of the hero to an appreciation of the ability to lead. He or she has to realize that while ownership provided the founder with power and experiential wisdom, the successor does not inherit the same authority to lead. Shares of stock transfer across generations, but the authority to lead has to be earned by each successive generation. It is more important to recognize that, over the generations, employees move from a dependent and loyal follower model to a more knowledgeable and mutually responsible partner model. And pulling employees toward the desired future is preferable to pushing them to achieve.

New leaders charged with evolution across generations face many traps (see Exhibit 10-1). The most notable is usually self-inflicted: assuming that the transfer of power implicit in being anointed as the successor confers on the successor the

---

| EXHIBIT 10-1 | COMMON TRAPS FOR THE NEW LEADER |

- Assuming that succession to a new management and ownership position vests the leader with the authority to lead. Authority is earned, not inherited.

- Becoming isolated from important others in the family and in the business. Staying in contact is important, even during conflict.

- Being distracted by key managers or other significant players in the family organization who have their own agendas.

- Having to always have the answer to any problem. It is a myth that "real leaders" know how to solve any and all problems.

- Keeping the existing management team too long. Fresh perspectives are necessary for the continuity of any business.

- Attempting too much too soon or too little too slowly.

- Being overly cautious or overly rebellious, depending on the new leader's historical relationship with the previous CEO-parent (or other relative).

---

authority to lead. But such authority can only be earned, slowly, by demonstrating competence, caring, and consistency and maintaining contact and communication.

Deciding what constitutes effective leadership is very much a judgment call. Too little too slowly can be just as ineffective as too much too quickly. How is a new leader to know? Self-awareness is a great skill that can be learned in some MBA programs and a variety of leadership development centers. Periodically requesting more objective and independent readings of any unique situations by others—a mentor, a consultant, members of the board, or members of the family council—can also be of help. Above all, successors need to avoid becoming isolated by the hard work new leadership requires. They need to continue to communicate with trusted others to ensure that their early judgment calls are as wise as is humanly possible.

THE RAW MATERIALS OF A NEW CULTURE

The materials with which the architect of a new culture works are financial and information systems, organizational structure, compensation, and, on the family front, the family constitution. (See Chapter 7 for more on family constitutions and a sample document.) Culture in the organization begins to change, however slowly, when a leader changes the information people receive, alters the way they get paid and what they get paid for, rearranges job responsibilities and reporting relationships, and adapts the mechanisms for coordination and accountability. By educating and informing both active and inactive family members and engaging them in developing a picture of their desired future relationship with the business, the leader can build shareholder loyalty and a culture of stewardship.

In order for any of these change initiatives to proceed, the architect must first earn the right to lead in a new direction; that is, the new leader must earn the respect of key nonfamily managers and family shareholders who are not active in management. The successor has to lead both the business and the family. This means that the new leader has to build a set of alliances, both in the business and in the family, that will allow her or him to begin to transform the "small things" that make all the difference in the overarching goal of making the changes needed for family business continuity. Unfortunately, many of the small things are important to people who feel much more comfortable with the status quo than with the prospect of change—and those people are in the majority. So, what can a new leader do? Exhibit 10-2 presents a formula for change, which many successors find helpful in understanding how to approach the change process.[3]

This change formula has proven quite useful to leaders whose mission includes bringing about the adaptation and rejuvenation needed for continuity. It guides leaders in determining the actions and steps that will yield the greatest return on energy and resources invested. The formula shows that change is a multiplicative function consisting of the product of three variables: dissatisfaction with the status quo, a vision of the desired future, and practical first steps to take to achieve the goal of change. Because it is a multiplicative function, if any one of these three elements is missing or has a value approaching zero, there will be no momentum for change. Hence, even if a clear vision and thorough knowledge of feasible practical steps are present, nothing will happen in the absence of sufficient dissatisfaction with the status quo. This simple diagnostic can help a leader prioritize activities to engage in in order to get employees' energy focused in productive and profitable ways.

The CEO of a highly visible consumer company was extremely dissatisfied with the performance of his company over the past several years. He had tried, through the employee newsletter, management briefings, company-wide state-of-the-business meetings, and meetings with the union leadership, to convince others of a need for concern, but to no avail. Frustrated at his inability to convey the sense of urgency that he and other key managers felt, he finally came to the

---

EXHIBIT 10-2   THE CHANGE FORMULA

$C = D \times V \times FS \gg RC$

where

C = Change.

D = Dissatisfaction with the status quo, making a clear case for change.

V = Vision of the desired future, providing a clear sense of direction.

FS = First steps in getting from "here to there," clearly outlining what must be done first.

RC = Natural resistance to change.

conclusion that employees believed management would cry wolf so as to get ever higher levels of productivity from the workforce. Aware that he could not drive the company where he thought it needed to go in the face of foreign competition, the CEO set about increasing dissatisfaction with the status quo. According to his assessment, it was the low level of this variable that most deflated the momentum for change and improvement. He decided to try something quite unconventional: He began to make some of the company's analyses of its competitive situation available to local media. These media were always interested in company news because the firm was a relatively large employer in the community.

The CEO was amazed at what a significant difference this approach made in increasing dissatisfaction with the status quo among employees and thereby increasing their readiness for change. Newspaper reports were being circulated and TV news stories retold in locker rooms, cafeterias, staff meetings, and union hall meetings. In the span of a couple of months, the CEO had achieved what had eluded him for a couple of years—the capacity to create a credible sense of urgency so that employees would join with him and top managers in changing and improving the business from the top down and from the bottom up.

Interestingly enough, family member shareholders not active in management, many of whom lived in the community, also displayed heightened concern about the state of the business. After all, employees who ran into them were asking them about the difficulties and their opinions on the prospects for improvement. This made the family much more ready to support the CEO's decisions (including approving capital investments in productivity-enhancing technology) than they were prior to his decision to increase dissatisfaction with the status quo by using the media.

THREE STATES OF EVOLUTION

Exhibit 10-3 shows the three states involved in the change process: the present state, representing the current situation of the family and the business; the transition state, where most of the change activities take place; and the future state, representing the direction in which the leader wants the organization to head. Let's begin with the future state, since, as Casey Stengel, former manager of the New York Yankees, once said, "If you don't know where you are going, you may end up somewhere else."

THE FUTURE STATE

Defining the future state of a business is equivalent to putting stakes in the ground around a set of results or changes expected in a one-, two-, or three-year period. The developer needs to bear in mind both the vision and the core mission of the enterprise and the owning family. Unlike a vision, which is usually somewhat abstract and longer range, the scenario for the future state should be

EXHIBIT 10-3   THE THREE STATES INVOLVED IN THE CHANGE PROCESS

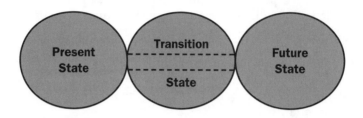

SOURCE: Adapted from Beckhard, R., and Harris, R., *Organizational Transitions: Managing Complex Change*, Reading, MA: Addison-Wesley, 1987.

precisely defined in financial, operational, and behavioral terms. It is best to write one scenario for the business and another for the family. New leaders should write the desired future state scenario as if that day had already arrived, describing the accomplishments and results that should be observable. For example, the business scenario could begin, "On November 1, 2010, Premier Corporation signed the papers acquiring a resort in Florida. At the same time, it announced third-quarter results showing a comparable properties revenue increase of 15 percent and a profit increase of 18 percent over the same period last year." The scenario should be as concrete as possible and should be a totally honest reflection of what the new leader wants for his or her future and the future of the family and business. The seven questions outlined in Exhibit 10-4 should be considered in creating a future state scenario. The bulleted items are suggested answers, included to provoke thoughtful consideration of the many aspects of the questions.

Compiling and discussing answers to the questions in Exhibit 10-4 in order to develop a shared definition of the desired future state is an ideal task for a family meeting or family retreat. Later, key nonfamily managers should also be involved in the process, particularly as it relates to questions 1 through 5. Building bridges between family shareholders' and nonfamily managers' views of the future of the corporation is essential. If the company has a board with independent outsiders, board members should be provided with these answers and engaged in a discussion of both the questions and the answers. Board members will be glad to get this direction from the owner-manager, shareholders, and key nonfamily managers, and it will make them better able to serve the company and its shareholders.

An advantage of having a precise definition of the future state is that it provides information to those not involved in the drafting of the statement and improves their ability to understand how they will fit into that future. Uncertainty

| EXHIBIT 10-4 | CREATING A FUTURE STATE SCENARIO |

1. What would I like to see as the core family business three years* from now?

   - Owning/operating existing businesses?
   - Owning/operating existing and additional like businesses?
   - Managing new ventures in related industries?
   - Owning/managing assets outside the industry (i.e., diversification)?
   - Other? Please explain.

   *The selection of a three-year time frame is arbitrary; pick the time frame most appropriate to your own situation.

2. What would I like to see the management structure of the business look like?

   - Similar to the current structure?
   - Sibling partnership?
   - Family CEO?
   - Outside CEO?
   - Other? Please explain.

3. What would I like to see as the governance structure?

   - A board with a mixture of independent outsiders and family members?
   - A board with a majority of outside directors?
   - A board with a majority of family directors?
   - An active family council that meets at least twice a year?
   - An annual shareholders' meeting, with extensive discussion of financial statements and other matters of shareholder interest?
   - A family office to manage the family's investments and provide shareholder services?
   - A combination of the above? Please explain.
   - Other? Please explain.

4. What do I want my own involvement in the business to be?

   - No role in the business—a successful life and career outside the family business?

   - Active shareholder and steward with a successful career outside the family business?
   - CEO?
   - Owner-manager, running one of the business units?
   - Owner-manager, working at the main office (e.g., CFO or VP New Ventures)?
   - Board member?
   - Other? Please explain.

5. What are my expectations for financial returns?

   - Dividends and distributions? (Specify percent or amount.)
   - Capital appreciation through the creation of long-term shareholder value?
   - Financial resources for my children?

6. How do I want my relationship with other members of the extended family to be?

   - Characterized more by collaboration than by competition?
   - One in which we all actively care for each other and are there for each other?
   - As positive as possible, given the usual differences of opinion and disagreements about the business?
   - Not too time consuming—I really want to give priority to my nuclear family?
   - One in which we all share the responsibility for upholding and updating the legacy via a family constitution or new policies (so that, for instance, next-generation girls can have the same opportunity the boys have had to eventually manage the corporation)?

7. How do I want our family to give back to the community at large?

   - Through philanthropy?
   - Through community involvement?
   - Through government service or politics?
   - Through education?

about and misperceptions of the implications of change on a person's future role are major sources of resistance. In addition, beginning the process with a definition of the future state allows management to take advantage of people's tendency to be more optimistic about their engagement in future opportunities than about their ability to fix current problems. Positive prospects, then, provide a positive tension. By pulling the organization and the family toward something desirable, the leader provides the fuel for the engine of change, particularly if there is a sharp contrast between the desired future state and the present state.

THE PRESENT STATE

The present state is where any dissatisfaction with the status quo must be found—and then promoted in the interest of continuity and perpetuation. Assessing the current situation is the key task of a leader trying to facilitate evolution to a new, more appropriate structure for the family and the business. It is in terms of the present state that the leadership defines the need for change. Many of the forces requiring change originate outside the business itself—competition, new technology, changes in consumer tastes, etc. Other forces of change may be more internally driven, as when a next-generation leader perceives the opportunity to turn a business that has relied primarily on its technical expertise into a more market-driven one or when a next-generation leader, after having been promoted to the presidency of the family business, experiences little increase in her ability to make decisions because of the presence of a CEO who will not let go.

Some of the need for change may also originate in the family. A younger daughter who has become president of the company, for instance, may be uncomfortably straddling two very different worlds. In the business, where she has been formally recognized as the president, she is at the top level of the hierarchy. In the family, where she is still "Daddy's little girl," the culture fails to reinforce her capacity to lead with appropriate power and influence.

Acknowledging differences and reaching accommodation on key issues are often necessary before a family and its business can mobilize for action and change. How can a leader tap that potential energy? The use of external consultants or "high-influence friends"[4]—whether board members, associates in the industry, or professionals available through educational venues like the Young President's Organization (YPO), The Executive Committee (TEC), or a business school or university—often helps in this process. Surveys can also provide feedback for action planning by the family and management group. For example, Case Western Reserve University has developed the Family Business Diagnostic Survey, which measures the current situation in both the business and the owning family. Other approaches to assessing the family's and the business's present state include: employee surveys, customer satisfaction surveys, family surveys, educational sessions with top managers to sense the state of the organization, "open-ear" meetings with different sections of the organization, and educational sessions with family members to sense the state of the relationship between the family and the business.

Finally, assessment of the present state has to include an evaluation of readiness for the particular change that is being contemplated. It is essential to identify the key subsystems, or parts of the organization and family, that will either have a bearing on the change or be affected by it. These key subsystems may be departments or divisions of the company, branches of the family, individual top managers, or shareholders/family members. Two factors are most relevant in the overall assessment of their readiness for changes that will begin to drive the company from its present to its future state: (1) their enthusiasm and support for the proposed changes and (2) their power or capability (what human resources, funds, and family or organizational influence they have available) to support or block the proposed changes.

The Raymond Corporation, then a medium-size, family-controlled materials-handling business, acquired a privately held company that had a technology it needed to add to its product line. The acquiring company, after performing a readiness assessment in preparation for the integration of the two companies, opted not to consolidate the companies at the same site by moving personnel halfway across the country, as had been previously decided. Instead, it created a project management organization and made the president of the acquired company its leader. The readiness assessment had exposed both the tremendous value of the individual contributors (the programmers) and their low readiness for such a dramatic move (their capability to walk out). The project management structure allowed for the gradual transfer of the technology and the eventual consolidation of key technology transfer agents, who moved east a couple of years later.

THE TRANSITION STATE

The work done during the transition period is quite different from the work associated with defining the desired future state and assessing the present state. It consists primarily of forming action plans, with unique temporary structures and systems to allow for follow-up and control of the process.

Having decided what needs to be changed, the leader now must decide where to begin the process:

- *With top management?* Should the leader begin by changing the make-up of the top management team, the roles of the individual members, the way the team operates, or the strategies it pursues?

- *With family?* Should the leader begin by convening the family, making more information available to its members, educating family members not active in the business about business matters, creating a family council, or developing policies to guide the desired relationship between the family and the business?

- *With ownership?* Should the leader begin by restructuring ownership, changing distribution of voting and non-voting stock, educating others about the estate plan, developing or updating buy–sell agreements, or rene-gotiating existing dividend or distribution expectations?

- *With the systems that are most ready?* Should the leader begin with those indi-viduals, departments, or groups of people most ready for the change—whether through their alignment with the desired future or out of dissatis-faction with the status quo—in order to create some early wins and develop momentum?

- *With new teams, units, or governance bodies?* Should the leader leverage the initial phase of the change process by using to advantage the lack of history of new bodies—like a third-generation (G3) team, a strategic planning com-mittee, a committee of the family council, or a newly formed advisory board?

- *With temporary project teams?* Should the leader create project teams with a limited lifespan in order to implement change? (Recall the project manage-ment organization created by George Raymond, the materials-handling company CEO, in order to successfully merge an acquired company.)

- *With the best practices for family business continuity?* Should the leader focus his or her attention on one or a combination of the governance and man-agement best practices discussed throughout this book?

CONTINUITY AND FAMILY-MANAGEMENT-OWNERSHIP STRUCTURES

The purpose of the transition state is to get family (F), management (M), owner-ship (O), and the relationship among the three from the present state to the desired future state (see Exhibit 10-5). The idea is to consider each subsystem both individually and in relation to the others: Do the criteria that family members need to meet in order to be considered for management positions in the company need to be renegotiated? Does the family need to go out of its way to support a younger next-generation member for leadership in the company, despite a history of using primogeniture as the determinant of future company leaders? On the management front, does the company need to initiate a strategic thinking/plan-ning process that "guns the engines" of growth? Does it need to hire new talent that better complements the skills the next-generation leader brings to the top team, further professionalizes management, and gives the new leader his or her own hire? And on the ownership front, does a buy–sell agreement need to be drafted? Do dividend policies need to be changed in order to support reinvest-ment in growth? Do vehicles for financing the execution of an estate plan need to be identified and insurance policies purchased? And how is all of this going to be coordinated and kept moving forward—through the use of temporary project teams or one of the new or existing governance bodies?

| EXHIBIT 10-5 | THE FAMILY-MANAGEMENT-OWNERSHIP RELATIONSHIP IN TRANSITION |

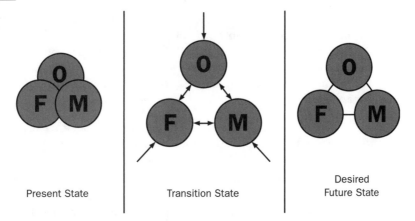

Present State   Transition State   Desired Future State

Various family business leaders recommend taking the following steps to ensure continuity across generations:

- Plan the estate and ownership transfer with business agility in mind.

- Assume, along with your spouse, appropriate leadership roles to assure trust and governance.

- Promote strategic growth by building on the firm's core competencies.

- Develop the leadership capability of the next generation and encourage its vision.

- Leverage the family's skills and abilities by hiring capable and dedicated nonfamily managers for leadership positions.

- Welcome the review of outside board members who continuously raise the bar for management and/or family shareholders.

- Promote communication and accommodation among family members through frequent family meetings and a family council.

Planning a family–business retreat or meeting is helpful early in the process. However, such gatherings are not for everyone. They are certainly not for families in conflict or for families in which some members are not on speaking terms. But where feasible, they represent an important investment in the future and a deposit in the family's emotional bank account. Family meetings are the best way to begin the process of creating a family business strategy and writing a family constitution that will guide the creation of a desired future state for the business, promote business continuity, and nurture family harmony.

COMMITMENT PLANNING

A simple methodology has been quite useful to leaders of change in diagnosing the nature of existing commitment and then gaining the commitment required for evolution of the complex family business system. The absence of such a commitment constitutes some form of resistance, passive or active, to change.

Commitment planning consists of identifying all key individuals in both the organization and the family and then asking the following questions:

1. Based on where he or she stands today, what is this key individual likely to do about the planned change? Block it? Let it happen? Help it happen? Make it happen?

2. In order for the process to be successful, where does the leader of the evolution need this key individual to be with regard to the planned change? Will it occur even if he or she is blocking it? Or does this person need to let it happen, help it happen, or make it happen?

3. What can the leader do to move this key individual from where he or she currently stands to where he or she must be in order for the planned change to be successful?

It is important to remember that, in many cases, all the leader needs from others in the organization or the family is a posture of neutrality toward change, just to let the change happen. While the leader of the evolution would clearly prefer to have everybody trying to make it happen, this is neither realistic nor necessary. Certainly, some key individuals may need to be prepared to let, help, or make some planned changes take place—for instance, changes in dividend policy may need the support of a majority of shareholders, and major changes in the make-up of the top management team may need at least a "let it happen" kind of support from the retiring or transitioning chairman and CEO of the corporation.

INSTITUTIONALIZING THE CHANGE

Change has often been defined as comprising an unfreezing stage, a "making the changes" stage, and, finally, a refreezing stage. Because evolution is often so difficult to bring about, the last thing any leader wants is retrenchment, or a sliding back to the "old ways," as soon as the planned change effort is completed.

In order to be effective, then, the changes implemented during a period of evolution need to be consolidated and institutionalized in such a way that what was envisioned as the desired future state becomes accepted as the present state. The most reliable tools available for this task are organizational structures, ownership structures, compensation, dividend policies, family involvement/employment policies, a family constitution, education, financial information, and information systems serving management and shareholders. Research and practice (as discussed in Chapters 8 and 9) have identified two governance bodies that are uniquely qualified to institutionalize the evolutionary process and provide continued governance of the family–business relationship: (1) frequent family meetings, or an ongoing family council, and (2) a board—statutory or advisory—with independent outsiders.

Leaders of change should use these tools thoughtfully but freely and in an ongoing fashion in order to ensure that the enthusiasm that went into the evolutionary process does not vanish after the campaign is over. Consistency as well as competency is required in bringing about change.

SUMMARY

1. Next-generation leaders have to be both leaders of change and growth and stewards of culture and values.

2. Leaders of a culture change must (a) create dissatisfaction with the status quo, (b) have an external (customer/competition) perspective, (c) have the capacity to forge a new direction, and (d) be able to generate a sense of urgency.

3. New leaders must not assume that the transfer of power implicit in being anointed as the successor also confers the authority to lead; such authority can only be earned.

4. The three states involved in the change process are the present, transition, and future states.

5. Commitment planning requires identifying all key individuals in both the organization and the family and then assessing these individuals' current positions on the change, where the leader needs each individual to be with regard to the change, and how the leader can move each individual to where he or she must be for the change to be successful.

6. Two governance bodies that are uniquely qualified to institutionalize the evolutionary process and provide continued governance in family–business relationships are (a) frequent family meetings, or an ongoing family council, and (b) a board with independent outsiders.

A SUCCESSION PLAN THAT ADDRESSES THE LEADERSHIP IMPERATIVES AND BEST PRACTICES FOR FAMILY BUSINESS CONTINUITY.[5]

Mike and Gabe Orazen drafted this preliminary succession plan in order to synthesize their learning from this textbook and create a platform for action in EPG, Inc., their family-owned business. Besides drafting the plan, Mike and Gabe, with their father's support, scheduled a mid-summer family meeting to discuss the plan. It is important to mention that prior to beginning the process of writing this plan (which they did in conjunction with CWRU's Family Business—The Next Generation: A Leadership Institute for Owner-Managers and Family-Controlled Companies), neither Mike nor Gabe felt confident that they could lead EPG successfully. They agreed very little as to the future organizational structure of the corporation and their individual roles in it. As a result, Michael Orazen, Sr., president and chief executive officer, also lacked confidence in the succession and continuity process and was delaying transferring power in the corporation to his two sons.

THE NEXT GENERATION'S VISION

Our goal in five years is to see EPG sustain the growth and profitability we experienced since 1996, a compounded 15 percent annual growth rate. This growth and profitability will come from an expanded product offering and more effective management styles, but with the same core mission:

- To become the leader in providing rubber extrusions for the architectural and other targeted custom markets, while furnishing unsurpassed service and response time.
- To do so for an appropriate profit and in a unified, focused, and fulfilling work environment.

In order to achieve this mission, EPG will have to have qualities and competencies that span the successful integration of several different func-

tions. Our vision is one that has and always should have an external focus on the customer.

We, as the leaders of EPG in the future, will have to continue raising questions of what we have yet to improve. When the employees and managers stop challenging each other and the status quo, the competitive advantage of our highly performing management team will quickly fade. It is important to maintain a culture of continuous improvement though employee training, team building, and continued education programs.

Building more business in our core market is the key to successfully achieving our mission. In order to reduce the risk of committing all our resources to one market, we should always look for opportunities and profit pools in other markets that complement our strengths and competencies. Our current effort to expand into plastic and TPE technology is to give our current customers more choices in architectural sealing applications.

Our external environment, primarily the competitive forces and the changes in our major supply chains, needs to be updated and kept in front of the management team constantly. We need to continue to add more to our current reporting capabilities to give the management the necessary information to make the decisions. Growth in the markets we participate in is becoming more difficult; the key to future growth is understanding that growth by itself is not healthy for EPG. We need to forecast how the growth will increase our cash flow and profit going forward.

The last important aspect of what EPG will be like in five years is our human resource strategy. The competencies we look for today and in the future should be teamwork, communications, responsiveness, and pride. Those qualities are very important for the leadership of the company. To meet the goal of creating a unified, focused, and fulfilling work environment, all of our employees should be striving to excel in these key competencies going forward. Fair base compensation, coupled with variable pay on the basis of company profitability for family and nonfamily employees, should remain a high priority within our human resource strategy. Promoting and compensating based on individual performance and company-wide profitability is the key to a successful human resource strategy in the future.

To forecast what our sales and product offerings will look like in five years would be in direct conflict with our need to stay in touch with the external environment as it changes. We have keys to improving every sector of our business strategy. Five years from now, we will have doubled our revenue, maintained a consistent net income of approximately 7 percent, while meeting ownership expectations of return on equity and dividends.

Our Family Council

EPG has a history of bringing the family together to keep everyone in and outside the business informed on ownership issues that need to be understood at all levels of the family. We still have to bring many family business issues to future family meetings. It is clear that communications in the past several years have not been effective in regard to the family business and issues a family council should be confronting. The need for a family council, for frequent family council and ownership meetings, is critical. We recently received feedback on the Family Diagnostic Survey from CWRU that the meetings have not been held for over two years and that, perhaps as a result of this, perceptions among the family vary greatly in all aspects of business, ownership, and family issues.

Our family will find being on the same page and sharing a vision of what the family and the company stand for will make the family feel more comfortable with the investment they're holding. We will find that the ambiguity that the last few years have fostered will be happily left behind when information starts flowing again. These renewed efforts to start routinely meeting as a family will help prepare the family for the challenges the transition into the new generation may bring.

We view this as an opportunity to improve the family, ownership, and business aspects of our family business. We cannot change the past, but have the opportunity to make a good family business even better and more prepared to deal with the ever-changing and increasingly complex issues that we will face in the future. Our next family council meeting will be attended by the founder and CEO, all of the children, and all of their spouses. Grandchildren will be going as well, but will not be attending the meetings until they reach the age of 16.

Family Meeting Agenda
(12 hours over 3 days of meetings)

1. Goals for this meeting and review of agenda

2. Case on the rise and fall of families in business

3. Present summary of best management and governance practices

4. Overview of the health of the business

5. Family council logistics

   a. Purpose

   b. Plan for continuation

   c. Family strategy and vision

   d. Family issues

   e. How to get involved

6. Discussion: Goals of the owners of EPG; develop a vision

7. Discussion: Ownership transfer

8. Succession and continuity plan

9. Board of Directors: Education

10. Discussion: Family employment policy; opportunity to get involved

11. Life insurance and buy–sell agreement; irrevocable trust

The priority goal of the family council is to promote communication amongst the family and ownership group on a consistent basis. The issues that we will be communicating to one another may change, but the communication and education efforts must remain constant and effective.

This meeting was the beginning of a tradition in this family business, because we believe in the

(continued)

(continued)

value that it provides our family, the ownership group, and the business. We also intend to continue having a great deal of fun together in these meetings, as well as engaging non-active family members in activities that involve the administration of the family council, as well as becoming more in tune with the business matters of EPG.

We are excited about the impact this will have on improved communication and ownership continuity.

ESTATE PLANNING AND OWNERSHIP TRANSFER WITH BUSINESS AGILITY IN MIND

The estate plan has been developed and driven by Michael Orazen, father and CEO. He has made all the wealth and ownership transfer decisions, with the advice of accountants and lawyers, and has kept the entire family and current owners well informed. He is currently working with a financial planning and insurance company to come up with a comprehensive wealth/ownership transfer plan that will satisfy his retirement needs when he chooses to become less active in the company. He will first exit his day-to-day role as president and eventually relinquish his role as CEO to become the chairman of the future advisory board. He will transfer more ownership at that time, giving the majority of his voting shares to those family members active in the business, yet keeping the total number of shares evenly distributed among all of the children.

Michael Orazen has structured a buy–sell agreement that controls the future transfer of ownership by the current owners. It gives the current owners and the company the first right of refusal if a bona fide offer is presented to an owner from outside the family. It allows gifting and transfer of ownership only to the owners' children, leaving the spouses with a cash portion of the ownership that the [owners'] will specifies, funded with life insurance, of which the company is the beneficiary. Each owner has a policy that will give the company the required funds to pay for the shares without crippling EPG. A sale of EPG Inc. would have to be evaluated and agreed upon by the entire ownership group.

NEXT-GENERATION LEADERSHIP DEVELOPMENT

It is clear that both of us [Mike Jr. and Gabe] have worked hard to achieve our individual development goals. We have both received bachelor's degrees and master's degrees from reputable universities. We both graduated from Family Business: The Next Generation Leadership Institute and now have the necessary knowledge and skills to successfully lead our organization and family through the transition.

The challenge we have now is preparing ourselves as a team to effectively lead this organization together. Understanding the strengths and weaknesses we have individually is a key to honest and open communications—being willing to listen and support the other's position, while making effective and prompt decisions. It basically comes down to mutually respecting what the other brings to the table and trusting that the information that needs to be transferred to one another is.

What our team leadership looks like on an organizational chart is undetectable. Mike Orazen, Jr. is now the president of the organization. Gabe works under him in the organizational chart, but together in leading and managing the organization daily. We see the success or failure of the organization with one president as a win-win or a lose-lose for both of us. As long as we communicate and continue to work on developing our team leadership strategy, we will be improving our ability to successfully lead the extended family and the organization.

GABE'S DEVELOPMENT PLAN

Individually, I have aspirations of improving the quality and quantity of communications with all my siblings and their spouses. Becoming a more effective leader will require learning everything I can from my father before he transitions away from EPG; measuring my development and progress in leadership and self-management competencies through peer and family reports; becoming more active in customer relations with our major accounts and potential accounts; and understanding our product application and being prepared to evaluate the market and the customers we serve. All of these developmental goals are important, but I must maintain the integrity and availability of the accounting and information systems at EPG as well, challenging others to defend or change their views, based on what the information is communicating. All of these efforts will be necessary to make my brother and myself successful in leading our generation to the success we are seeking to accomplish together.

MIKE JR.'S DEVELOPMENT PLAN

My individual development goals are complementary to Gabe's. According to many of the self-assessment tools we used in the Next Generation Leadership Institute, as well as my knowledge of myself, I have several key areas to improve on. Most of the areas can be placed somewhere in the following categories:

- Improve goal setting and monitoring of progress.
- Improve my ability to use and analyze objective financial and numeric indicators of progress of self, others, and business.
- Improve reliability by following through with things I say I will do.

In most respects, my weaknesses are Gabe's strengths. I believe Gabe's statements about the importance of us working together as a team to lead this generation of the business to be very true. We can only truly be successful if that is the case. That means that both Gabe and I must also always work on our teamwork and communication skills. They will be important for our leadership ability, and they will be critical for our interaction with one another.

I also believe both Gabe and I need to work in the near term on continuing to expose ourselves to both our internal and our external customers. We must work harder at being seen and heard within our company and within our industry, without acting or being perceived as anything but what we are: intelligent, educated, prepared, grounded leaders of EPG for the next generation—leaders with a respect and dedication to the past, but ideas for improvement in the future, committed to continue building a company that lasts.

LEADERSHIP BY THE CEO AND THE CHIEF TRUST OFFICER

Up until about five years ago, if you would have asked us how difficult it would be for Mike Orazen, Sr. to begin transitioning leadership of EPG from him to the next generation, I think we both would have had doubts that it would be a smooth process. EPG is his creation—some would say his fifth child. But just as he raised his own children, and then let them go and watched them grow into adults, we believe he desires the same with EPG.

We are certain that Mike Sr. will transition out of power as an ambassador for EPG. [See Chapter 2 for a definition of the ambassador exit strategy and the other five strategies.] He will continue to nurture internal and external relationships with employees and customers. He will take them fishing and golfing, he will drop in on a mock up or a job site to provide technical expertise and create and enhance his relationship with others in the industry, and he will coach employees within EPG. Most importantly, he will continue to be a mentor and a resource for the next-generation leaders of EPG.

Just as letting go of his kids couldn't have been easy, it will likely not be easy to transition out of the leadership position at EPG. There will be tests for the next generation of leaders at EPG. There will be economic downturns that will impact our company. There will be mistakes made by Gabe and Mike Jr. These times will define the ultimate exit strategy of Mike Orazen, Sr. There will be times when he may instinctually become "the old general" that feels the company is going in the wrong direction in the absence of his guidance. Though these times will be trying for him, he will ultimately keep these feelings in check and contribute in a positive manner as ambassador and mentor for EPG and for the next-generation leaders.

The chief trust officer, Barb Orazen and our mother, has held many roles at EPG over the years. She has always been Mike Sr.'s partner and confidante. She held a position in the HR department in the first 10 years of EPG. Over the past five years, she has become less involved with the business aspect of our family business and more of the glue that keeps the family together, listening when members are troubled and keeping things in perspective.

(continued)

(continued)

Over the next several years, her role may change again. She may find that with Mike Sr. spending less time at EPG and becoming less involved in day-to-day operations, she will be spending more time with him. There may be times that she will need to be sensitive to the difficulty and emotions that he will inevitably face, particularly early on. She has also expressed an interest in helping out at EPG, particularly with the two of us, several hours a week.

Both of our spouses seem to take the same approach to EPG. They view it as a good job and an excellent opportunity for a career for their respective husbands, and they respect the complexities of the family business, but neither of them believes at this point that they have a compelling responsibility or role within the family business. At this point, there is not really a problem with this. In fact, it is quite understandable. But we hope that as we assume the lead role in the family and the business, they will understand that their roles can be very important. And that, hopefully, their skills in those roles will be as complementary as our skills are to one another.

THE CONTRIBUTION OF KEY NONFAMILY EXECUTIVES

Our mission/vision and values statement states, "Most of all we will recognize and reward achievements based on merit for those who create and innovate and also those who continually support the day-to-day business requirements." The key to this statement is "based on merit." Clearly, the two of us have been "given" an opportunity at EPG due to our relationship with the founder. But it is just as clear that we have taken the opportunity and run with it. We have prepared ourselves for leadership through formal education and our experiences. Our results can be objectively measured by clear impacts we have made on the organization. In many respects, our stripes were more difficult to earn than if our last name was something other than Orazen. We recognize that this is O.K., and serves to assure others that nepotism for nepotism's sake is not a practice that EPG condones. The Family Business Diagnostic Survey that we participated in confirms

that EPG rewards based on merit. The key nonfamily executives were comfortable that the succession plan would promote leaders that were prepared, regardless of family ties.

We fully realize that key nonfamily executives have played, and will continue to play, a very important role in EPG's growth and success. Gabe is talented and connected in the finance side of the business. Mike Jr. has substantial experience in operations as well as skill in leading people. But there are critical contributions that are uniquely made by key nonfamily members. Mike Scanlon has and will continue to play an important role in sales and marketing. The same is true with Smith McKee in production, Eugene Gormley in engineering, and Stacy Friedman in human resources. And as the organization continues to grow, there will be more areas that need to be led by talented individuals.

As with everything, perception is often reality. We need to be sensitive to the fact that we cannot fill all the top positions at EPG with relatives for two primary reasons. First, we don't have the talent in our family to run a top-notch organization without nonfamily members bringing skills, experience, and a different way at looking at an issue. Second, if the top of the organization were full of people from our family, a reasonable person would assume that there was a cap to their ability to rise to or near the top if they have "the wrong last name." Our organization's success to date is a result of good leadership and followership at all levels of the organization, and our success will only have a chance of continuing if we commit to "recognize and reward achievements based on merit. . . ."

ACCOUNTABILITY TO AN ADVISORY BOARD

To date, EPG has not realized the potential value of an advisory board and the positive impact it could have on our company. Through our education at the program at CWRU, we, along with Mike Orazen, Sr., are convinced that an advisory board, if chosen correctly, will add a great deal of value. As seen on the agenda for the family meeting, we will attempt to educate the family on the need and role of an advisory board. We will also begin to discuss potential board members.

Mike Orazen, Sr. will head up the project of establishing a board of advisors. He will ultimately determine the members of the board; however, we are confident that he will consult us on our thoughts and ideas on members and logistics of EPG's board of advisors. Our goal is to have our first quarterly board meeting in the second quarter of 2002. Mike Orazen, Sr. will likely remain CEO and chairman of the board of EPG for the next three to five years. We realize that the value the board offers will be contingent on the decisions we make in choosing its members. The board will aid in the transition of power in many ways. From Mike Sr.'s perspective, he will have the opportunity to put a board together that creates accountability and provides insight to the next generation as they assume the leadership role. From our point of view, the board will help Mike Sr. work through the issues that he may be dealing with during the period of time he is exiting the business as the leader. This can be very valuable assistance. This, along with financial performance review and strategy review, will help EPG continue its success through the next generation.

CONCLUSION

We must remember that the learning doesn't stop with this plan. We will continue to learn through our experiences. We must continue to study other suc-cesses and failures of family businesses. We will learn from teaching other family members and third-generation members. We will continue to learn from our mentor, Mike Sr., for our job is to understand and appreciate the factors that have created success so far and to make changes that are required to fine-tune the organization and adapt us to the changing environment. We intend to follow up on the seven best practices, build wealth in our generation, and pass on to the next generation a better business than when we took it over. This is our goal of stewardship and continuity, one worth our continued best efforts.

QUESTIONS:

1. What leadership imperatives and best practices are Mike and Gabe Orazen counting on to assist them in dealing with the generational transition and business continuity challenges that EPG and the Orazen family face? Discuss briefly.

2. Do you think that Michael Orazen, Sr., should feel more confident in transferring power to the next generation now?

3. What is the key to the ultimate effectiveness of this plan?

4. What do you predict will happen to EPG and the Orazen family?

11

THE FUTURE: CAN THE FAMILY
BUSINESS COMPETE AND THRIVE?

In 1998, the Follett Corporation faced the bleak prospect of disintermediation in the industry it had dominated until the advent of the Internet. Follett was 125 years old and moving to a fourth generation of family leadership. Ranked among *Forbes* magazine's 200 largest privately held firms, it consisted of 640 brick-and-mortar college bookstores and strong brand equity, founded on a solid franchise with colleges and schools that preferred to have someone else manage and operate their bookstores.

Follett had enjoyed 45 continuous years of sales growth. It distributed primarily college, high school, and elementary school textbooks; audiovisual materials; teaching aids for educators; and systems and services for libraries through wholesale and retail channels. It serviced its 640 locations out of one main distribution center and its corporate headquarters in the Midwest. In the late 1990s, new entrants in the industry, which perhaps had visions of becoming the Amazon.com of the textbook market, were challenging the company. While lacking Follett's expertise, gained through years of experience and customer orientation, they were backed by money from the public market and venture capitalists who subscribed to the e-commerce vision. With no need to show a profit and with every incentive to grow market share to support their stratospheric market valuations, they discounted textbooks by as much as 50 percent. The excessive optimism about new technologies and the Internet had not yet peaked, as it would in March 2000 with new all-time highs for NASDAQ stocks.

"The Internet has literally shaken and totally transformed the vision and strategy at Follett," said Mark Litzsinger, the fourth-generation family member elected chairman of Follett Corporation in 2001. "The immediate worry was the possibility of being disintermediated in the distribution process—in other words, that our suppliers could go direct to our customers, students, teachers, librarians and school districts without any need for us."[1]

CHAPTER 11 ■ THE FUTURE: CAN THE FAMILY BUSINESS COMPETE AND THRIVE?

234

Follett was one of the first companies to establish a "clicks and bricks" strategy. Faced with a challenge, it launched eFollett.com to complement the reach it had already established through its 640 stores. This web presence allowed Follett to sell business to business, business to consumer, and business to education. But to get there, it had to approve a significant investment in new technologies. The problem was that this multi-million-dollar expenditure, a sizable single investment without precedent in the history of the company, had not even been budgeted—such was the speed with which change had arrived.

The board took up the request of the next-generation members of management, who wanted to be proactive in the face of accelerated change in their industry. It had to consider the risks associated with the initiative, as well as those associated with not acting promptly. It had to ensure that shareholder, and not just management, interests were being addressed. Family shareholders had to confirm a strategic consensus and commitment to the strategy before the company could move ahead.

Quick approval by the board of directors led to rapid implementation of the e-commerce initiative. In short order, Follett had the premier college bookstore web site, where students and teachers could order all their textbooks, reading materials, and logo wear.

AGILITY IN THE FACE OF CHANGE

It often takes a bold vision, crafted out of a sense of urgency by the next generation, to spur rapid action toward change. The next generation is often most sensitive to the need for change immediately after assuming leadership from the previous generation. Aware that the competitive environment does not hold back out of respect for the hard work done by a previous generation of owner-managers, next-generation leaders take the baton and run. Follett Corporation was a winner precisely because it appreciated the competitive strengths that had led to its success while, at the same time, attending to the need for change posed by new competitive conditions. Confronted with the challenges presented by e-commerce, Follett did not choose to sell out, turning a successful company into an investment vehicle for the owning family. Nor did it abandon its "bricks" in favor of the Internet. Instead, when faced with competition from web-based companies, it intelligently added "clicks" to its channel strategy and thus retained control of its market.

The unique and sustainable competitive advantages family businesses often enjoy can serve them well in competition against larger and often better-capitalized management-controlled firms. Their speed and flexibility, long-term strategies, strategic focus on somewhat protected niches, customer orientation, and patient capital in the presence of practices that safeguard trust and family unity constitute advantages that are not easy to replicate.

The dot-coms that made headlines in the late 1990s were pursuing strategies that were intensely digital. But as a result of all the cash generated by investors with an

EXHIBIT 11-1   THE BUSINESS REJUVENATION MATRIX

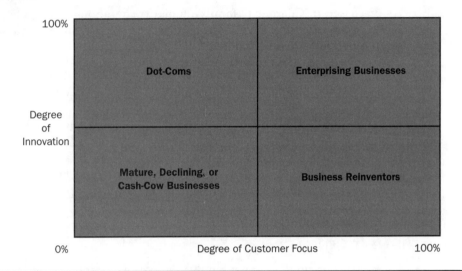

SOURCE: Adapted from Slywotzky, A., and Morrison, D., *How Digital Is Your Business?* New York: Crown Business/Random House, 2000.

appetite for digital companies, they were more focused on raising equity capital than on satisfying customer needs. Given the abundance of readily available investment capital, a focus on creating value for customers seemed archaic and irrelevant.

Of course, the enthusiasm for tech upstarts did not suspend the laws of economics for long. Other competitive advantages rooted in unique (non-Internet) organizational capabilities soon demonstrated their capacity to make a difference. As a result, many family businesses—even those at the crossroads between generations, which often are mature and/or declining businesses—got an opportunity to reinvent themselves and set out on a new growth path for the next generation. Some of these companies, like Follett, consolidated their traditional strengths and then rejuvenated the company by reengineering the processes that help them integrate their suppliers and their customers with the business. By implementing new digital strategies, they added value through channels like e-commerce.

Other family businesses (like Cemex, which is discussed later in this chapter), invested in people and organizational capabilities so as to consolidate their relationships with their customers and reinforce their high level of service and customer support orientation. By taking unique steps, leaders of these businesses guided their companies to the lower right-hand and upper right-hand quadrants in the matrix shown in Exhibit 11-1, thereby reinvigorating their business and improving its competitive fitness through value creation for customers.

CHAPTER 11 ■ THE FUTURE: CAN THE FAMILY BUSINESS COMPETE AND THRIVE?

236

COMPETITION AND VALUE CREATION

As discussed in Chapter 6, family-owned corporations can create competitive advantage by adopting a unique combination of seven sources of value—physical assets, financial resources, product price/performance, brand equity, organizational capabilities, customer–supplier integration, and the family–business relationship.

The capacity of family businesses to deploy a unique combination of assets or competencies in order to gain a competitive advantage is rooted in the unique profile of a family-controlled company. Positive interactions between the owning family and the business make certain strategies and managerial practices more likely, less costly, and easier to implement and sustain over time than they would be in larger, publicly held companies. When this positive, unique family–business interaction contributes to patient capital and innovative strategies and supports continued customer focus, the enterprising family ends up with a business that is built to last.

TAPPING THE NEXT GENERATION

Over the generations, younger family members have tended to be more fascinated by and more inclined to accept new technologies than have their older relatives. Members of business families are no exception. If their chosen profession is management, next-generation members are much more likely to want to engage in strategic planning, redesign information/financial systems, and pursue new products and e-commerce opportunities. Do next-generation members have to migrate from the family business in order to pursue their dreams, or can their skills and visions be usefully tapped by the family enterprise?

The business reasons for welcoming the next-generation's ideas is that their complementary skills and perspectives are precisely what the family business often needs as it struggles to update itself in order to continue to create value for its customers. Sidney Printing Works in Cincinnati, Ohio, is a case in point. Instead of dashing off to work for or start their own online company, fourth-generation family members joined the family company and provided it with the skills the firm needed to become a strong contender in the new competitive reality. Besides printing labels, signs, maps, and product literature in its plant, Sidney Printing Works could now assist customers with web materials, help them submit designs digitally for production in multiple media, and customize and archive those designs for multiple end uses. An acknowledgment of the value of the innovations contributed by the fourth generation was the creation of a new business unit called SpringDot, Inc.[2]

Indeed, if there is a disagreement worth having in a family-controlled company, it is the disagreement about vision and future direction for the firm. Implicit in the difficulty of conversing about this issue across generations is the tension between fully appreciating and respecting what has made the business successful so far and fully accepting that change is unavoidable. Leaders must recognize that unless the firm is willing to create the variety required to thrive in the presence of accelerating change, it will be overtaken by the competition and eventually driven to extinction. The Follett Corporation board of directors, for example, realized that this was the issue at stake.

This tension is not new, and it is not exclusively a product of e-commerce. As discussed in Chapter 4, when Samuel Curtis Johnson III was a young chemist working in the company's lab, he tried to convince his father, S. C. Johnson II, that he had the formula for a breakthrough product—an insecticide. His idea was rebuffed on several occasions, because of S. C. Johnson II's belief that the company should stick to the wax business. After several more attempts to convince his father of the invention's value—and not oblivious to the often repeated words of his father, "Remember, son, we are a wax company"—young Samuel Curtis reportedly added a tiny amount of wax as an inert ingredient to his formulation for the insecticide. This time he received the go-ahead for his now wax-based product. SC Johnson: A Family Company grew from $171 million in annual revenues to $6 billion, with much of the growth and the lion's share of the profits coming from the new insecticide products Raid and Off!

THRIVING THROUGH COMPETITION

Competition today is all about procuring and deploying new products and new product/service combinations in new supply-chain channels, including the Internet. Businesses are effectively creating new arrangements and new links in the value chain daily. Almost two decades ago, glimpses of this development could be gleaned from an influential article in the *Harvard Business Review*, which reported on three family-controlled companies that operated on a high-trust model supported by detailed procurement and inventory replenishment policies. These family businesses—Milliken, Levi Strauss, and Dillard's—agreed to update and coordinate their processes in order to increase the value-adding capacity of the entire chain. The electronic coordination was handled through an electronic data interchange, or EDI system.[3]

Faced with increased competition and smaller margins, the companies wanted to reduce overall inventories and inventories of obsolete items and their associated costs, increase inventory turnovers, and still have products available for customers. The idea was to have Dillard's immediately and automatically update the number of stock-keeping units, or SKUs, in the chain. Information about the purchase of a pair of Levi Strauss blue jeans in any Dillard's store would be recorded at the cash register and then sent via the EDI network to Levi Strauss and Milliken, which would proceed, based on agreed-upon replenishment policies, to manufacture additional jeans and fabric for jean production, respectively.

More recently, another owner-managed company bearing the founder's name—Dell Computer—created a choiceboard, where a customer can design his or her own computer and pay for it before Dell has to so much as pay for the components that will go into it. By digitizing both internal and customer relationship processes, Dell is able to provide customization and differentiation for its customers, who get a computer that meets their precise requirements. But

CHAPTER 11 ■ THE FUTURE: CAN THE FAMILY BUSINESS COMPETE AND THRIVE?

238

more importantly, the company is able to reduce its total costs, a reduction that it can then pass on to its customers, creating further customer value without sacrificing margins. Michael Dell insists that what is happening in the computer industry is not a price war but rather a cost war that Dell can easily win against the likes of Compaq, Hewlett-Packard, and IBM.[4] Dell has turned the value chain on its head. Whereas most companies must raise capital to fund the purchase of raw materials and then must manufacture products, put them in the distribution channel, sell them, and collect on them in order to replenish their capital, Dell collects money from the customer first, before purchasing raw materials, making the product, or putting it in the distribution channel. In this way, Dell has significantly reduced total costs, increased inventory turnovers, and enhanced its return on capital.

It is the value chain that Bill Ford, chairman of the Ford Motor Company, is targeting when he talks about bringing digital strategies to bear on his business. Ford's dealers do not like that kind of talk. For the most part, they believe that the rationale for the change is much like that for recent changes in the travel industry—go directly to the customers and save on commissions by not passing sales through an agent. But Bill Ford has much higher returns in mind than an extra few percentage points. He would like to do in the automotive industry at least some of what Michael Dell has done in the computer industry. Imagine how much more value that kind of an arrangement could provide for the customer and for Ford family shareholders.

Cemex, a family-controlled company founded in 1906 in Hidalgo, Mexico, is one of the top three producers of cement worldwide. It has reengineered internal and customer relations processes through CEMEXNET. This digital network, coupled with the new workforce skills needed to make it work, and a new logistics infrastructure with smaller decentralized plants have enabled the company to reduce the time needed to deliver cement in traffic-congested Mexico City from three hours to twenty minutes, on average. Because its customers, usually general contractors, face tremendous unpredictability in their work schedules from sources they cannot control—for example, environmental and workplace regulation by the government, weather conditions, union requirements, and traffic congestion—they appreciate the reliability and shorter lead times that Cemex can offer them. Decreased delivery times allow contractors to place an order for cement only when they need it and still not leave crews idle, thereby reducing their costs. For its trouble, Cemex is rewarded with a higher selling price for its cement and ready-mix concrete and returns on investment that are double the industry average.

Because this organizational capability is now embedded in Cemex, the company has been able to acquire competitors throughout the world and quickly realize gains from implementing a digital strategy that allows these plants to achieve better returns. Cemex manufactures and distributes cement in 30 countries and sells cement in 60 other countries; worldwide sales reached over $5 billion in 2000.[5] If an asset-intensive, low-margin business with slow growth rates and highly cyclical market demand can do it, other family-controlled companies can as well.

ORGANIC COMPETENCIES AND THE BUSINESS'S FUTURE

Family-owned companies seldom enjoy a comparative advantage over their publicly traded counterparts with regard to physical and financial assets. A source of value that family firms have more traditionally commanded is a unique set of organizational capabilities—people, skills, and systems—that, in combination, may produce higher quality products/services, quicker response, deeper relationships with customers and suppliers, more agile customization, and lower total costs.

Innovating through new digital technologies is another strategy that may open new arrangements within the value chain, such as that developed by Milliken, Levi Strauss, and Dillard's. Family companies can restructure channel dynamics, take on strategic partners in the value chain, and get closer to the end customer in this way.

Product/service performance and reputation also have been a differentiating feature of many family companies. Over time, a product's or service's performance creates brand equity, which has been effectively deployed by family businesses, including such well-known companies as Marriott, Kohler, Hallmark, Cargill, the *Wall Street Journal*, Nordstrom's, the *New York Times*, and Anheuser-Busch in the United States and Hermés, Roca, Deusto, El Corte Inglés, Ferrovial, *El Nuevo Día*, Grupo Femsa, Harrod's, Toyota, and BMW in other countries.

Sony (which is not a family company) provides a great example of the importance of brand equity to a company's growth and continued competitiveness. To his board members' consternation, Akio Morita, representing the Sony Corporation, on one of his first trips to the United States, turned down an order from Bulova Watch Company's purchasing agent because the agent insisted that the transistor radios be branded Bulova. Although the board advised him to take the order, Morita instead committed to several smaller sales of products that would be branded Sony. At the time, Sony was an unknown brand in the United States—but its name would not remain unknown for long. Years later, Morita celebrated this decision as his best one during his long and successful career at Sony.

Most intangible assets, such as brand equity, caring and skilled employees, and committed ownership, are difficult to replicate. Thus, they offer family companies a greater probability of sustainability over time. (See Exhibit 11-2 for a list of

---

EXHIBIT 11-2   POTENTIAL ORGANIC COMPETENCIES OF A FAMILY COMPANY

- Organizational Capabilities: People, Skills, and Systems

- Customer–Supplier Integration: Relationships and Systems

- Product/Service Price and Performance

- Brand Equity: Reputation

- Concentrated Ownership Structure

- Family Unity and Business Opportunity

CHAPTER 11 ■ THE FUTURE: CAN THE FAMILY BUSINESS COMPETE AND THRIVE?

240

potential organic competencies.) But nothing lasts forever, so the top management of family companies, with the assistance of the board of directors or advisory board, should annually review company strategy to ensure that changes in the firm's competitive environment are not rendering organic competencies useless in customers' eyes. Only those competencies valued by customers can provide the family firm with competitive advantages.

INTERPRENEURSHIP: INTERGENERATIONAL GROWTH IN ENTREPRENEURIAL FAMILIES

Intergenerational entrepreneurial activity, or interpreneurship, keeps the family-controlled company young and provides entrepreneurial opportunities for next-generation members. Interpreneurship is often driven by new products, product line extensions, new markets for existing products, exports, joint ventures, or strategic alliances with other members of the value chain.[6]

Intergenerational growth through entrepreneurial activity improves the odds that the family enterprise will continue across generations. But as in the SC Johnson story discussed earlier in this chapter, disagreements about vision often make this kind of growth a difficult proposition. Answering the questions in Exhibit 11-3 can help a next-generation leader determine the family business's potential for intergenerational growth and his or her role in it.

Growth for its own sake without a unique strategy to support the growth effort is to be avoided. Putting a product that creates little value for customers on the Internet or in another new distribution channel only glorifies an undifferentiated product; it does nothing to improve its competitive fitness. Just such an approach led to the tragic fate of many online businesses. Toys and groceries are commodities; the Internet has not changed that. A growth opportunity needs to be supported by competitive and economic factors that combine to create the most value for customers. Only then will the family business be able to share in the value creation process and its next-generation leaders contribute to maintaining competitive fitness and, over the long term, create shareholder value.

EXHIBIT 11-3   FOCUSING ON INTERGENERATIONAL GROWTH

- How can innovation be exploited to offer a better deal to customers, create a better-functioning organization for employees, and generate better returns for shareholders?

- What in the nature of the family–business interaction may represent a unique core competence that can be turned into a competitive advantage?

- What will be the company's next unique, differentiated value proposition for the customer?

- What can the next-generation leadership do to convince top management and/or the board of directors to financially support this unique, differentiated value proposition?

GLOBAL OPPORTUNITIES

The future holds many growth opportunities in other parts of the world. Family companies have often been reluctant to grow internationally because of a conservative approach to fiscal management and a propensity for risk avoidance. It is true that, except in select open economies, there has not generally been a compelling rationale for going global. Family enterprises in Latin America, Europe, the Middle East, and Asia have found that business risk was more easily managed by diversifying domestically than by going overseas. If the owning family had a good relationship with the government, an established reputation in the local market, and access to skilled nonfamily managers well versed in other industries, diversification in the protected market was a lower-risk growth option.

As local economies have opened up to global trade, opportunities for diversification no longer seem as compelling. In Chile, for instance, the fast-tracked opening of the local economy to global trade in the 1980s produced significant restructuring of the country's economy. Many family companies closed down, unable to compete with global competitors. Other companies that either already enjoyed advantages or began to pursue comparative competitive advantages thrived. A similar process took place in Mexico in the 1990s, with widely diversified "grupos" selling entire companies or divisions to foreign competitors and at the same time redeploying assets to businesses that continued to enjoy comparative advantages after the North American Free Trade Agreement went into effect.

Among U.S. family companies, the large size of domestic markets and a tendency toward risk avoidance have slowed overseas growth, except by very large and professionally managed companies like SC Johnson, Mars, Cargill, and Ford. Other companies have grown comfortable with global expansion opportunities by seeking alliances with family companies in foreign countries. Partners in these new ventures may be families they have known for years in a more unstructured, personal context. Consider the case of Simpson Investments, of Seattle, Washington. After being friends with a business family in Chile and doing some pilot tree farm projects with them over the years, the family decided to partner with the Chileans in a $100 million pulp mill operation in southern Chile.

While expanding overseas will likely seem a more compelling opportunity for many family companies in the future, the management of risk will continue to be an important item. For those family businesses that do decide to enter the global marketplace, here are some suggestions: First of all, it is wise to abandon the myth that the company can remotely exercise managerial control through sophisticated financial information and control systems. When it comes to foreign operations, there really is no substitute for being there. Different reporting practices, cultures, competitive dynamics, compensation and incentive policies, and even general business practices render management through detection of financial variances useless. Identifying such discrepancies often amounts to too little too late.

Second, networking through travel is a sound practice when growing globally is the strategy. Meeting with business, business school, and government leaders, as well as the leaders of the competition, provides much intelligence on the appropriate adaptation of strategies for the local market. SC Johnson: A Family

CHAPTER 11 ■ THE FUTURE: CAN THE FAMILY BUSINESS COMPETE AND THRIVE?

242

Company, for instance, has a board of directors with independent outsiders in most of the countries in which it operates. The company recruits smart, well-networked business, academic, and social leaders, who help it revise and customize its strategies and practices, infusing them with local content. Members of the SC Johnson family and top nonfamily managers travel often to various business locations, managing the risk of distance by adding some personal proximity to their global management portfolio.

POSITIVE-SUM DYNAMICS THROUGH FAMILY AND ENTERPRISE LEADERSHIP

Family companies moving between generations are particularly vulnerable to zero-sum dynamics. In the absence of growth or the perception of future business opportunities, there is a great propensity among family members to see winning only in terms of defeating someone else. In family companies, of course, that someone else is often a relative—the next-generation successor who patiently awaits his or her turn to lead, the branch of the family that has no members in the management of the enterprise, the impractical cousin who is an incurable romantic. If the enterprise is growing, there is no reason why a gain for one person or family branch has to come at the expense of another. However, in the absence of growth, both the perception of opportunity and family harmony are likely to suffer.

Family unity and business opportunity, as the Discovery Action Research Project so clearly indicated, are good predictors of the use of appropriate managerial and governance practices. These practices, in turn, are good predictors of family unity and the family's perception of growth opportunities. This virtuous cycle is an important one for family-controlled corporations to achieve.

Given the accelerating speed of change, next-generation members in a family company are an important asset in the adaptation of the business to new competitive conditions. They can also be contributors to the creation of loyalty and goodwill, rooted in opportunity, among shareholders and family members. With respect to the outside competitive environment, they have to be leaders of change, promoting dissatisfaction with the status quo and communicating a vision of a better future ahead. In dealing with shareholders and family, these next-generation leaders have to accommodate the growing diversity of preferences of wealthier family members and inspire shareholder loyalty.

Next-generation leaders need to understand, firsthand, the value to the extended family of helping the business family achieve its non-economic goals. These leaders must craft their own approach to meeting economic and non-economic family goals, similar to the way in which managers at the firm level must learn to improve both productivity and employee satisfaction and governments at the country level must learn to promote economic growth and simultaneously improve the quality of the environment. It is a huge assignment, but one that many next-generation members experience as their calling—the very personal and unique way they can create value for the family business and make a difference.

SUMMARY

1. It often takes a bold vision, crafted out of a sense of urgency by the next generation, to spur rapid action toward change.

2. Younger family members often offer the complementary skills and perspectives needed by the family business to update itself and continue to create value for its customers.

3. Competition today is based on procuring and deploying new products and new product/service combinations in new supply-chain channels, including the Internet.

4. Through the use of new digital technologies, family companies can restructure channel dynamics, take on strategic partners in the value chain, and get closer to the end customer.

5. Intangible assets, such as brand equity, caring and skilled employees, and committed ownership, are difficult to replicate and thus offer family companies a greater probability of creating sustainable competitive advantages over time.

6. Interpreneurship, or intergenerational entrepreneurial activity, is often driven by new products, product line extensions, new markets for existing products, exports, joint ventures, or strategic alliances with other members of the value chain.

7. Putting a product that creates little value for customers in a new distribution channel only glorifies an undifferentiated product; it does nothing to improve its competitive fitness. A growth opportunity needs to be supported by competitive and economic factors that combine to create the most value for customers.

8. Family companies have often been reluctant to grow internationally because of a conservative approach to fiscal management and a propensity for risk avoidance.

CHAPTER 11 ■ THE FUTURE: CAN THE FAMILY BUSINESS COMPETE AND THRIVE?

244

DEFENDING THE
COMPANY'S
POSITION IN THE
MARKETPLACE

Please answer the following questions about the Follett Corporation case, using the facts and ideas presented in this chapter.

QUESTIONS

1. What did the management of the Follett Corporation do when faced with a new type of competition from the dot-com industry?

2. What role did the company's board of directors and family shareholders play in acknowledging the threat and leading efforts for adaptation? Can you think of anything else they might have done?

3. What would you recommend that Mark Litzsinger, family member and chairman of Follett Corporation, personally do to successfully defend the company's position in the marketplace?

CASES

CASE 8:
GOLF AND GARDENS, INC.

In late 1948, Dick Strong, president and CEO of Golf and Gardens, Inc., arrived in Pennsylvania after serving in World War II. He had saved a little money, and he and his father bought a piece of property and developed it into a golf course together. Eventually, Dick decided to build a golf course and real estate development business. His father wanted to limit his personal involvement, so he eventually sold all his interest in the property to Dick. Thus, none of Dick's brothers or sisters were ever part of the family-owned business. The company grew at a rate of approximately 9 percent annually and enjoyed annual revenues of approximately $28 million in 2002. It also saw the value of its assets—mostly undeveloped land—skyrocket.

Over this same time period, several national measures of economic activity in the industry indicated considerably lower growth rates in both revenues and asset values of other companies. In fact, Golf and Gardens seemed to be growing at twice the rate achieved by the average performers in the industry.

Although he was very pleased with the company's record, Dick felt that he had two major unresolved issues. First, he questioned whether, given the size of his estate and his age, he could do enough to avoid extraordinarily high estate taxes. Second, he was uncertain as to whether his five sons and daughters would get along well enough to allow the family-owned business to continue to a third generation (see Exhibit 1). He felt very strongly about keeping the business together. Because of the expertise and economies of scale that he had been able to build into the business, he was disinclined to divide it into smaller business units that the sons and daughters could separately own and manage.

This case was prepared by Professor Ernesto J. Poza as the basis for a class discussion rather than to illustrate the effective or ineffective handling of a family business management situation. This case was revised in May 2002.

EXHIBIT I STRONG FAMILY TREE

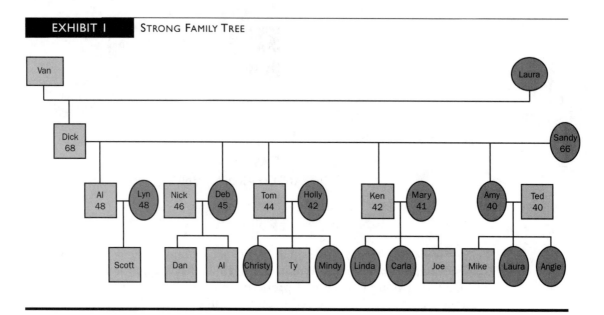

Al, the eldest son, had worked in the business ever since he was eight years old. Along with his two brothers, Tom and Ken, Al had learned the business from the bottom up by doing mostly odd jobs, especially during the summer months. They mowed lawns, dug ditches, picked up trash, and repaired clubhouses. The three sons were busy in "the house that Dick built." Their sisters, Deb and Amy, on the other hand, always seemed to be protected from toil in the male-dominated industry in which Golf and Gardens operated.

Notwithstanding their early experiences in the business, not all the boys went into the family-owned business. One decided to go work for a *Fortune 500* company after graduating from college and developed his career there for over a decade. He had recently returned to the family-owned business, citing a desire to be closer to his family and to work in a more caring corporate culture, too. Amy and Deb also went to work for other companies. Amy had returned recently and assumed responsibilities in the marketing department. Thus, four of the five siblings (all except Deb) were now working in the firm. They had very different positions and, as managers, limited interdependence. Most of the need for communication and coordination seemed to emerge around strategic and ownership issues, not the day-to-day running of the business.

Dick thought that there were three major ways the company might grow in the future. First, the company could begin operations in Florida, where it already had developed some expertise with smaller real estate investments. Second, it could convert several of its golf club properties into more lucrative commercial developments. Population growth surrounding several of the company's older properties was pushing office complexes and retail shopping centers right up to the eighteenth hole. Finally, the company could grow in the property management area, effectively providing management of properties for other owners and investor groups. In their industry, the service contract side of the business was growing significantly.

THE DISCOVERY ACTION RESEARCH PROJECT AND THE STRONG FAMILY

Because of Dick Strong's concerns regarding the future of the family-owned business, he approached the Weatherhead School of Management Partnership with Family Business program. He had read an article about educational programs serving family businesses and wondered if they could be of help to him. After several conversations, he agreed to participate in the action research effort. His goal was to discover just how ready he and his family were to transition the business across generations of owner-managers. Given his dream of continuity, he had to decide what issues to address on a priority basis.

A faculty member and a couple of Weatherhead students visited the offices of Golf and Gardens, distributing copies of the Discovery study to family members active in the business, several key nonfamily managers, and several family members who were spouses or direct-line descendants and shareholders but did not work in the business. The data collection meeting ended on a positive note, with all participants expressing their desire to receive the feedback and begin to take constructive steps. Participants were reminded that individual responses would be kept confidential and the feedback would come in the form of averages and ranges of responses, without ever identifying who said what.

Several weeks after this meeting, when the family business survey data and the family survey data had been analyzed, the faculty member and students in the feedback team met to discuss the results. (See Exhibit 2 for a summary of the findings.) There was concern about the impact that sharing some of these findings might have on individual Strong family members. But, ultimately, the team decided to provide the family business survey results to both the family and the nonfamily managers who had participated. The family survey results were then presented to the family members in the second phase of the meeting, after nonfamily managers had been excused.

CASE QUESTIONS

1. Based on the data collected and the facts presented in the case, what are the key issues, problems, or opportunities facing Golf and Gardens and the Strong family?

2. How might this feedback process influence future prospects for continuity in this family-owned business? What constructive changes do you see the Strongs making in response to the survey?

3. What is your prediction of what will happen in this family-owned business over the next three years? Use the survey data and the facts in the case to support your prediction.

| EXHIBIT 2 | ACTION RESEARCH RESULTS FOR GOLF AND GARDENS |

Family Business Survey Results

1. The CEO is very satisfied with the company's current results and its track record and believes he has only two major issues in front of him: estate planning and planning for succession.

2. There is a large gap between family managers and nonfamily managers in the extent to which they perceive the organization to be operating with a reasonable plan for where it is going and how it will get there. Nonfamily managers are much less satisfied than family managers in this regard.

3. Family managers, in particular, do not see themselves as having regular reviews of their performance on the job.

4. Neither family nor nonfamily managers know the length of time the present owner-manager will continue as CEO.

5. Family and nonfamily managers agree that those who would be involved do not know the standards and processes through which succession will occur.

6. Family managers do not perceive the company as having an effective board of directors or advisors.

7. Nonfamily managers do not perceive the CEO as delegating authority and responsibility and letting people do their jobs.

8. Both family and nonfamily managers agree the company is market-driven in its activities.

9. Both family and nonfamily managers consider it important that this company remain a family business.

10. Unlike nonfamily managers, family managers do not believe that career paths to senior positions are equally available to men and women.

11. Nonfamily managers feel that they are compensated fairly and equitably and have career paths to senior positions.

12. Nonfamily managers do not perceive that family members working in the company are maintaining helpful and cooperative relationships.

Family Survey Results

1. Family members (both active and inactive in management) agree that the family does not hold family meetings on a regular basis. But there was a wide range of answers.

2. Family members do not agree that the standards and processes through which family firm employment occurs have been established.

3. Family members do not agree that how ownership of the family firm will be transferred between generations of the family has been established.

4. Family members differed significantly in the extent to which they agreed with the statement "Family differences are addressed in a constructive way."

5. Family members disagreed that the standards and processes through which CEO succession will occur are known to them.

6. Family members strongly agreed that they are free to seek their own careers.

7. Family members agreed that they needed to have better communication and meet as a family more frequently to discuss issues and resolve problems.

CASE 9:
FASTENERS FOR RETAIL:
A QUESTION OF SUCCESSION (PART B)

At the same time Paul Conway decided that he did not want to continue his career at FFr, the company's senior management finalized its strategic plan. The plan made a strong case for developing fulfillment and manufacturing capabilities, expanding sales internationally, and increasing the sales force. Gerry recalled,

> It was apparent from the strategic plan that the management team saw many opportunities for growth. I didn't want to make the size of investment that was needed to broaden the product line and increase sales growth. I wanted to hand over the company, and there was no one in the second generation who was interested in it. Their career goals led them in different directions.

A joint meeting of the family owners and advisory board was held to discuss the future of FFr. The advisory board had significant experience in valuing and selling private firms. Its broad experience supported discussion of a wide array of options as the Conway family considered the future of FFr. The Conway children were the largest shareholders, but only Marty and Gerry held voting shares in the company. Stuart recalled the meeting, as follows:

> The agenda question was "Do we want to continue the business without a family member running it?" From the start, Paul and Gerry Jr. believed that selling the business was the best course of action. Initially I felt a strong desire to keep FFr as a family business, as did Kevin. My thinking was partially sentimental—the company had been part of our lives for so long. The advisory board helped us consider all our options. Our discussion was interesting and very involved. After reviewing the options it became apparent that a sale was the best course of action, and we quickly reached agreement about it. Looking back, I'd say that going through the process around the sale made us closer to one another—it was an important experience that we shared.

During the meeting, the board also encouraged Gerry to define his objectives for the company:

> I wanted to keep the company in Cleveland because I wanted my employees to be able to continue to work for FFr. Staying in Cleveland meant that we would be looking for a financial buyer. While we could get more money from a strategic buyer, there was a strong likelihood that a strategic buyer would move the company out of the area. Selling to a financial buyer served the shareholders and the key employees whose efforts helped build the company.

Research Associate Tracey Eira Messer prepared this case under the supervision of Professor Ernesto J. Poza as the basis for a class discussion rather than to illustrate the effective or ineffective handling of an administrative situation. For permission to publish this case, grateful acknowledgment is made to Gerald Conway, chairman emeritus of Fasteners for Retail.

The decision was made to explore selling FFr to a financial buyer. As part of the marketing process, Gerry prepared a memo reflecting on the reasons for the company's success (see Exhibit 1). Five groups participated in the bidding process. Eight months after the owners made the decision to sell, the company was sold to a local investment firm. As part of the sale, the Conway family gave current executives and key managers the opportunity to own equity in the new company. A generous gift from the shareholders, the offer of low-interest loans, and a small investment by each employee allowed key personnel to participate in ownership. In addition, the investment firm awarded senior management team members two sets of options that vested over periods of two and three years.

TRANSITIONS

The transition to new ownership was very smooth. Senior management remained in place after the sale, and FFr's revenues continued to grow. The new owners provided an infusion of capital that enabled FFr to make several company and product acquisitions, improve systems capabilities, and hire new personnel. The president, Don Kimmel, drove the strategic vision. Gerry Conway served as an internal cheerleader, an ambassador to the trade industry and to customers. Gerry also played an ongoing role in new product development.

The transition for the Conway children was uneventful, though some family routines were temporarily disrupted. Around the time of the sale, family meetings that had previously included spouses were limited to Gerry, Marty, and the Conway children. One of the children recalls,

> It was awkward not having the spouses present; it felt funny to involve them in some conversations but not others. They knew how much money we were talking about . . . and the change in status after the sale was uncomfortable for us at first— going from not having enough money to having an inheritance now. At first, the change felt a bit daunting, but eventually, we became comfortable with our new choices and responsibilities.

Paul's transition to teaching may have been the biggest change in the family. While at FFr, Paul took over a year to think about his future before deciding to become a teacher rather than the president of FFr. He was confident in his decision, but leaving a 10-year career at FFr and preparing for a teaching career represented a big life change. Following the sale of FFr, Paul and his wife, Natalie, moved to Arizona, where he began his second career.

> When I said that I did not want to stay at FFr, some of my siblings were surprised, but no one had trouble with it. Everyone accepted my decision, and I never felt uncomfortable. My mom was great. She wanted her children to be happy, and she wanted her husband to be happy. She was supportive of my decision and probably worked behind the scenes to help the family adjust.
>
> The other piece that made it okay was that we had learned how to communicate pretty well. In family meetings, we shared our dreams and ambitions. My family understood why I needed to make this change and why we decided to move. In fact, my parents came to visit us, and they fell in love with Arizona too.

EXHIBIT I	GERRY CONWAY'S PERSONAL VIEW ON THE SUCCESS OF FFR

Following are some of the entrepreneurial policy decisions that explain the growth, profitability, and absence of debt at FFr:

- Specialize in inexpensive products and maintain a larger average order size.

- Stay within the niche of display accessories. Aggressively develop new products to stay ahead of competition and to enhance revenue.

- Patent new proprietary products.

- Keep tool cost out of product price; amortize it over time.

- Don't compete with your customers; keep out of their business lines.

- Use multiple sales channels: catalogs, trade shows, mail, direct sales, telephone solicitation, and the Internet.

- Outsource manufacturing and subcontract assembly as long as possible.

- Form alliances and share development costs.

- Hire smart specialists (consultants).

- Attend family business seminars.

- Have an advisory board and use it.

- Complement entrepreneurship with a resourceful management team.

- Don't reveal the secrets of your success.

The following principles form the core of my entrepreneurial philosophy:

- Always look for creative ways to do things. Use talent for innovation and understanding of the market.

- Question the status quo mentality. Foster a sense of urgency and encourage change.

- Cheerlead. Be an ambassador of good will.

- Delegate.

Since selling FFr, Gerry has enjoyed a more relaxed pace. The Conways increased their involvement in the Fairfax Foundation, a family philanthropic project focused on mental health issues. While Gerry and Marty initially led the foundation's efforts, Fairfax is a family foundation, and the second generation has become involved in its activities. In Gerry's words,

> We sold most of the company to a local investment firm, but kept some shares. My brother Bill and I remained on the board and I remained chairman for a few more years. I continued to work on new products, though I spent more time with community activities, family involvement, traveling, and playing sports.
>
> Before this experience, I would not have said that selling the family business was a good outcome, but it was for us. After the sale, we continued to have family meetings and got together regularly to talk about our shared interests, like the family foundation.

CASE QUESTIONS

1. Please review Case 5, Fasteners for Retail: A Question of Succession (Part A) in the case section of Part 3. You will notice that both Fasteners for Retail and the Conway family utilized many of the best practices discussed in this textbook. Are you surprised by the decision to sell the family-owned company to a financial buyer? Why, or why not?

2. Does this turn of events represent a success or a failure for FFr and the Conway family? Whom do you think won—or lost—the most in this transaction? Why?

3. Is family business continuity within the founding family always a desirable goal? What might be equally or even more desirable goals? Under what circumstances would these other goals be more desirable?

ENDNOTES

CHAPTER 1

1. Astrachan, J., & Carey, M., "Family Businesses in the United States Economy." Paper presented to the Center for the Study of Taxation, Washington, D.C., 1994.

2. Rottenberg, D., ed., *Family Business Magazine*, Winter 2002, p. 44.

3. Ward, John, *Keeping the Family Business Healthy: How to Plan for Continued Growth, Profitability and Family Leadership*, San Francisco: Jossey-Bass, 1987.

4. Chrisman, J., Chua, J., & Sharma, P., *A Review and Annotated Bibliography of Family Business Studies*, Boston: Kluwer Academic Publishers, 1996.

5. Gomez-Mejía, L., Nuñez-Nickel, M., & Gutierrez, I., "The Role of Family Ties in Agency Contracts," *Academy of Management Journal 44*, pp. 81–96, 2001.

6. Schulze, W., Lubatkin, M., Dino, R., & Buchholtz, A., "Agency Relationships in Family Firms," *Organization Science 12*(2), 2001.

7. Astrachan, J., Klein, S., & Smyrnios, K., "The F-PEC Scale of Family Influence: A Proposal for Solving the Family Definition Problem," *Family Business Review 15*(1), 2002.

8. Chua, J., Chrisman, J., & Sharma, P., "Defining Family Business by Behavior," *Entrepreneurship Theory and Practice 23*(4), pp. 19–37, 1999.

9. Porras, J., & Collins, J., *Built to Last*, New York: HarperCollins, 1997. Note that while the authors do not identify the businesses that are family-owned or family-controlled, many of the enterprises chosen as exemplary are (or until recently were) family businesses.

10. Danco, Léon, *Beyond Survival: A Guide for the Business Owner and His Family*, Cleveland, OH: The University Press, 1975.

11. Burke, W. Warner, ed., *Organizational Dynamics*, New York: American Management Association, 1983.

12. Lansberg, I., ed., *Family Business Review 1*(1), 1986.

13. See Astrachan & Carey, op. cit.; Kleiman, R., Petty, W., & Martin, J., "Family Controlled Firms: An Assessment of Performance," *Family Business Annual 1*, pp. 1–13, 1995; and Poza, E., *A la sombra del roble*, Cleveland, OH: Editorial Universitaria, 1995.

14. See Danco, op. cit.; Poza, E., *Smart Growth: Critical Choices for Family Business Continuity and Prosperity*, San Francisco: Jossey-Bass, 1989; and Ward, op. cit.

15. Daily, C., & Dollinger, M., "An Empirical Examination of Ownership Structure in Family and Professionally Managed Firms," *Family Business Review 5*(2), pp. 117–136, 1992.

16. See Schulze et al., op. cit.; and Gomez-Mejía, Nuñez-Nickel, & Gutierrez, op. cit.

17. See Daily & Dollinger, op. cit.; and James, H., "Owner as Manager, Extended Horizons and the Family Firm," *International Journal of the Economics of Business 6*(1), 1999.

18. See Davis, P., "Realizing the Potential of the Family Business," *Organizational Dynamics 11* (Summer), pp. 47–56, 1983; and Lansberg, I., "Managing Human Resources in Family Firms," *Organizational Dynamics 11* (Summer), pp. 39–46, 1983.

19. Alderfer, C., "Change Processes in Organizations," in M. Dunnette, ed., *Handbook of Industrial and Organizational Psychology*, New York: Rand, 1976.

20. McCollum, M., "Integration in the Family Firm: When the Family System Replaces Controls and Culture," *Family Business Review* 1(4), pp. 399–417, 1988.

21. Schulze et al., op. cit.

22. Gomez-Mejía, Nuñez-Nickel, & Gutierrez, op. cit.

23. Ibid.

24. Schulze et al., op. cit.

25. Cabrera-Suarez, K., De Saa-Perez, P., & Garcia-Almeida, D., "The Succession Process from a Resource-and-Knowledge–Based View of the Firm," *Family Business Review* 14(1), pp. 37–47, 2001.

CHAPTER 2

1. Poza, E., Hanlon, S., & Kishida, R., "Does the Family-Business Interaction Represent a Resource or a Cost?" *Family Business Review* (in press).

2. See Sonnenfeld, J. A., & Spence, P. L., "The Parting Patriarch of a Family Firm," *Family Business Review* 2(4), pp. 355–375, 1989; Gomez-Mejía, L., Nuñez-Nickel, M., & Gutierrez, I., "The Role of Family Ties in Agency Contracts," *Academy of Management Journal* 44, pp. 81–96, 2001; and Poza, E., *Smart Growth: Critical Choices for Family Business Continuity and Prosperity*, San Francisco: Jossey-Bass, 1989.

3. Collins, J., *Good to Great: Why Some Companies Make the Leap . . . and Others Don't*, New York: Harper-Collins, 2001.

4. Barboza, D., "At Johnson Wax, a Family Hands Down Its Heirloom," *New York Times*, August 22, 1999, p. B1.

5. Ibid.

6. Sonnenfeld & Spence, op. cit.

7. Barnes, L. B., *The Precista Tools Case*, Boston: Harvard University Publishing Clearinghouse, 1988.

8. Danco, L., *Beyond Survival: A Guide for the Business Owner and His Family*, Cleveland, OH: The University Press, 1977.

9. Zuckerman, G., & Calian, S., "George Soros Alters His Style, Making a Role for Son Robert," *Wall Street Journal*, June 16, 2000, p. C1.

10. Personal communication between Antonio L. Ferré and Ernesto Poza, October 2002.

11. Personal communication between Jack Bares and Ernesto Poza, March 2000.

12. Barboza, op. cit.

13. Daily, C., & Dollinger, M., "An Empirical Examination of Ownership Structure in Family and Professionally Managed Firms," *Family Business Review* 5(2), pp. 117–136, 1992.

CHAPTER 3

1. See, for example, Barboza, D., "At Johnson Wax, a Family Hands Down Its Heirloom," *New York Times*, August 22, 1999, p. B1; Wells, M., "Are Dynasties Dying?" *Forbes*, March 6, 2000, pp. 126–131; and Cohen, D., "The Fall of the House of Wang," *Business Month*, February 1990, pp. 23–31.

2. Jones, A., "The Fall of the Bingham Dynasty," *New York Times*, January 19, 1986, p. 1.

3. See Poza, E., & Messer, T., "Spousal Leadership and Continuity in the Family Firm," *Family Business Review* 14(1), pp. 25–35, 2001; and LaChapelle, K., & Barnes, L., "The Trust Catalyst in Family-Owned Businesses," *Family Business Review* 11(1), pp. 1–17, 1998.

4. Ibid.

5. Poza, E., Alfred, T., & Maheshwari, A., "Stakeholder Perceptions of Culture and Management Practices in Family and Family Firms," *Family Business Review* 10(2), pp. 135–156, 1997.

6. LaChapelle & Barnes, op. cit.

7. Graham, K., "Journalistic Family Values," *Wall Street Journal*, March 20, 2000, p. 18.

CHAPTER 4

1. Ward, Leah, "Passing the Perot Torch," *Dallas Morning News*, March 19, 2000, p. 1H.

2. Lohse, Deborah, "At AIG, Son Is (Nearly) Spitting Image of CEO Father," *Wall Street Journal*, June 15, 2000, p. C1.

3. McLean, Bethany, "Growing Up Gallo," *Fortune Magazine*, August 14, 2000, p. 211.

4. Poza, E. J., Alfred, T., & Maheshwari, A., "Stakeholder Perceptions of Culture and Management Practices in Family and Family Firms—A Preliminary Report," *Family Business Review* 10(2), pp. 135–155, 1997.

5. Sulkes, Stan, "Old-Fashioned Business of Printing Meets Dot-Com World at SpringDot," *The Cincinnati Post*, August 29, 2000.

6. Gregersen, H., & Black, S., "J. W. Marriott, Jr., on Growing the Legacy," *Academy of Management Executive 16*(2), pp. 33–39, 2002.

7. Davis, J. A., & Tagiuri, R. "The Influence of Life-Stage on Father-Son Work Relationships in Family Companies," *Family Business Review* 2(1), pp. 47–76, 1989.

8. Dumas, Colette, "Preparing the New CEO: Managing the Father-Daughter Succession Process in Family Businesses," *Family Business Review* 3(2), pp. 169–181, 1990.

9. Barnes, Louis B., *Organizational Transitions for Individuals, Families and Work Groups*, Englewood Cliffs, NJ: Prentice-Hall, 1991.

CHAPTER 5

1. Arthur Andersen/Mass Mutual Family Business Survey, 1997.

2. Arthur Andersen/Mass Mutual Family Business Survey, 1993.

3. Dawson, P., personal conversation with the author, June 2002.

4. Ibid.

5. Davis, J., personal conversation with the author, June 2001.

6. Danco, L., & Nager, R., "The Ten Most Common Mistakes in Estate Planning," *Family Business Magazine*, Spring 1993, p. 36.

7. Adapted from Jonovic, D., *Family Philosophy Questionnaire*, Cleveland, OH: Family Business Management Services, 2000; and Fithian, S., *The Legacy Questionnaire*, Quincy, MA: The Legacy Companies, 1998.

CHAPTER 6

1. Graham, K., "Journalistic Family Values," *Wall Street Journal*, March 20, 2000, p. A18.

2. Poza, E., *Smart Growth: Critical Choices for Family Business Continuity*, San Francisco: Jossey-Bass, 1989; Cleveland: University Publishers, 1997.

3. Cameron, K., Whetten, D., & Kim, M., "Organizational Dysfunctions and Decline," *Academy of Management Journal* 30(1), pp. 126–138, 1987.

4. Boulton, R., Libert, B., & Samek, S., *Cracking the Value Code*, New York: HarperCollins, 2000.

5. See, for example, Gallo, M. A., & Sveen, J., "Internationalizing the Family Business," *Family Business Review* 4(2), Summer 1991, pp. 181–190.

6. Davis, S., & Meyer, C., *Future Wealth*, Boston: Harvard Business School Press, 2000.

7. Personal conversation with Ernesto Poza, June 2001.

8. Hoover's Company Profile, http://www.hoover.com, July 2002.

9. Johnson, F., personal conversation with the author, June 1996.

10. Poza, E., Johnson, S., & Alfred, T., "Changing the Family Business Through Action Research," *Family Business Review* 11(4), pp. 311–323, 1998.

11. Habbershon, T., & Astrachan, J., "Perceptions Are Reality: How Family Meetings Lead to Collective Action," *Family Business Review* 10(1), pp. 37–52, 1997.

12. de Visscher, Francois, "When Shareholders Lose Their Patience," *Family Business Magazine* 11(4), Autumn 2000, pp. 9–12.

13. See Poza, op. cit.; and Ward, J., *Keeping the Family Business Healthy*, San Francisco: Jossey-Bass, 1987.

14. Litz, R., & Kleysen, R., "Your Old Men Shall Dream Dreams, Your Young Men Shall See Visions: Toward a Theory of Family Firm Innovation with Help from the Brubeck Family," *Family Business Review* 14(4), pp. 335–351, 2001.

15. Gloyd, R., "Notes from the Producer," from the Telarc recording *In Their Own Sweet Way*, CD-83355.

16. Ward, J., *Keeping the Family Business Healthy: How to Plan for Continued Growth, Profitability and Family Leadership*, San Francisco: Jossey-Bass, 1987.

CHAPTER 7

1. Nelton, Sharon, "Lessons from Katharine Graham," *Family Business Magazine*, Autumn 2001, p. 12.

2. Dyer, W. G., *The Entrepreneurial Experience*, San Francisco: Jossey-Bass, 1992.

3. Hersey, P., & Blanchard, K., *Management of Organizational Behavior: Utilizing Human Resources*, 5th ed., Englewood Cliffs, NJ: Prentice-Hall, 1988.

4. Gregersen, H., & Black, S., "J. W. Marriott, Jr., on Growing the Legacy," *Academy of Management Executive 16*(2), pp. 33–39, 2002.

5. Werner, S., & Tosi, H., "Other People's Money: The Effects of Ownership on Compensation, Strategy and Managerial Pay," *Academy of Management Journal* 38(6), pp. 1672–1691, 1995.

6. Cole, P. M., "Women in Family Business," *Family Business Review 10*(4), pp. 353–371, 1997.

CHAPTER 8

1. Poole, C., "Family Ties," *Forbes*, April 26, 1993, pp. 124–126.

2. Judge, W., & Zeithaml, C., "Institutional and Strategic Choice Perspectives on Board Involvement in the Strategic Direction Process," *Academy of Management Journal*, October 1992, pp. 766–794.

3. Cadbury, Adrian, "Family Firms and Their Governance: Creating Tomorrow's Company from Today's," Egon Zehnder International, 2000.

4. Harvey-Jones, J., *Reflections on Leadership*, New York: HarperCollins, 1988.

5. Foster, R., & Kaplan, S., *Creative Destruction*, New York: Currency/Doubleday, 2001; and Ward, J., *Keeping the Family Business Healthy*, San Francisco: Jossey-Bass, 1987, p. 2.

6. Cadbury, Adrian, op. cit.

7. Schwartz, M., & Barnes, L., "Outside Boards and Family Businesses: Another Look," *Family Business Review 4*(3), 1991, pp. 269–285.

CHAPTER 9

1. Jones, Alex, "The Fall of the House of Bingham," *New York Times*, January 19, 1986; and Jones, Alex, "The Binghams: After the Fall," *New York Times*, December 21, 1986.

2. Fancher, M., "Coming Together After Strike to Rebuild Relationships, Trust," *The Seattle Times*, January 21, 2001.

3. Poza, E., Alfred, T., & Maheshwari, A., "Stakeholder Perceptions of Culture and Management Practices in Family and Family Firms," *Family Business Review 10*(2), 1997.

4. Habbershon, T., & Williams, M., "A Resource-Based Framework for Assessing the Strategic Advantages of Family Firms," *Family Business Review 12*(1), 1999, pp. 1–25.

5. Churchill, N. C., & Hatten, K. J., "Non-Market-Based Transfers of Wealth and Power: A Research Framework of Family Businesses," *American Journal of Small Business 11*(3), 1987, pp. 51–64.

6. Poza, E., Alfred, T., & Maheshwari, A., op.cit.

7. Habbershon, T., & Astrachan, J., "Perceptions Are Reality: How Family Meetings Lead to Collective Action," *Family Business Review 10*(1), pp. 37–52, 1997.

8. Poza, E., & Messer, T., "Spousal Leadership and Continuity in the Family Firm," *Family Business Review 14*(1), pp. 25–35, 2001.

9. Quoted in Brigid McMenamin, "Close Knit," *Forbes*, December 25, 2000.

10. Cadbury, Adrian, "Family Firms and Their Governance: Creating Tomorrow's Company from Today's," London: Egon Zehnder International, 2000.

CHAPTER 10

1. http://www.scjohnson.com.

2. Slater, R., *The New GE: How Jack Welch Revived an American Institution*, Homewood, IL: Business One Irwin, 1993, p. 261.

3. Beckhard, R., & Harris, R., *Organizational Transitions: Managing Complex Change*, Reading, MA: Addison Wesley, 1987.

4. Barnes, L., "Incongruent Hierarchies: Daughters and Younger Sons as Company CEOs," *Family Business Review 1*(1), pp. 9–21, 1988.

5. Orazen, M., & Orazen, G., "Next Generation's Succession Plan Addressing The 7 Best Practices for Family Business Continuity." Paper presented to Family Business—The Next Generation: A Leadership Institute, June 2000.

CHAPTER 11

1. Litzsinger, M., personal conversation with the author, September 2001.

2. Callison, J., "A Family Looks to the Future," *The Cincinnati Enquirer*, June 13, 2001.

3. Abernathy, F., Dunlop, J., Hammond, J., & Weil, D., *A Stitch in Time*, New York: Oxford University Press, 1999.

4. De Lis, P., "La Fusion de HP y Compaq nos da una gran oportunidad," *El Pais*, Negocios, Barcelona, No. 832, October 14, 2001, p. 7.

5. Slywotzky, A., & Morrison, D., *How Digital Is Your Business?* New York: Crown Business/Random House, 2000.

6. Poza, E., *Smart Growth, Critical Choices for Family Business Continuity*, Cleveland, OH: University Publishers, 1997.

INDEX